Slum Tourism

Slum tourism is a globalizing trend and a controversial form of tourism. Impoverished urban areas have always enticed the popular imagination, considered to be places of 'otherness', 'moral decay', 'deviant liberty' or 'authenticity'. 'Slumming' has a long tradition in the Global North, for example in Victorian London when the upper classes toured the East End. What is new, however, is its development dynamics and its rapidly spreading popularity across the globe. Township tourism and favela tourism have currently reached mass tourism characteristics in South Africa and in Rio de Janeiro, Brazil. In other countries of the Global South, slum tourism now also occurs, and providers see huge growth potential.

While the morally controversial practice of slum tourism has raised much attention and opinionated debates in the media for several years, academic research has only recently started addressing it as a global phenomenon. This book provides the first systematic overview of the field and the diverse issues connected to slum tourism. This multidisciplinary collection is unique in both its conceptual and empirical breadth. Its chapters indicate that 'global slumming' is not merely a controversial and challenging topic in itself, but also offers an apt lens through which to discuss core concepts in critical tourism studies in a global perspective, in particular 'poverty', 'power' and 'ethics'.

Building on research by prolific researchers from ten different countries, the book provides a comprehensive and unique insight into the current empirical, practical and theoretical knowledge on the subject. It takes a thorough and critical review of issues associated with slum tourism, asking why slums are visited, whether they should be visited, how they are represented, who is benefiting from it and in what way. It offers new insights into tourism's role in poverty alleviation and urban regeneration, power relations in contact zones and tourism's cultural and political implications.

Drawing on research from four continents and seven different countries, and from multidisciplinary perspectives, this ground-breaking volume will be valuable reading for students, researchers and academics interested in this contemporary form of tourism.

Fabian Frenzel is Lecturer at the School of Management, University of Leicester.

Ko Koens is a postgraduate researcher and part-time lecturer at the International Centre for Research in Events, Tourism and Hospitality, Leeds Metropolitan University.

Malte Steinbrink is Senior Lecturer of Social and Cultural Geography at the Institute of Geography and the Institute of Migration Research and Intercultural Studies (IMIS), University of Osnabrück, Germany.

Contemporary Geographies of Leisure, Tourism and Mobility

Series Editor: C. Michael Hall

Professor at the Department of Management,
College of Business & Economics, University of Canterbury,
Private Bag 4800, Christchurch, New Zealand

The aim of this series is to explore and communicate the intersections and relationships between leisure, tourism and human mobility within the social sciences.

It will incorporate both traditional and new perspectives on leisure and tourism from contemporary geography, e.g. notions of identity, representation and culture, while also providing for perspectives from cognate areas such as anthropology, cultural studies, gastronomy and food studies, marketing, policy studies and political economy, regional and urban planning, and sociology, within the development of an integrated field of leisure and tourism studies.

Also, increasingly, tourism and leisure are regarded as steps in a continuum of human mobility. Inclusion of mobility in the series offers the prospect to examine the relationship between tourism and migration, the sojourner, educational travel, and second home and retirement travel phenomena.

The series comprises two strands:

Contemporary Geographies of Leisure, Tourism and Mobility aims to address the needs of students and academics, and the titles will be published in hardback and paperback. Titles include:

1. **The Moralisation of Tourism**
   Sun, sand . . . and saving the world?
   Jim Butcher

2. **The Ethics of Tourism Development**
   Mick Smith and Rosaleen Duffy

3. **Tourism in the Caribbean**
   Trends, development, prospects
   Edited by David Timothy Duval

4. **Qualitative Research in Tourism**
   Ontologies, epistemologies and methodologies
   Edited by Jenny Phillimore and Lisa Goodson

5. **The Media and the Tourist Imagination**
   Converging cultures
   Edited by David Crouch, Rhona Jackson and Felix Thompson

6. **Tourism and Global Environmental Change**
   Ecological, social, economic and political interrelationships
   Edited by Stefan Gössling and C. Michael Hall

7. **Cultural Heritage of Tourism in the Developing World**
   Edited by Dallen J. Timothy and Gyan Nyaupane

8. **Understanding and Managing Tourism Impacts**
   An integrated approach
   C. Michael Hall and Alan Lew

9. **An Introduction to Visual Research Methods in Tourism**
   Edited by Tijana Rakic and Donna Chambers

10. **Tourism and Climate Change**
    Impacts, adaptation and mitigation
    C. Michael Hall, Stefan Gössling and Daniel Scott

Routledge Studies in Contemporary Geographies of Leisure, Tourism and Mobility
is a forum for innovative new research intended for research students and academics, and
the titles will be available in hardback only. Titles include:

Slum Tourism

Poverty, power and ethics

**Edited by
Fabian Frenzel,
Ko Koens and
Malte Steinbrink**

Routledge
Taylor & Francis Group

LONDON AND NEW YORK

First published 2012
by Routledge
2 Park Square, Milton Park, Abingdon, Oxon OX14 4RN

Simultaneously published in the USA and Canada
by Routledge
711 Third Avenue, New York, NY 10017

*Routledge is an imprint of the Taylor & Francis Group,
an informa business*

British Library Cataloguing in Publication Data
A catalogue record for this book is available from the British Library

Library of Congress Cataloging in Publication Data
Frenzel, Fabian, 1975–
    Slum tourism : poverty, power and ethics / Fabian Frenzel,
    Malte Steinbrink, Ko Koens.
    p. cm.
    Includes bibliographical references and index.
    1. Tourism–Environmental aspects. 2. Tourism–Moral and ethical
    aspects. 3. Slums. I. Steinbrink, Malte. II. Koens, Ko. III. Title.
    G156.5.E58F74 2012
    338.4'791–dc23
    2011046944

ISBN: 978–0–415–69878–8 (hbk)
ISBN: 978–0–203–13675–1 (ebk)

Typeset in Times New Roman
by Florence Production Ltd, Stoodleigh, Devon

Contents

Illustrations

Figures

Tables

Contributors

João Afonso Baptista holds a PhD in Social Anthropology from the Martin Luther University, Germany. He is a lecturer and researcher in the Department of Social and Cultural Anthropology at the University of Hamburg, Germany. His main research and theoretical interests are political ecology, tourism and ethical consumption.

Kanika Basu is an urban planner and her current work engagements relate to slum improvement, housing for the urban poor and micro-finance for livelihood promotion. Her areas of research interest are people's perspectives and participation in development processes, and tourism-led development.

Shelley Ruth Butler teaches at the Institute for the Study of Canada at McGill University, Montreal. Trained as a cultural anthropologist, her ethnographic research and publications focus on critical museology and alternative tourism in Canada and South Africa.

Yannan Ding is a PhD candidate in Human Geography at the University of Leuven, Belgium. He has been working on urban history, urban geography and regional development, with a focus on informal settlements. His research interests include sociological and planning discourses on the 'urban village'.

Kim Dovey is Professor of Architecture and Urban Design at the University of Melbourne, where he has published widely on social issues in architecture, urban design and planning. His books include *Becoming Places* (Routledge, 2010), *Framing Places* (Routledge, 2008) and *Fluid City* (Routledge, 2005). He currently leads a series of research projects on place identity, urban intensification, informal settlements and creative cities.

Bianca Freire-Medeiros is Senior Lecturer of Sociology at Getulio Vargas Foundation, Rio de Janeiro, Brazil. She has published extensively on the relationship between tourism, poverty, consumption and audio-visual culture.

Fabian Frenzel is a lecturer at the School of Management, University of Leicester. He studied political science at Freie Universität in Berlin and wrote his PhD on political and activist mobilities and protest camps at the Centre for Tourism & Cultural Change, Leeds Metropolitan University. He has published research on alternative media networks, slum tourism and participant action research.

Ross King is a professorial Fellow in the Faculty of Architecture, Building and Planning at the University of Melbourne, Australia, researching social issues pertinent to architecture and urban conditions with a focus on Southeast Asia. Recent publications include *Kuala Lumpur and Putrajaya* (NUS Press, 2008) and *Reading Bangkok* (NUS Press, 2011). He is also affiliated with the Silpakorn and Kasetsart Universities in Thailand.

Ko Koens is a PhD candidate at the International Centre of Responsible Tourism at Leeds Metropolitan University, England. Currently he is writing a PhD on small-business involvement in township tourism. He has also published on the sustainability of tourism in other regions and has a particular interest in small businesses and policy development.

Palloma Menezes is a PhD candidate in Sociology at the Rio de Janeiro State University, Brazil. Her research focuses on urban sociology and reflects upon possible intersections between heritage, tourism and public policies with regard to the Rio de Janeiro favelas.

Julia Meschkank is a research assistant at the Institute of Geography, University of Potsdam, Germany. In her current PhD project, she is focusing on recent tourism to Berlin's Neukölln district – a socially deprived area and Turkish neighbourhood.

Tony Seaton is is MacAnally Professor of Travel History and Tourism Behaviour at the Centre for Irish Tourism Policy Studies, Department of Economics, Kemmy Business School, University of Limerick, Ireland. His main research interests are in tourism behaviour, literary and historical aspects of travel, and thanatourism.

Malte Steinbrink is a senior lecturer and researcher of Social Geography at the Institute of Geography and at the Institute of Migration Research and Intercultural Studies (IMIS), University of Osnabrück, Germany. His research and publications focus on the nexus of mobility and development, social network research and tourism studies.

Kisnaphol Wattanawanyoo is a lecturer and researcher at the School of Architecture and Design, King Mongkut's University of Technology Thonburi, Thailand. His research focuses on community housing, urban community, informal urbanism and architectural activism.

Preface

The slum is a reality that few of us reading this book will have experienced, though I would suggest we will, at some point, have felt its presence, maybe as a sense of concern, perhaps as a distant feeling of guilt and even fear, but all easily buried under our normative sense of comfort and conformity. While slums may seem distant, as with some perverse five degrees of separation, we are never far from them, indeed they are closer to us than ever. Occasionally we catch sight of a slum; fleetingly from the window of a train as it cuts through the messy peripheries of major cities, or from a glanced television news report or documentary reflecting on the plight of its inhabitants. Other than this, for many in the developed world, the slum is consigned to the realms of another's imagination, expressed as a setting in a novel or a backdrop to a film.

The word 'slum' holds an imprecise power. While there is an official and rather unfeeling United Nations definition for a slum, which refers to an ostensibly urban area characterized by sub-standard housing and 'squalor' where the population lacks security of tenure, the word conjures up far more of a disturbing picture and taps into an imaginary that has grown out of the worst excesses of the grand projects of the last three centuries: industrialization, urbanization and capitalism. The slum is certainly a physical reality, apparently unplanned and disorganized, informal and lacking in basic services. It is seen to be the opposite of ordered society and of that more problematic concept of 'civilization'. The slum is offensive to the trained aesthetic of the developed world, which seeks formal clean lines, symmetry, and the neat and the tidy. The slum perverts our evolved common understandings of sanitation and hygiene with evocations of dirt, filth, disease and decay. The association of disorder with manifest problems of being 'dirty', and extended still to being inherently unhealthy, has its roots in nineteenth-century European urbanization. Engels' celebrated descriptions of the Irish quarter of Manchester in the mid-nineteenth century moves between his revulsion of a dense and unplanned physical form and its biological consequences. For Engels, the slum defied 'all considerations of cleanliness, ventilation, and health'.

That urban planning and building control emerged throughout the twentieth century as a response to the concept of the slum is well documented. Planning works to regulate space and impose order within consensual and cultural frameworks of aesthetics and standards of health. The slum, without precision of shape and process, signifies a place where development has not reached, as if somehow defiant of the progressive processes of social ordering and public planning. And while most places are 'lived in', reflecting almost a joy of life, the populations of slums are seen to 'dwell', as if dwelling is a sort of code for mere existence. The slum is a focal point for social problems – illiteracy, unemployment, crime, drug abuse etc. – which are defined in, and by, their very concentration. By virtue of where they are, and almost irrespective of the causes and conditions of their location, slum dwellers are the wretched of the earth deemed to exist between the immoral and the wholly forgotten. The slum is a manifestation of poverty and inequality and stands, in the real and the imaginary, as a powerful warning of where society does not wish to be.

Historically, we can understand the slum. The poetic, evocative and poignant descriptions of life in mid-nineteenth-century London slums in Dickens' novels are echoes of sad moments in history, but history nonetheless. We can point to such moments as part of a wider process of development, almost as a necessary, if distasteful, by-product. In an imagined grand narrative of global development, now almost exclusively authored by capitalism, the slum is destined to be a negative side-effect capable, in theory at least, of being eliminated and yet tolerated. So too can we understand the slum geographically. Favelas, shanty towns, ghettos and the like speak of *global* processes – national and international patterns of development and trends in population flows. Also, sociologically we can understand the workings within a slum, the processes of marginalization and exclusion, the social relationships formed and the strategies of existence that are developed. What is decidedly more challenging is how we can understand the slum emotionally and, indeed, in a moral sense. That slums persist, that over one billion of the world's population live in slums, that they remain sadly defiant of the optimism of 'development', and that they continue to grow, are all sad reflections on the ways in which societies value the concept of humanity.

These dangerous, dirty and desolate places would appear to be the very antithetical tourist destination and yet we find ourselves dealing with the phenomenon of 'slum tourism'. As this book makes clear, this is a complex and challenging practice. At one level touring the kingdoms of the poor has a history at least to the eighteenth century. Writers, philanthropists, politicians and scientists, for various reasons, toured slum areas, throughout the nineteenth and twentieth centuries and into the present. Gazing on the poor, and amid the squalor observed, they have been inspired to seek reform, lead rebellion or at the very least bring the plight of slum dwellers to a wider audience. Such forms of specialist engagement continue today, but it is only relatively recently that this has developed into a significant and more organised activity. Visits have become increasingly structured, indeed creatively packaged, and have found some degree of understanding under the label of 'slum tourism'. Touring the poor is increasingly and variously organized by local slum communities, non-governmental organizations and tour operators. It is sanctioned by tourist agencies, is promoted on websites and appears within established guidebooks as something to experience. The slum has joined the realm of 'attractions' – a sight to see.

As this volume exemplifies, such a category covers different formats and, beneath these formats, a host of different motivations and experiences. Considering the motivations for slum tourism takes us into some disturbing territory. It plays with notions of the romantic sublime, almost celebrating a type of inverted aesthetics where the tourist wishes to see the drama of shanty towns, both literally and metaphorically, precariously and haphazardly holding on to the very margins of society. The slum has taken on a sense of the spectacular, a place that unconsciously impresses. Even in its physical being, and from a distance, the slum impacts upon the eye and provides a counterpoint for the more established urban form within which the majority of tourist activity takes place. And now, more than ever, the tourist is able to be guided into the fabric of the slum. This allowed access forms a powerful narrative in tourism. It is the narrative of revelation and it works on a sense of having been granted permission to go backstage, to those places that are normally closed off from view. The attraction of the slum is rooted in the starkness of the difference it displays. The distance between the ways of life as normally experienced by tourists wealthy enough to be visiting, say, Johannesburg or Mumbai in the first place, and the ways of life of slum dwellers is of course vast, and it is this distance that provides a perverse power of attraction. The tourist would seem to experience a sense of privilege, a feeling of exceptionality, arguably a feeling of authenticity, not as some remote objective quality but rather as a sense of authenticating one's own humanity. Slum tours can be framed by wider processes of socio-cultural change that have driven growth in what has clumsily been termed 'adventure' tourism, where the motivation is partially active sensation seeking, taking on risk (largely in controlled settings), and a genuine exploration of unorthodox environments, and partially the desire to feed the ego and to accentuate one's social standing in a Bourdieurian sense. At the same time, there is no doubt that there is a genuine desire among some social groups to visit slums as part of a wider political action to draw attention to the sad persistence of slum conditions and to challenge their very existence. The problem is that these drivers are not mutually exclusive, making for an ethical blurring. Unlike other forms of touristic activity, slum tourism allows for moral and political ambiguity that is difficult to address. Indeed, it goes with the territory.

There is also an opaqueness relating to what the wider impacts are of slum tourism. What are its consequences? What outcomes does engaging in a tour of a township or favela have? It would seem that, for some slum tourists, the emotional experiences and emotional legacy of the tour do induce some form of later political action, whether this leads to further activism or remains as mere awareness raising. For other slum tourists, engagement is more passive, and the slum can quickly and easily be relegated to just another leisure experience. For slum dwellers and the various bodies that seek to represent their interests, tourism is truly a mixed blessing. Not only can tourism bring attention to the realities of slum conditions, it can bring, it is argued, and depending upon how it is organised, direct and much needed financial benefit to slum dwellers or, more precisely, to *some* slum dwellers. If born from the slum itself, tourism allows for a line of development that displays genuine creativity and enterprise, while other economic opportunities are closed off. If imposed solely from an outside opportunist operator, the slum becomes exploited in the cruellest of ways. Either way, tourism can encourage a form of objectification and othering and act to embed the condition of the slum as a reality to be preserved rather than to be changed.

The experience of tourists visiting slums is not particularly well researched; partly because the phenomenon is relatively recent, partly because the conditions of close observational research are problematic and bear risk, and partly because such research carries with it a series of weighty ethical issues. This book paves the way for tackling these issues and developing a challenging research agenda that is able to provide some intellectual and empirical underpinning for what will always be a difficult area. It is difficult for it displays some of the ugly continuities of humanity, not only in the slums themselves but in the way that leisured societies can continue to voyeuristically extract some pleasure, passive as it may be, from the existence of squalor and human degradation. It is also difficult because the reality of the slum is shaped and maintained by a complex global system that we find hard to address, indeed understand. However, such difficulties should not deter us from attempting to eradicate the clearly morally wrong condition of the slum. Through gaining a deeper understanding of slum tourism we are, in effect, engaging in a process of self-analysis that can only contribute to the ultimate goal of eradicating slum conditions and the poverty that creates them. Slum tourism is hopefully a means to an end and not an end in itself.

Professor Mike Robinson
Chair of Cultural Heritage
Director, Ironbridge Institute
University of Birmingham

Acknowledgements

Our gratitude goes first to all the authors who contributed their research to this edition for their constructive cooperation and their patience and flexibility in helping us in preparing this book. We would also like to thank our editors at Routledge, Emma Travis and Carol Barber, for encouraging us to pursue this edition and for their professional support in realizing it. Many thanks go to Jeremy Lowe for his concise work on proofing the texts and for Ute Dolezal (Potsdam) for the help with designing a map of global slum tourism destinations. Also, many thanks to Andreas Pott (Osnabrück) and Louise Dixey (Leeds Metropolitan University) for some great ideas. In addition, we would like to thank Manfred Rolfes in Potsdam for his continuous support and encouragement during the project. We would also like to thank all participants at the conference 'Destination Slum' in December 2010 for the discussions and debates that encouraged us to compile this publication. This also holds true for the members of the slum tourism research network (slumtourism.net) – an increasingly lively community in which to advance slum tourism research. Many thanks also go to the University of the West of England for supporting the production of this book and the conference through its early career research grant scheme. Finally, many thanks to our families, partners and friends for the support that made this book possible.

1 Development and globalization of a new trend in tourism

*Malte Steinbrink, Fabian Frenzel
and Ko Koens*

Over the last two decades, we have witnessed the development of slum tourism in an increasing number of destinations in the Global South. Slum tourism is unmistakably gaining in importance in terms of both economics and the numbers of tourists. It takes place in various ways, but the most obvious and established practices are guided tours – be they coach, van, jeep, quad, bicycle or walking tours. In some cities guided slum visits already constitute an important element in the range of offers made by the urban tourism industry.

Arguably, every new trend in tourism allows wider reflections on tourism itself. Questions arise as to why it emerges precisely at a particular point in time and in a particular social context, and as to how and with what consequences it develops in different local settings. Slum tourism in the Global South is one such new trend in international tourism. We argue that the main characteristic of this phenomenon – often also called 'slumming' – is the touristic valorization of poverty-stricken urban areas of the metropolises in so-called developing or emerging nations, which are visited primarily by tourists from the Global North.

At first sight, slum tourism may look surprising and startling since it contradicts common notions of what tourists do during their holidays. The wish to see and experience 'something else' and to 'distance oneself from everyday life', as expressed in common holiday motives, usually refers to beautiful and relaxing encounters. Slum tourism doesn't seem to correspond with these notions. This astonishment is often mirrored in the media. In order to find explanations for this 'extraordinary form of tourism' (Rolfes 2010), journalists especially tend to come up quickly with speculations about the tourists' motives, and these presumptions are often the starting point of ethical debates and judgements about slum tourism (Schimmelpfennig 2010). Academic research has started to reflect on slum tourism, and this book aims at advancing the debates developing in the field.

There are two principal ways to try to understand the new trend. The first is to analyse current practices and the ongoing construction of the 'destination slum' in the Global South. The second is to look at historical processes of destination-making and at comparable tourist practices in the past. Most of the chapters in this book follow the first path and reflect on slum tourism on the basis of recent case studies. We therefore start this book by providing a brief overview of the origins and development of slum tourism.

How it started: early slumming in the Global North

The creation of every new destination or type of destination draws upon more or less established images and ideas about unfamiliar and distant regions and their inhabitants (Pott 2007). These images refer to stocks of standardized, long-standing ascriptions that arise in discursive processes occurring both within and outside tourism. Tourists and the tourism industry seek for discursive connectivity, reproduce these ascriptions and/or create new meanings and images, while reacting to social structures and their changes. New forms of tourism often have historical forerunners. This also holds true for the new destination type of the slum in the Global South.

Curiosity about slums appears to be as old as the slum itself: the term 'slum' evolved in eighteenth-century London. Originally, 'slum' was a slang word – presumably of Irish origin – coined by slum dwellers. It only found its way into standard English around 1840, and was then used by upper-class Londoners to describe the East End. During the same period, the word 'slumming' evolved in London's 'West Side Lingo' (Steinbrink 2012). The term described a burgeoning practice of members of London's higher classes visiting the East End, often guided by police officers in civilian attire, journalists and clergymen. These early slummers were frequently wrapped in the cloak of concern, welfare and charity; however, this changed in the second half of the nineteenth century, when slumming developed into a more purpose-free leisure-time activity (Koven 2004).

In the 1880s, slumming emerged in New York, marking an increasing 'touristification' of the phenomenon. Wealthy tourists from London had imported slumming, eager to visit the poorer areas in New York (e.g. Bowery) in order to compare them with 'their' slums at home. Tourist guide books included routes for walking tours through various impoverished areas (Keeler 1902; Ingersoll 1906). Additionally, the first commercial tour companies specializing in guided slum visits were established in Manhattan, Chicago and San Francisco. In the early twentieth century, 'slum tourism' in a more narrow sense emerged for the first time, and slumming became an integral part of urban tourism (Cocks 2001: 174ff.).

The historic cases of slumming in London and the United States are quite well documented (Conforti 1996; Cocks 2001; Koven 2004; Ross 2007; Dowling 2009; Heap 2009; Steinbrink 2012; Seaton in this volume). These studies also point to continuities in the development of slum tourism, for example in the way that tourists gaze (Urry 2002) on slums seeking the 'low', the 'dark' – the 'unknown side of the city'. The examples demonstrate that the slum was discursively construed as well as touristically staged and experienced as 'the other side of the city', and as the 'place of the "Other"'. At the same time, they illustrate that this ascribed 'Other' had often been a lot more than just the 'economic "Other"' – the slum was more than just the 'place of poverty'. The slum was also a surface for the projection of a 'societal "Other"'. Dominant modes of social distinction were negotiated through the topography of urban landscapes. However, these dominant modes and characteristics of the 'Other' varied from one historical period to another and depended on the respective social context.

Steinbrink's (2012) reconstruction of the genesis of slum tourism discusses these changes: in the industrializing Victorian London, shaped by extremely rigid moral values and norms, the slums were seen as places of moral decay and libidinal liberty. The slum was socially constructed as the place of the 'immoral "Other"' ('moral slumming'). In the 'modern' US of the early twentieth century slumming took a different form. Between 1880 and 1920, millions of immigrants from eastern and southern Europe and from Asia entered the US, challenging the predominant understanding of the American identity as 'white, Anglo-Saxon and protestant'. The guided slumming tours of the time can be seen as a response to this. They predominantly visited ethnic urban enclaves and constructed immigrant communities as 'ethnic (pre-modern) "Other"' (with the most popular examples being 'China towns' and 'little Italies'). Through this 'ethnic slumming', the immigrant groups were symbolically assigned to their place – both spatially (i.e. within 'their' quarters) and socially (i.e. at the margins of society) (ibid.).

While slum tourism in the Global South has forerunners in the North, its occurrence and its remarkable dynamism in many so-called developing countries and emerging economies is new. The present globalization of this form of tourism can be understood as a further stage of development of slum tourism. The two examples of historic slumming in the North already indicate certain continuities and changes. The territorial ascription of the 'Other' in the slum seems to be a constant, whereas the formation of the respective 'Other' is subject to alteration depending on the social context. This insight might help when dealing with the recent phenomenon. It could mean examining slum tourism against the background of a globalized world society. Steinbrink and Pott (2010) point out that slumming in the Global South is no longer merely about 'the other side of the city', but essentially seems to concern the 'other side of the world' ('global slumming'). This brings the process of constructing a 'global or world-societal "Other"' to the foreground. Hence, the globalization of slum tourism needs further explanation. Questions arise regarding the interplay of the new global form and the local practices of slum tourism in different places, pointing at the importance of local factors in this process of 'glocalization' (Robertson 1995) of slumming.

In the next section, we briefly trace the occurrence of the phenomenon in different places in 'the South' and at different points in time in order to show how slum tourism spread across the globe and how it developed in different local settings. It can be seen as an attempt to illustrate the dynamics of its globalization.

The recent phenomenon: slumming in the Global South

To answer the question of when slum tourism in the South actually started evokes reflections about the definition of tourism. Already in Victorian London, pioneer 'slummers' went into slums for other reasons but leisure: there were journalists in search of a good story, academics looking for an interesting research field, and social reformers, political activists and 'helpers', either by profession or by altruism (Koven 2004). Such 'professional and altruist slummers' played an important role in the development of slum tourism historically. Professional slummers today continue to significantly shape the image of slums in the Global South through their photos, films and reports, contributing to the discursive production of the slum as an attraction. They are also actively involved in the development of the actual practice of slum tourism by taking other visitors into 'their' slums. While professional and altruist slummers pave the way for slum tourism, they can be differentiated from people who visit poor urban areas as a leisure-time activity ('leisure slummers'). We propose talking about slum tourism in a more narrow sense when the visits take place within the organizational context of tourism. Once the (slum) tourism infrastructure has developed in a particular destination, professional slummers will be likely to use this as well (e.g. researchers who stay in B & Bs situated in a slum or journalists who use commercial tour guides for their inquiries), and the lines between professional slummers and slum tourists blur.

The presence of professional and altruist slummers is not the only precondition for the development of slum tourism. While professional slummers are found in uncountable slums all over the world, organized slum tourism has only evolved in particular places. In the following section we present a list of slum tourism destinations that developed since the early 1990s, highlighting preconditions and initial impulses of their emergence. It is only a first step to trace the development in a comparative perspective and it remains a central research question for slum tourism research to better understand the specific conditions that enable slum tourism development in particular destinations (Frenzel in this volume).

It is widely accepted that the more recent form of slum tourism started in *South Africa* (Rogerson 2004; Mowforth and Munt 2009; Butler 2010; Rolfes 2010). During the time of apartheid, tours were already conducted in 'non-white group areas', both by the apartheid regime (as official tourist attractions), and by critical NGOs (non-governmental organizations) and political groups for international solidarity activists (Dondolo 2002; Frenzel in this volume). After the end of apartheid legislation and international sanctions, township tourism has expanded across all major cities in the country (with the main township destinations situated in Cape Town, Johannesburg and Durban). In Cape Town alone, tours are offered by forty to fifty operators. We estimate that, altogether, around 800,000 tourists currently participate in organized tours. Township tourism has become an integral part of city tourism in South Africa.

Parallel to the development of township tourism in post-apartheid South Africa, slum tourism also started in *Brazil*. The occurrence of favela tourism is linked with the United Nations Conference on Environment and Development (UNCED) in Rio de Janeiro in 1992, where journalists and political activists were the first to tour Rocinha, a settlement known as the largest favela in the city (Freire-Medeiros 2009; Frisch 2012; Frenzel in this volume). From these first informally guided tours a commercial tourism branch has grown, and about eight different commercial favela tour companies and about twenty independent guides are operating in the city today. We estimate that, in 2011, more than 50,000 tourists participated in organized favela visits in Rio. And this number will probably increase with the coming FIFA World Cup in 2014 and Olympic Games in 2016. More recently, favela tours are also offered in São Paulo and Salvador de Bahia.

The figures from Brazil and South Africa indicate that slum tourism is already a highly professionalized business in these two countries. This includes increasing diversification, particular in Cape Town and Rio de Janeiro. Apart from guided tours, both destinations now offer elements of adventure tourism (e.g. quad, bicycle and motorbike tours and even bungee jumping), accommodation in the slum and specialized tours focusing on music, food or ecological aspects.

In the meantime, slum tours have also emerged in other countries of the Global South, and this development is gaining in pace. It is difficult to give precise evidence of all different locations in the Global South where slum tourism is practised. Nevertheless, in the following paragraphs we have tried to provide a chronological overview of the places where slum tourism has been conducted in an organized form (see Figure 1.1).[1]

During the 1980s, the 'Smokey Mountains' in Manila in the *Philippines* had become a symbol for urban poverty in the Global South. In the early 1990s, a tour operator started offering tours to this huge garbage dump, where thousands of people lived and worked. To our knowledge these tours stopped in 1993, when the dump was closed. Most inhabitants had to move to Payatas, another dump, which collapsed in 2000 in a landslide that buried hundreds of people.

Another example of tours visiting a garbage dump is in Mazatlán, *Mexico*. From around 1997 an evangelical North American church community has offered 'garbage tours' to tourists from various resort zones and even from cruise ships stopping in Mazatlán. Half-day excursions are provided that start by driving through some of the city's poorer neighbourhoods and end with a visit to a local garbage dump and the people living and working there as garbage collectors (Dürr 2012). More recently, commercial slum tours have also started to be offered in impoverished neighbourhoods in Mexico City. Using names like 'undercover tours' or 'safari tours', the tours take tourists around feared 'barrios' such as Tepito.

Inspired by the experiences in South Africa, township tours have been offered in *Namibia* since the turn of the century. The main destination is

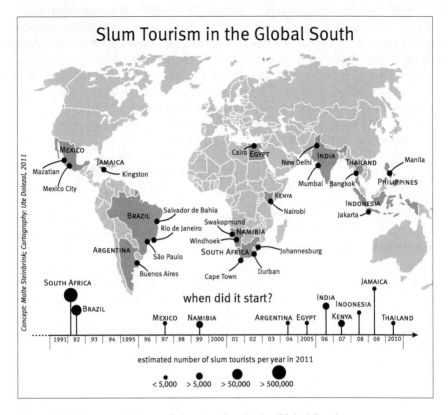

Figure 1.1 Times and places of slum tourism in the Global South.

Katutura, Windhoek – a settlement founded during the apartheid era after forcible evictions of African town dwellers in 1959. There are at least ten companies (including an official tour offered by the city council) specializing in township tours in Windhoek and two in Swakopmund (de Bruyn 2008).

In December 2004, slum tourism started in Argentina. A former movie location scout, Roisi Martin, started to offer visits to 'Villa 20' and 'Trava tours' (visits to a transvestite brothel in the red-light district in Buenos Aires) (Marrison 2005). Another company, 'Villa Tours', takes tourists to villas miserias on the outskirts of the city for US$70 a person. Since very recently, aerial tours have also been offered by a flight company:

> to allow a peek inside these mysterious communities, and to give people an idea of the 'miseré' in which the inhabitants live. This is the only safe, secure and unobtrusive way to get a glimpse of this gritty side of Argentina.
>
> (Buenos Aires Air Tours 2011)

In *Egypt*, slum tourism emerged in 2005 when American eco-activists T.H. and Sybille Culhane started 'Solar CITIES Urban Eco Tours'. Inspired by their experiences of urban eco tours in Rio's favelas and of eco township tours during the Earth Summit 2002 in Johannesburg, these urban planners developed an inner-city eco tour through the slums of Darb al-Ahmar and Manshiyat Nasser ('Garbage City') in Cairo, which is guided by local tour guides (Solar CITIES 2008).

One year later, in January 2006, English social worker Chris Way and his Indian counterpart Krishna Poojari started 'Reality Tours and Travel' in Mumbai, *India*, after Way had got to know of the concept of favela tourism in Rio de Janeiro in 2003. Slum tourism in India is noticeably expanding at present. A driving force for this development has been the huge media attention in the wake of eight-times Oscar-awarded Hollywood film *Slumdog Millio*naire (2008), which uses Dharavi, apparently the largest slum in Asia, as a backdrop (Meschkank 2010; Dyson 2012; Basu and Meschkank in this volume). Currently, an estimated 8,000 tourists take part in the slum tours annually, and several new tour operators have slowly started to enter the market in Mumbai and elsewhere in India (e.g. 'Be a Local Tours & Travel'; 'Mumbai Magic').

Slum tourism in *Kenya* started at the World Social Forum (WSF) that took place in Nairobi in 2007. Similar to the development of favela tourism in Rio, the first tours were provided for political activists, this time by NGOs that were active in the Kibera slum. This formed the basis of a growing slum tourism industry, and today a variety of commercial tour operators are active in Kibera, which is often labelled as the biggest slum of Africa (Mowforth and Munt 2009; Frenzel in this volume).

In Jakarta, *Indonesia*, Ronny Poluan was the first to start commercial slum tourism. After a period of unemployment, the former documentary filmmaker founded his company 'Jakarta Hidden Tours' in 2008. For a fee of US$56 for two people, the company offers one of five different tours leading to the slums of Ciliwung, Tanah Abang, Papango, Galur or Luar Batang (Febrina 2009). To our knowledge he is still the only one who offers organized slum tours in Indonesia.

In Kingston, *Jamaica*, organized slum visits have also recently emerged. The notorious slum area of Trenchtown is widely credited as being the root of ska, rocksteady and reggae music. Despite the prevailing poverty of the area, this neighbourhood has emerged as one of the most famous parts of Kingston. During the Cricket World Cup in 2007, informal local guides offered tours to the 'government yard' or the public housing project that Bob Marley made famous in his hit song 'No Woman, No Cry'. Expectations are that Trenchtown will increasingly attract international visitors, and that the touring business will be more professionalized now that the Trench Town Culture Yard was designated a Protected National Heritage Site in February 2009.

An entirely new development in slum tourism destination-making can be observed in Bangkok, *Thailand*. In all the other destinations in the Global South, individuals, small businesses or NGOs were the pioneers in organized slum tours, and bigger firms only later joined the market (e.g. in Cape Town). Contrastingly, in Bangkok it is the renowned tour operator 'Asian Trail', owned by Luzi Matzig (one of the most prominent personalities in Asian tourism), which opened up the market for commercial slum tourism. The Asian Trail proposes a tour to embark on a journey into Khlong Toei district, home to the largest slum in the capital city (Citrinot 2010).

As large and internationally operating destination management companies like Asian Trail enter the slum tourism market and start up opening up new destinations, the development of 'the slum' as a universal type of tourist destination reaches a further stage: slum tourism seems to have entered the realm of mainstream global tourism.

About this book: poverty, power and ethics

In December 2010, a conference called 'Destination Slum' was held in Bristol. It was the first academic conference to bring together researchers who currently work in the area of slum tourism. The event was attended by academics from thirteen countries and various disciplinary backgrounds. The idea was to explore a variety of cases of historical, recent and emerging slum tourism destinations, and to start conceptualizing and situating this phenomenon on the basis of interdisciplinary comparisons.

The conference in Bristol mainly set out to ask questions and to start the process of answering them. The chapters in this book, as well as special issue 14(2) of the journal *Tourism Geographies* (Frenzel and Koens 2012), offer a selection of the presented papers. In choosing the chapters for this book we have reflected on the main issues that were discussed at the conference and have sought to find the dialogue between the different papers.

The subtitle of this book, 'poverty, power and ethics', highlights the importance of these three concepts – mirrored in most academic work on the subject – when dealing with slum tourism (see Figure 1.2).

In broader tourism research, poverty, power and ethics are core issues. They are in the centre of a wide range of academic debates, each with long traditions. This introduction is not the place to display these debates, but the chapters of the book refer to them from a variety of angles. By explicitly pointing at the nexus between these three terms, we would like to draw attention to their relevance to the emerging field of study. We use them for structuring some emerging questions concerning the phenomenon of slum tourism.

Poverty's relevance for the study of slum tourism results first and foremost from the fact that poverty is the defining feature and lowest common denominator of what is usually defined as 'slum' (UN 2003). And poverty also seems to be the main attraction: it appears plausible to assume that the attractiveness of slums as tourist destinations is often directly connected with conceptions and associations tourists have of the places they intend to visit (tourists want to see what they expect to see). Confirmed by empirical studies on the expectations of slum tourists, 'poverty' is in the centre of the semantic

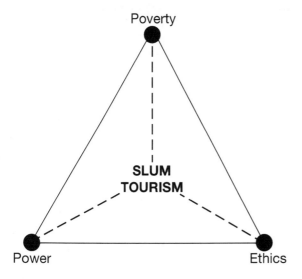

Figure 1.2 Slum tourism: poverty, power and ethics.

field evoked by terms such as 'township' and 'slum' (Rolfes *et al.* 2009; Meschkank 2010; Rolfes 2010). Is it therefore appropriate to talk about slum tourism as a kind of 'poverty tourism'?

Poverty is also central for slum tourism because slum tourism is often viewed and marketed as having the potential to stimulate local entrepreneurship and local economic development, and to support poverty alleviation. Is slum tourism then a kind of 'pro-poor tourism'? And do we then have to deal with a paradox that this kind of tourism actually tries to overcome its own attractiveness?

The desire to see people living in poverty immediately raises concerns about the *ethics* of slum tourism. The accusation of voyeurism is often levelled against slum tourists. Slum tourism is heavily criticized in public discourses and morally judged in the media. Slum tourists from the North are criticized as immoral gawkers, and the tourist gaze on poverty is compared to a visit to a zoo and judged as distasteful. This judgement seems to be so fundamentally evident that the question of why it is considered as ethically wrong to look at the poor is rarely asked, nor is the question of how such a moralizing view on slum tourism influences its form and practice.

The ethical dimension also touches on the topic of representation. First, questions arise in regard to slum tourism's relationship to what has been called 'literary' slumming (Williams 2008). Slums are not only displayed in tourism but in a variety of other forms, such as films, literature and fashion (Freire-Medeiros 2009; Linke 2012). These representations discursively shape the image of the slum, and thereby create the tourists' curiousness and interests.

In some cases, films and books even directly trigger the occurrence of slum tourism (Mendes 2010). The ethics of these representations are often as deeply contested as those of slum tourism; and the ethical scepticism concerning representations shows similar patterns. This leads to two other sets of questions: first, how are slums portrayed in slum tourism? Who decides what and how to showcase? Are the slum destinations represented in ways that are 'objective' or 'fair', or are they shown in a distorted manner, romanticized or dramatized? And what are the reasons and dynamics behind these practices and representations? Second, is the touristification of slums a form of exploitation of the poor? As the slum tours are sold to tourists they have value and, according to Freire-Medeiros (2009), commoditize poverty. But how is this done, and how is poverty valorized? Where is the value coming from; who has created it? If the slums are sold as a sight, who may profit from it? What value do tour operators add that justifies their role in the supply chain? Do they share the profits, do they support or initiate social projects or do they pay the slum dwellers for using the resource that is 'the slum' for the production of a tourist site? And if economic or social opportunities would arise from this form of tourism, would that be the end that morally justifies the means, if the means itself is considered as immoral?

All these questions directly relate to the concept of *power*. Indeed, poverty is often associated with powerlessness, and poverty definitions that go beyond quantitative monetary income-indicators usually involve notions of disempowerment in political, cultural and social terms (Scheyvens 2007; Mowforth and Munt 2009). The particular relevance of the question of power in slum tourism derives from the assumption of relative powerlessness of slum dwellers vis-à-vis the visiting tourists and the tour operators. Underlying the notion of social voyeurism seems to be the idea that tourists are more powerful than the poor they visit. It is for that reason that watching the poor is considered problematic. What are the mechanisms in which slum tourists and operators deal with this issue? How do tourists justify watching the poor in the light of these accusations? And how do slum tour operators respond? Furthermore, to what extent does power become relevant in the exchanges created in slum tourism? In the same context, slum tourism and the valorization of slums also relate to the broader discussion of urban governance, urban renewal and gentrification. How far are urban politics involved in that issue? Can slum tourism be a kind of an urban development tool, and who uses it, with what intentions? But reflections of power are not reducible to the practice on the local scale. Global power relations have been theorized in a variety of ways in respect of international tourism, in particular third-world travel. This concerns the ways in which certain narratives and imaginaries, including notions of the poor (or the South), are constructed, circulated, negotiated and modified in the practice of slum tourism. Core issues presented in this book are the power of narratives and imaginaries in shaping the slum tourism encounter, as well as the ways in which slum tourism functions as a means of reproduction or modification of these narratives.

Structure of the book

In the first section of the book, a range of chapters is assembled in order to situate slum tourism research in other fields of tourism research.

The chapter by Seaton, 'Wanting to live with common people . . .? The literary evolution of slumming', discusses a history of slumming that includes what has been called 'literary slumming' (Williams 2008) – the production and consumption of representations of slums. Drawing our attention to curiosity about the 'low life' evidenced as early as in the seventeenth-century literature on slums and poverty, Seaton sheds new light on the historical significance of the phenomenon. Following Seaton's argument, slum tourism can be situated as a specific form of the perception of poverty and slums, often comical, deriding and riddled with procedure and bigotry. His work shows that poverty has made good entertainment for some time and that, educational and political aims aside, the intentions of this entertainment were often rather unethical. Through extensive evidence from writers' descriptions of English and French slums over two centuries, Seaton sheds light on the aesthetics that govern slum perception. The political concerns that arise towards the social question in the nineteenth century are preceded by a perception of slums and poverty as an entertaining and natural part of life.

Frenzel's chapter, 'Beyond "Othering": the political roots of slum tourism', picks up on the question of how slum tourism relates to the social question – the political demand to deal with and end poverty. He does so by situating slum tourism in relation to political and justice tourism. Based on three case studies, he proposes a developmental model of slum tourism in which political events and specific contexts attracting political tourists seem to work as preconditions for slum tourism development. As political tourists enter the slums in three discussed cases, they create infrastructures that enable more mainstream tourists to follow in their footsteps. Observing the discursive changes from the early visits of political tourists to the development of slum tourism, Frenzel claims that, in the development of slum tourism in the three cases, the slums were increasingly displayed and discursively constructed as sites of cultural difference. This shift in discourse equally appeals to slum tourists, providers and local elites who are all concerned with the political and ethical implications of poverty. Local elites often reject slum visits by international visitors in the initial phases of slum tourism development. Tourists and providers must answer ethical accusations levelled against them as exploiters of the poor. Once slums are considered culturally different they can be seen as valuable and visitable. In this sense, slum tourism appears to be a response to the social question. Frenzel doubts that slum tourism provides a sufficient or appropriate answer, but argues that it indicates the development of a global social question.

The negative perception of (local) authorities is further discussed in Basu's contribution, 'Slum tourism: for the poor, by the poor'. She focuses on tourism to the Dharavi slum in Mumbai. Indian authorities strongly denounce these slum tours. Often this is done on ethical grounds, as tour operators are said to 'abuse' local people. Basu relates this response to the 'zeitgeist' in India, where the rapid proliferation of slums is seen as a blotch on India's success story of development and its rise as an international economic and political power. To highlight such parts of India through tourism is seen as problematic, particularly when tours market themselves with the concept of showing the 'reality' or 'authenticity' of India. This further irks authorities who feel it devalues the cultural and social heritage of other tourism attractions in the country. Basu questions the logic of an outright rejection of slum tourism on ethical grounds. She points to the conflict between criticizing slum tourism on ethical grounds, while at the same time endorsing it as a tool for economic development and poverty alleviation. Instead, she chooses to view slum tourism as a learning experience. By recounting a personal narrative of a visit to Dharavi, she provides examples of ways in which slum tourism could contribute to the debunking of myths, create a greater understanding of slums and increase appreciation of its inhabitants. When it comes to the question of how slum tours should be organized and/or regulated, Basu argues against prescribing unilateral recommendations. Instead, she advocates a participatory approach that goes beyond sharing some of the profits of the operations. She acknowledges the great difficulties in creating some sort of consensus from various extreme and diverse views, but argues that, 'if organized with a participatory, pragmatic and efficient approach, slum tourism can be made pro-poor and can also make significant contributions in slum development'.

Koens's contribution, 'Competition, cooperation and collaboration: business relations and power in township tourism', picks up from the question of how tourism might contribute to poverty relief. He looks closely at the theme of making tourism pro-poor in his investigation of using township tourism in and around Cape Town as a tool for local economic development through small-business participation. The location of South Africa is interesting, due to the emphasis officials put on small-business ownership for reducing poverty and achieving the social goal of empowering formerly disadvantaged individuals through black economic empowerment. Government views tourism as having great potential for achieving these goals, and has created a comprehensive, responsible tourism policy to support formerly disadvantaged individuals with small tourism businesses in order to build business relations with the existing tourism industry.

Using a framework that in turn focuses on competition, cooperation and collaboration, Koens draws attention to the ways in which frictions between small businesses hinder possibilities to create sustainable business relations. Intense competition disjoints relations of trust among small-business owners, and has created a 'fractured' business community in which power is an important asset. These issues can be grounded in the historical, structural and socio-economic position of small township business. In dealing with businesses from outside the township, small-business owners are acutely aware of their lack of business acumen and perceive difficulties in competing with established ('white') tour operators from outside the townships. Koens concludes that, although township tourism has certainly brought individual benefits that should not be underestimated, its total impact on local economic development is limited, and that township tourism should not be seen as a panacea.

The second part of the book looks at techniques, practices and problems of representation of poverty in slum tourism.

Menezes' chapter, 'A forgotten place to remember: reflections on the attempt to turn a favela into a museum', takes the case of a museum proposed to represent Rio de Janeiro's oldest favela. She discusses the difficulties of representing heritage, and the paradoxes that the museum comes up against in attempting to freeze authentic aspects of the favela in time. In negotiating techniques to make a whole area into an open-air museum, classical notions of what a museum is supposed to be are transcended. However, this becomes a problem for the museum itself, which is forgotten not only by tourists, but also by the residents themselves. With limited participation in the process of museum creation, residents expect a museum building to emerge, as they remain puzzled by the concept of an open-air museum. The tourists stay away as the project runs up against persisting security issues in the favela. Multiple politics of heritage and representation, conflated with trends in museum aesthetics and urban regeneration, overlap and end in failure. The irony of a forgotten place of memory can't escape the reader. The example of the forgotten museum should be carefully studied to avoid similar failures of more recent attempts by Rio de Janeiro's policy makers to valorize favelas for tourist consumption in a large-scale development project in preparation for the Summer Olympics and Soccer World Cup (*Tourism Review* 2010).

Baptista's chapter, 'Tourism of poverty: the value of being poor in the non-governmental order', looks at the power of discourses of poverty in creating spaces for intervention for 'moral tourists' and development agencies. Looking at a community-based tourism project in the village of Canhane in Mozambique, he considers the ways that poverty becomes valuable – a resource harnessed by international development agencies and tourism operators alike. Baptista's ethnographic study shows in detail the ways in which poverty becomes a discourse that enables tourists to assert their problematic role vis-à-vis the poverty they encounter as 'moral consumers' who contribute to the development of the visited sites. Tourism in Canhane is carefully orchestrated to maintain the image of the village as a 'development case'. Displayed to tourists are only those parts of the village that either confirm preconfigured notions of poverty and underdevelopment or have seen development that was enabled by the tourists and their developmental impact. Baptista shows how the case of Canhane relates to the current trend of community-based tourism (CBT). While CBT is broadly praised as a tool to enable democratic community-based development, Baptista's evidence suggests that CBT might much rather be a new form of powerful development discourse, by which the Canhane villagers find themselves in the need to reproduce the logic of this discourse in order to access funds. The power of tourism as a development tool, then, is not so much to eradicate poverty but to homogenize the notions of poverty and development with a clear bias that places tourists and development agencies in a position to solve these problems.

Meschkank's chapter, 'Negotiating poverty: the interplay between Dharavi's production and consumption as a tourist destination', studies the semantic transformation of dominant representations that slum tourism operators perform to make slum tourism work in the case of Dharavi, Mumbai. Thereby, the initial associations that tourists have with slums ('squalor, desperation, stagnation, crime and disease') need to be appealed to and confirmed in order for the tour to work as a business as well as a transformative experience. Indeed, the tour becomes a linguistic tool to reread the slum as a place that is positively valued ('enterprise, humour and non-stop activity'). Meschkank dissects this transformation in detail, and places it in a theoretical context of Niklas Luhmann's systems theory and its application to tourism studies (Pott 2007). This systems theory perspective not only opens up new insights into the particular case and on slum tourism in general, but also provides slum tourism research with a new theoretical apparatus to observe the logic in which its representational practice works.

A similar and yet stylistically radically different attempt is offered by the collaborative photo essay of King and Dovey, 'Reading the Bangkok slum'. The authors reject approaching the issue of representation purely linguistically, and instead provide a chapter about imageries and reactions to them. In displaying images of slum settlements in the Asian metropolis, they hope to provoke thoughts about the ways one might think about the slums, whether they are purposefully or accidentally confronted. As spectators tend to place their own interpretations on what they see, their images are not meant to provide straightforward answers to the issue of power in representation. Instead, they intend to highlight the contestability of every interpretation by way of provoking disagreement. Replicating the 'accidental' nature of many tourists chancing upon the slums of Bangkok, King and Dovey intend to make us consider the concept of slum tourism visually, without reverting to the much-rehearsed literature on the tourist gaze.

The third part of the book discusses potential interventions and other attempts to use slum tourism as a tool of empowerment.

Freire-Medeiros's contribution, 'Favela tourism: listening to local voices', is one of the first to provide a voice to the local population. In particular, she investigates the perspective of inhabitants of the favelas in Rio de Janeiro with regard to favela tourism. It is remarkable that the various debates with regard to slum tourism have until now taken so little account of local inhabitants, in particular as the ethical debates often deal with perceived negative consequences for them. As she argues, 'only a few researchers take into account the expectations, opinions and reactions expressed by the very population that they accuse others – in this case, tourism promoters and tourists – of objectifying'. This holds the danger they will essentialize and fetishize those that are affected by and are part of tourism in such areas.

She points out that favelas (and other slums) are diverse rather than uniformly poor. People also interpret and deal with favela tourism differently. Overall, the local outlook of local inhabitants may be best seen as a continuum rather than a dichotomy. On the one hand, they have a positive outlook as they recognize that tourism helps improve awareness of the favelas after a long history of discrimination and stigmatization. On the other hand, they are critical of the way Rocinha has been exploited as a tourist destination and can be suspicious of tourists' intentions or behaviour. Their 'reverse gaze' is important, as it influences not only the ethical dilemmas but also the way favela tourism is expressed. Residents and other parties involved in favela tourism constantly renegotiate their individual perspectives in dealing with each other, creating a shared space between each other.

A very different representation of the phenomenon of slum tourism is investigated by Ding's 'Slum tourism and inclusive urban development: reflections on China'. He views slum tourism as a form of niche tourism and claims that this perspective can help move it beyond moral critiques. To further his point he takes the reader to China and discusses three types of tourist interactions in the 'chengzhongcun' ('villages amid the city'), which can best be described as the Chinese equivalent of slums. The Chinese experience brings to the foreground interesting questions regarding the definition of slum tourism in different cultural and relational settings around the world. The Chinese case is different from slum tourism elsewhere in that all examples regard domestic slum tourism and show a great diversity of expression. In Hefei, an attempt has been made to use the slum as a medium to critically convey the conditions of poverty in China to a domestic audience of better-off Chinese through an art exhibition. Dafen village has become a popular tourist attraction due to the many artists who have gathered in the area (possibly due to the low rents). It has been heavily developed and may not even be seen as slum anymore. The third example that Ding investigates deals with the Times Museum of Guangzhou. Although the Times Museum is not built in a 'chengzhongcun' itself, it is strongly related to the surrounding 'chengzhongcuns'. Again a gaze can be observed, as the museum may be considered an 'urban observatory' of the dynamism between the city and the 'Other', that is, the 'chengzhongcun'.

Wattanawanyoo, in 'Poverty tourism as advocacy: a case in Bangkok', introduces a case study of advocacy on behalf of urban poor in the Thai capital. He presents the case of the Fort Maklon squatter community and its attempt to stay put in the old town of Bangkok. Wattanawanyoo engages in the field both as a researcher and as an urban activist, reporting on using tourism in an intervention to support a traditional community to be able to remain when threatened by increasing city development. His case provides an interesting inroad to reflect on the political role slum tourism can play in urban development conflicts and as an understanding of how what constitutes a valuable site differs between local elites and visiting international tourists.

Butler's 'Curatorial interventions in township tours: two trajectories' investigates the nature of contemporary township tours around Cape Town and Johannesburg. She discusses how township tours are complex cultural productions that have not only economic but also symbolic consequences, for both locals and visitors. The aim of the current tourist economy is to provide a good tourist experience, and this implicates township tours with regard to representation even when operators have good intentions. Difficult issues in encounters with poverty are suppressed, and initiatives to diffuse tourism voyeurism (e.g. walking tours) may intensify problems of exposure for poor communities. Butler proposes two 'curatorial interventions' that may serve to make these issues visible.

The first intervention deals with reversing the power dynamics involved in township tours by enabling township residents to photograph and interview tourists and exhibit the results. Such a project could serve to counter the proliferation of romantic and exotic representations of the 'Other'. At the same time it provides township residents with the opportunity to ask questions about their reasons for visiting and initiate discussions about difficult issues, such as their reasons for visiting marginalized communities while on holiday. The second intervention incorporates the unmarked 'white' world into a township tour. Current township tours inadvertently confirm spatial arrangements of apartheid, and create a binary opposition between blacks and whites and African and European heritage. By showing the inherent linkages between townships and other areas (e.g. by following the route of a local domestic worker on a township tour) it may be possible to break through this narrative. Furthermore, in this way it may be possible to show how communities are increasingly separated by class rather than by race. Butler recognizes that practical difficulties may prevent her proposed interventions from coming into existence. However, her chapter serves a purpose in questioning existing narratives of slum tourism and the way they represent slums, as well as showing possibilities for other ways of representation that view townships as integral to the city.

This book, and the special issue 14(2) of *Tourism Geography* on slum tourism (Frenzel and Koens 2012), present a broad section of slum tourism research that is currently taking place. They give an overview of the phenomenon, but many questions remain open or indeed will hopefully develop when reading this book. We hope that the variety of perspectives presented in this book provide useful insights that stipulate future discussions about this 'extraordinary form of tourism'.

Note

1   The authors would be very grateful for any further information concerning other (and new) slum tourism destinations in the Global South.

Bibliography

Buenos Aires Air Tours (2011) 'Villa Tours'. Available online at http://buenosaires airtours.wordpress.com/tours/villa-tours (accessed 21 October 2011).

Butler, S.R. (2010) 'Should I stay or should I go? Negotiating township tours in post-apartheid South Africa', *Journal of Tourism and Cultural Change*, 8(1–2): 15–29.

Citrinot, L. (2010) 'Asian Trails proposes another vision of Bangkok', *eTN: Global Travel Industry News*. Available online at www.eturbonews.com/15443/asian-trails-proposes-another-vision-bangkok (accessed 21 October 2011).

Cocks, C. (2001) *Doing the Town: The Rise of Urban Tourism in the United States, 1850–1915*, Berkeley, CA: University of California Press.

Conforti, J. (1996) 'Ghettos as tourism attractions', *Annals of Tourism Research*, 23(4): 830.

de Bruyn, E. (2008) 'Township tours – the other Africa', *Allgemeine Zeitung*, 23 May. Available online at www.az.com.na/tourismus/reiseberichte/township-tours-the-other-africa.67399.php (accessed 21 October 2011).

Dondolo, L. (2002) *The Construction of Public History and Tourism Destinations in Cape Town's Townships: A Study of Routes, Sites and Heritage*, Cape Town: University of the Western Cape.

Dowling, R.M. (2009) *Slumming in New York: From the Waterfront to Mythic Harlem*, Champaign, IL: University of Illinois Press.

Dürr, E. (2012) 'Encounters over garbage: tourists and lifestyle migrants at a Mexican dump', *Tourism Geographies*, 14(2): forthcoming.

Dyson, P. (2012) 'Slum tourism: representing and interpreting "reality" in Dharavi, Mumbai', *Tourism Geographies*, 14(2): forthcoming.

Febrina, A.S. (2009) 'Taking a tour on the poor side', *The Jakarta Post*. Available online at www.thejakartapost.com/news/2009/06/09/taking-a-tour-poor-side.html (accessed 21 October 2011).

Freire-Medeiros, B. (2009) 'The favela and its touristic transits', *Geoforum*, 40(4): 580–8.

Frenzel, F. and Koens, K. (2012) 'Slum tourism: developments in a young field of interdisciplinary tourism research', *Tourism Geographies*, 14(2): forthcoming.

Frisch, T. (2012) 'Glimpses of another world: the favela and its transformation from a "social exclusion area" into a touristic attraction', *Tourism Geographies*, 14(2): forthcoming.

Heap, C. (2009) *Slumming: Sexual and Racial Encounters in American Nightlife, 1885–1940*, Chicago, IL: Chicago University Press.

Ingersoll, E. (1906) *Handy Guide to New York City*, Chicago, IL: Rand McNally.

Keeler, C. (1902) *San Francisco and Thereabout*, San Francisco, CA: California Promotion Committee.

Koven, S. (2004) *Slumming: Sexual and Social Politics in Victorian London*, Princeton, NJ: Princeton University Press.

Linke, U. (2012) 'Mobile imaginaries, portable signs: the global consumption of iconic representations of slum life', *Tourism Geographies*, 14(2): forthcoming.

Marrison, J. (2005) 'Wise to the streets', *The Guardian*. Available online at www.guardian.co.uk/travel/2005/dec/15/argentina.buenosaires.darktourism (accessed 21 October 2011).

Mendes, A. (2010) 'Showcasing India unshining: film tourism in Danny Boyle's *Slumdog Millionaire*', *Third Text*, 24(4): 471–9.

18 *Malte Steinbrink, Fabian Frenzel and Ko Koens*

Meschkank, J. (2010) 'Investigations into slum tourism in Mumbai: poverty tourism and the tensions between different constructions of reality', *GeoJournal*, 76(1): 47–62.

Mowforth, M. and Munt, I. (2009) *Tourism and Sustainability: Development, Globalisation and New Tourism in the Third World*, 3rd edn, Abingdon: Routledge.

Pott, A. (2007) *Orte des Tourismus: Eine raum- und gesellschaftstheoretische Untersuchung*, Bielefeld: Transcript.

Robertson, R. (1995) 'Glocalization: time-space and homogeneity-heterogeneity', in M. Featherstone, S. Lash and R. Robertson (eds) *Global Modernities*, London: Sage.

Rogerson, C.M. (2004) 'Urban tourism and small tourism enterprise development in Johannesburg: the case of township tourism', *GeoJournal*, 60(1): 249–57.

Rolfes, M. (2010) 'Poverty tourism: theoretical reflections and empirical findings regarding an extraordinary form of tourism', *GeoJournal*, 75(5): 421–42.

——, Steinbrink, M. and Uhl, C. (2009) *Townships as Attraction: An Empirical Study of Township Tourism in Cape Town*, Potsdam: Universitätsverlag.

Ross, E. (2007) *Slum Travelers: Ladies and London Poverty, 1860–1920*, Berkeley, CA: University of California Press.

Scheyvens, R. (2007) 'Exploring the tourism-poverty nexus', *Current Issues in Tourism*, 10(2): 231. Available online at www.informaworld.com/10.2167/cit318.0 (accessed 14 July 2010).

Schimmelpfennig, S. (2010) 'The poverty tourism debate', *Good Intentions Are Not Enough*. Available online at http://goodintents.org/aid-debates/poverty-tourism (accessed 19 October 2011).

Solar CITIES (2008) 'Coming to Egypt? Why not take the Solar CITIES Tour!?' Available online at http://solarcities.blogspot.com/2008/03/coming-to-egypt-why-not-take-solar.html (accessed 21 October 2011).

Steinbrink, M. (2012) '"We did the slum!" Urban poverty tourism in historical perspective', *Tourism Geographies*, 14(2): forthcoming.

—— and Pott, A. (2010) 'Global slumming. Zur Genese und Globalisierung des Armutstourismus', in H. Wöhler, A. Pott and V. Denzer (eds) *Tourismusräume. Zur Soziokulturellen Konstruktion eines Globalen Phänomens*, Bielefeld: Transcript.

Tourism Review (2010) 'Rio offers a new tourist attraction: a tour to the slums'. Available online at www.tourism-review.com/rio-top-tour-welcome-to-the-slums-news2405 (accessed 8 August 2011).

UN (United Nations) (2003) *The Challenge of Slums: Global Report on Human Settlements, 2003*, London: Earthscan.

Urry, J. (2002) *The Tourist Gaze*, 2nd edn, Thousand Oaks, CA: Sage Publications.

Williams, C. (2008) 'Ghettourism and voyeurism, or challenging stereotypes and raising consciousness? Literary and non-literary forays into the favelas of Rio de Janeiro', *Bulletin of Latin American Research*, 27(4): 483–500.

Part I

Situating slum tourism

2 Wanting to live with common people[1] . . .?

The literary evolution of slumming

Tony Seaton

Introduction

How often in fairy tales do we hear of a poor person whose life is transformed after servants, sent forth by a king to search the land to find a subject who can accomplish a seemingly impossible task, return with news that the only one they can find to do it is a social nobody living in sub-prime accommodation? The lowly one is transplanted from hovel to palace, is royally rewarded and lives aristocratically ever after. Two aspects of this traditional narrative are worth noting. First, the king does not initially move out of his palace to lead the search party; he delegates the task to servants. Second, hardly ever is he looking for more than one subject – certainly not lengthy encounters with representative members of a whole underclass on their home ground.

In these reflections we can see how apparently untraditional is slumming. In the past, people of higher status did not go out of their way to consort with those of lower status. The word 'slum' is comparatively recent, and was first used as a slang term in the 1820s to mean 'street, alley, court etc. situated in a crowded district of a town or city and inhabited by people of a low class or by the very poor' (*OED* 1990: 2024). The activity of 'slumming' is even more recent, defined as 'visitation of slums, especially for charitable and philanthropic purposes' (ibid.).

These definitions suggest that slumming – contact between rich and poor in the territory of the latter – is a modern phenomenon, and that philanthropy is, at least nominally, a main motivation. This is the underlying premise in Koven's seminal study of slumming in nineteenth-century England and America (Koven 2004). His book narrates the history of social policy interventions by government departments, philanthropic agencies and charitable groups to ameliorate poverty in overcrowded cities, and the abusive practices (sexual exploitation, physical cruelty and neglect) that could accompany their operation. This essentially socio-political conception is one that applies to some, not all, of modern slum tourism, even though in the twenty-first century it may take place, not just in western capitals, but in shanty towns and townships within, or on the fringes of, expanding cities in developing countries (e.g. Rolfes *et al.* 2009; Meschkank 2011).

But this philanthropic conception of slumming is not the only way of viewing it. An alternative dictionary definition offers a less altruistic 'take' on slumming as: 'an excursion into slums out of curiosity or pleasure' (Merriam-Webster 1971: 2147). This hedonistic interpretation would seem at least as credible as the philanthropic view, given that slum tourism is a leisure activity – a province in which most people seek personal enjoyment. It is also an interpretation with a longer history than philanthropic slumming.

The purpose of this chapter is to sketch out a brief chronology of the origins and progress of slumming, and the connections between hedonism and philanthropy. It draws attention to the conditions of urban development in which slumming occurred, and how they were not just a problem for impoverished underclasses, but, at a socio-psychological level, conditions that affected everybody. It seeks to show how slumming involved issues of social control, ideology, cultural acquisition and existential performance that had their origins in urban representations and changing mythologies.

The chapter focuses mainly on literary and artistic sources of slumming history because, until late in the nineteenth century, it was writers and illustrators who were the slum travellers, and who recorded in newspapers, magazines and books what they saw in words and visual images. Through these representations they shaped public perceptions of slum dwellers and the lives they led, perceptions that persisted into the age of photography and the broadcast media.

Slumming in pre-industrial society

The history of slumming may broadly be divided into two major phases – pre-industrial and afterwards.

The beginnings of slumming

The first evidence of slumming occurs in literary texts that began to appear in sixteenth- and early seventeenth-century London (*c.*1540–1640). These were books and pamphlets that purported to describe the low life of the capital and the floating populations of vagabonds and unemployed itinerants who gravitated to it to find work and/or to pursue criminal careers. They comprised discharged serving men, ex-soldiers, evicted labourers, gypsies, seasonally unemployed artisans and people who had illegally left their parishes to seek a livelihood in the city. There were believed to be as many as 72,000 such itinerant 'rogues' in Henry VIII's reign (Judges 1930: xv).

The texts were written mainly by men we would today call 'hack' journalists and freelance writers, trying to make a living by using their encounters with underclasses as literary material. They revealed the scams, crimes and confidence tricks practised by 'vagabonds, thieves, rogues and cozeners', sometimes seeking credibility for these revelations by parading their familiarity with knowledge of the 'vulgar tongue, the coded slang spoken in the Elizabethan and Jacobean underworld (ibid.: xiii). A specimen of these works was *Caveat for Common Cursitors* (1567), by Thomas Harman, a country magistrate in Kent with professional knowledge of the 'Fraternity of Vagabonds'. His book identifies twenty-five types of low-life 'knave' who conned or robbed people on the streets. They included such exotic figures as the Abram Man, Palliard or Clapperdudgeon; the Upright man; the Frater; and the 'morts and doxies' of confidence tricksters. Harman has been praised for his 'determination to be . . . accurate and to document each of his exhibits as scrupulously as possible' (Delgado 1972: 23).

Harman's work was plagiarized and emulated by other writers in the same genre, including Robert Greene (*A Notable Discovery of Cozenage*, 1591; *The Second Part of Cony-catching*, 1591; *The Third Part of Cony-catching*, 1592; *A Disputation Between a He-cony-catcher and a She-cony-catcher*, 1592; and *The Black Book's Messenger*, 1592), Thomas Dekker (*The Seven Deadly Sins of London*, 1606; *The Bellman of London*, 1608; and *Lantern and Candlelight*, 1608) and Samuel Rid (*Martin Markwall, Beadle of Bridlewell*, 1610; and *The Art of Juggling*, 1612). Appraisals and examples of their work can be found in a seminal study by Aydelotte (1913), and compilations of early low-life texts have been edited by Judges (1930) and Delgado (1972 and 1992). Aydelotte and Judges have excellent introductory overviews of the economic and social conditions that made such large populations travel the country, fetching up in cities to find work and live on their wits.

These cautionary tales were aimed partly at Londoners and partly at visitors – the bumpkin up from the country or the foreign traveller in town on business. In both cases the aim was to alert them to the risks of crime and violence from strangers on the streets – a sort of printed 'Crime Watch' for the visitor. They were also almost certainly consumed, like true crime coverage today, as voyeuristic entertainment.

Augustan low life in London, 1690s–1720s: the world of Ned Ward and Tom Brown

Journalistic slumming and low-life narratives ended in the 1630s and 1640s with the English Civil War and the puritanical regime of Oliver Cromwell that followed it. The questionable pleasures of London (theatres, dancing, gaming, whoring) were censored and largely suppressed, and with them low-life travelogues. But after the Restoration of Charles II in 1660 there was a reaction to the repressive society of the Puritan interregnum and a revival of pleasures that were not just liberal, but often libertine. With them came literary slumming and cautionary tales of low life in the Tudor tradition, which persisted late into the following century. One of the most notorious of these productions was *The Tricks of the Town Laid Open*, an anonymous work first published in the 1690s but still in print in the 1740s. It purported to be a 'companion for country gentlemen' coming to town, written by a concerned Londoner attempting to dissuade them from making the trip. The book describes the perils that awaited them: gaming house confidence tricksters, whorehouse bawds and street conmen. Another work, *A Trip Through Town* (1735), begins: 'The town of London is a kind of large Forest of Wild-Beasts', and describes the 'real Causes of Debaucheries practis'd upon the Fair Sex' and the criminal activities that landed people in Newgate Gate prison, or got them hanged at Tyburn (Straus 1927: 111–13).

The king of post-Restoration, low-life travelogues was Ned Ward, a hack writer who published a series of sketches of the metropolis that were to be influential for two centuries. The series was called the *The London Spy* and was serialized in eighteen monthly parts between 1698 and 1700, and then issued in book form (Ward 1701). It was partly an entertainment guide to sights and events in London, including playhouses, fairs, music shops, the Old Bailey and so on. But its main content was a tour of disreputable dives of pleasure and low-life encounters, described in a vivid, bombastic style. One section was called 'Night-Accidents, the Whims and Frolicks of Staggering Bravadoes and Strolling Strumpets'. Ward's tours included a night in Billingsgate Fish Market, trips to the mad house of Bedlam and observations of punishments inflicted in the Bridlewell House of Correction. There he watched prison inmates on the treadmill, and voyeuristically deplored the sight of 'bare breasted young girls ... [more] design'd to feast the Eyes of the Spectators, or stir up the Beastly Appetites of Lascivious Persons, than to Correct Vice, or Reform Manners'. Ward set precedents for low-life reporting for the next two centuries and, in his biographer's judgement, he was the first writer who 'discovered the city of London for the journalist' (Troyer 1946: 59).

A contemporary of Ward was Tom Brown, who also travelled on foot through London and offered a kind of *Time Out* guide to its sights. They included respectable ones, such as Westminster Abbey, St James's Park, Presbyterian and Quaker meeting houses and coffee houses for the old and young. But he also reported on bawdy houses and low taverns, including one described as 'a little Sodom, where as many vices are daily practis'd, as ever were known'. He recounted prurient tales of vice and tragedy, including that of '. . . a harlot in St James, that hang'd herself for an Irish Captain, and was unluckily cut down by her maid'. Both Ward and Brown reported on what today would be called 'sex tourism' – a pursuit that was particularly rife in poor areas, as is still the case today.

By the mid-eighteenth century London was infamous for its low-life culture, in which vice and crime were widespread, and corporal punishment and public executions were available as tourist spectacles. Hogarth's engravings depicted this world. In the 1780s there appeared multi-volume works of *The Newgate Calendar* – containing biographies of criminals with engravings of their crimes or executions – that enjoyed popularity for several decades.

Regency low life of the 1820s: Tom and Jerry 'on the town'

The last throws of this robust and largely amoral tradition of literary slumming came in the first two decades of the nineteenth century, with the sensational success of a work called *Life in London or, the Day and Night Scenes of Jerry Hawthorn, esq., and his elegant friend, Corinthian Tom, accompanied by Bob Logic, the Oxonian, in their rambles and Sprees through the Metropolis*. It was written by Pierce Egan (1772–1849), a journalist born in the London suburbs, who knew the criminal and sporting world of the metropolis – including its appeal to young aristocrats (Reid 1971). *Life in London* was a monthly serial publication, published as a book in 1822, illustrated by thirty-six coloured, aquatint engravings by George Cruikshank (1792–1878). The protagonists were Tom and Jerry, two young gentlemen about town, who roistered their way around London, taking in high-class joints (Piccadilly, Tattersall's), sporting gaffs, low dives in Billingsgate fish market and districts of prostitution (Low 1999: 99–122). The book was a great popular success and started a craze that was exploited in theatrical adaptations, commercial merchandizing (which included ceramic mementos and printed ephemera) and literary plagiarisms with titles such as *Real Life in London*, *Life in Ireland* and *Life in Paris* (Hindley n.d.). The rumbustious world of picaresque touring it depicted has been said to prefigure Dickens' *Sketches by Boz* and *The Pickwick Papers*.

Almost contemporaneous with Egan's work was a pseudonymous one, unashamedly copied from Ned Ward's work a hundred years earlier: *The English Spy*, by Thomas Malloy Westmacott ('Blackmantle' 1826). A two-volume work illustrated with seventy-two coloured plates, it was a prurient exposé of vice and intrigue in London and other fashionable haunts where the rich took their pleasures, including Cowes and Brighton.

Industrialization and nineteenth-century slumming in London and Paris

All the instances of literary slumming just considered involved no agendas of philanthropic action or social reform. Even accounts apparently offering cautionary warnings of crime and vice could equally be read as titillating accounts, or even as tour guides. The works of Ned Ward, Tom Brown and Pierce Egan were not solemn in tone, but knockabout and farcical.

But, from the 1830s onwards, slumming in London and another great European capital, Paris, began to assume a new moral dimension (Steinbrink 2012). Both cities were undergoing geographical and socio-cultural crises and transformations that were qualitative and quantitative, the effects of which were to alter the nature and variety of encounters between classes, and with them the practice of slumming. Three main social developments affected both cities: rapid population growth; high levels of urban poverty; and interventions by public agencies, governmental and charitable, in managing urban dysfunctions that were physical and moral.

Nineteenth-century population growth

In 1809, London had a population just touching one million; Paris had just over half of that. By 1850, London had over two million and Paris more than one million. A decade later, London had three million inhabitants and Paris two million. By 1901, London had more than four million and Paris just under three million. Both cities had grown in a century by between four and five times. In Britain there was also an exponential growth in cities outside London. In 1800, there was not one town outside London with a population of 100,000; by 1891 there were twenty-three (Keating 1971: 11).

The effects of these urban population explosions were both psychological and physical. The psychological effect was to induce a kind of imaginative paralysis in the face of the numbing impact of population numbers, density and geographical dispersion. Citizens in towns of 10,000 to 30,000 inhabitants can form some coherent view of the town, but once the total reaches a million, and the urbanization spreads for miles, then the world becomes less and less decipherable. For long-time residents, incomers and temporary visitors from other less populous places, the enormity and anonymity of the spreading city were astonishing, stressful and exhausting. Simmel, the first sociologist to theorize the micro-phenomenology of urbanization, compared city life with rural life, and concluded that rural impressions used up:

> less consciousness than does the rapid crowding of changing images . . . and the unexpectedness of onrushing of impressions [in cities] . . . The metropolis exacts from man as a discriminating creature a different amount of consciousness than does rural life.
>
> (1950: 410)

A mid-century historian of London, marvelling at its relentless growth, spoke in less abstract terms of:

> new manners and customs, new diseases, new follies, new social complications [that] would arise, from the fact of three millions of men silently agreeing to live together on eleven square miles of land; when fish would cease to inhabit the poisoned river, when the roar of traffic would render it almost impossible to converse; when in fact, London would get too large for comfort, safety, pleasure or even intercourse.
>
> (Thornbury 1865: 2)

Poverty and pathology: the Victorian city as problem

In the wake of population increases came poverty and overcrowding that produced appalling living conditions and disease for many across several English industrial cities – Manchester, Leeds, Wigan, Sheffield and the capital. The reasons were a combination of unemployment and low wages, particularly among unskilled workers arriving from the countryside. In France, Paris was the main centre of urban distress, since it did not have the regional industrial development of Britain's northern cities.

And as these urban conditions worsened with time there was another consequence, more marked in London than in Paris – a growing social segregation. The classes became polarized geographically as workers concentrated in places of intensive economic activity, while those who could afford it moved away from such areas due to the industrial ugliness and health hazards they produced. There was what a leading historical demographer has called a move 'from multi-purpose to single-purpose neighbourhoods' that produced a residential climate in which 'strict social segregation became a prerequisite for success in any new development' (Olsen 1973: 266–8).

Both the psychological and physical effects turned the city into a great unknown – a spreading wilderness of endless streets and numberless people, in which segregated groups existed in their own world, some in strange and terrible circumstances of poverty, degradation and criminality. But nobody was quite sure to what extent. Such a picture awakened humanitarian feelings, but it also cast a political shadow. In France and Britain, concern for the welfare of the urban poor went hand in hand with fears about social unrest and the threats to public order possibly incubating among them, particularly during the 1840s and 1850s.

Public policy, governmental investigations and social surveys

In London and Paris, the social problems associated with rapid urbanization were taken up by national and regional governments, and by religious and philanthropic agencies. Both set about engaging with the lower orders in order to relieve their suffering and manage them.

The first need was diagnostic – to anatomize and measure the extent of the problems. The 1830s saw the first widespread application of social science methodologies, using surveys and statistics to track social conditions in France and England. In England these took the form of government reports and commissions into problems of health, housing, working conditions, sanitary arrangements and crime. One of the first great governmental inquiries was the Poor Law report of 1834, which comprised twenty-two volumes on social conditions (Checkland and Checkland 1974). Throughout the century the quantity of statistics on the condition, health and sanitary conditions of the poor continued (see Stedman-Jones 1971; Koven 2004).

Philanthropic bodies, comprising charities, religious groups and individual activists, also attempted to diagnose and alleviate social suffering in London and elsewhere. Their number and activities increased as the century wore on. They included Dr Barnado's, the Salvation Army, inner-city missions (Howat and Nicholls 2003), pro-social private initiatives by figures such as Charles Booth, and organizations such as the Rowntree Trust. These philanthropic initiatives were reported in several contexts: Annual Reports of the Charity

Organization Society and District Committees from the 1870s (Stedman-Jones 1971), and book-length narratives by individual members (e.g. Weylland *c.*1875; Smith 1889). In France, worsening social conditions for the labouring classes in Paris, particularly in the 1840s and 1850s, provoked similar initiatives, including surveys into the extent and dimensions of poverty. Sheon has called the 1830s and 1840s in France 'the first modern statistical age' (1984: 139).

All these initiatives brought middle-class reformers and policy makers into cross-class encounters with the poor on a scale that had never previously existed. For the first time, there were significant numbers of comfortably off people slumming through conviction and a desire to relieve social distress.

Growth of the press, journalism and writers

There was also a quite different social development that provoked literary slumming in France and Britain. This was the rise of the press and the development of the journalistic role, and with them the evolution of new urban ideologies and myths. From the early years of the nineteenth century, technology increased the speed and volume, and reduced the cost, of printing. Newspaper circulations increased every year and, by the 1840s, daily newspapers were joined by mass-circulation, weekly illustrated magazines, comic and serious (Fox 1977). Reading them became a national habit in both countries. In England, editors discovered that one of the subjects that consistently appealed to readers was content on what came to be called 'the condition of England question', and the urban suffering and criminality often involved. In response to this, public interest reporters began to evolve as social truth-tellers, seeking out facts and stories about low life. Naturally peripatetic, they would go anywhere and associate with all sorts, haunting law courts, drinking in pubs and clubs and spending time pounding the streets. Some, mainly young, writers started as 'penny-a-liners', who lived a hand-to-mouth existence without a fixed position on a single newspaper, paid by the line by whomever they could sell a story to. It was in their interests to seek out the odd, the sensational and the socially harrowing to keep this precarious income flowing.

Some journalists made names as low-life specialists, representing their slum travels as voyages of social exploration and themselves as forensic investigators trawling the lower depths, dredging up terrible realities for the armchair reader at home in Peckham, Holloway and Norwood. The titles of some collections – *Sinks of London Laid Open* (Anon. 1848) and *The Night Side of London* (Ritchie 1858) – reflected a sensational spin that did not necessarily mean that they served no useful purpose in exposing social evils and even proposing remedies. A book by the editor of *The Builder* magazine, *Town Swamps and Social Bridges* (Godwin 1859), despite its extravagant title, anatomized the terrible living conditions of the poor, but tabled innovative solutions for improvement. This question – whether cross-class encounters by journalists represented humanitarian concern or sensationalistic exploitation for voyeuristic readers – is one posed by many, if not all, literary slumming texts. This can be gauged by sampling texts of some of the writers who achieved celebrity in Victorian literary slumming.

Engels and the English city

Karl Marx and Friedrich Engels have commonly been represented as aging, bearded patriarchs fulminating on class war and revolutionary theory. But in 1844 Engels was a young, radical student in his twenties, despatched to Manchester by his father to learn the family business in the cotton mills of Lancashire. Instead of paying attention to business, he spent most of his time mixing with, observing and recording the lives of urban workers in Manchester, exploring London, and gathering information on other British industrial cities. The result of his observations was a path-breaking book, *The Condition of the Working Class in England in 1844*. In it he described the evil conditions in which labourers lived and worked, tracing the reasons back to the effects of the capitalistic economic system. His first impression of London was its vast extent: 'London is unique, because it is a city in which one can roam for hours without leaving the built-up area and without seeing the slightest sign of the approach of open country' (Engels 1844/1928: 30).

Thereafter, it was the impenetrable squalor of the metropolis that affected him, with its:

> thousands of hidden alleys and passages where the houses are so bad that no one with an iota of self-respect would live in them unless forced to do so by dire poverty. Such dens are often to be found close to the splendid mansions of the wealthy.
>
> (Ibid.: 34)

And there were people even worse off – the homeless. 'Every morning', commented Engels, 'fifty-thousand Londoners wake up not knowing where they are going to sleep at night' (ibid.: 37–8).

But it was Manchester that Engels described at greatest length and with greatest indignation, recounting personal observations gleaned from his explorations made over a period of twenty-two months: 'I know Manchester as well as I know my native town and I know more about it than most of its inhabitants' (ibid.: 51). He documented how 40,000 people, about a quarter of the population of Greater Manchester and its suburbs, lived in cellars he regarded as unfit for human habitation. He saw working people in populous districts cheated by unscrupulous retailers, and their children running around without shoes (ibid.: 78–85). He also noticed in his walks that, due to the segregated layouts of the middle-class and working-class districts, it was possible for well-off people to travel without ever seeing a slum (ibid.: 54).

His descriptions of industrial labour in other British towns and cities – Birmingham, Leeds, Dublin, Edinburgh, Nottingham and Glasgow – were more heavily based on secondary sources such as newspaper articles and official surveys. In nearly all cases he ended with indictments of the 'barbarous indifference' and 'selfish egotism' he saw everywhere, and the evidence of 'social conflict' and 'class warfare open and shameless'. Anticipating accusations of exaggeration he added to his account of Manchester:

> On re-reading my description of the Old Town I must admit that, far from having exaggerated anything, I have not written vividly enough to impress the reader with the filth and dilapidation of a district which is quite unfit for human habitation.
>
> (Ibid.: 63)

For many years, Engels' work was relatively ignored, but in 1973 Marcus published a notable reclamation that asserted its status as social document and literature (Marcus 1973).

Henry Mayhew and the London poor

Henry Mayhew was one of three brothers who began their literary careers writing theatrical entertainments, charades and sketches for comic magazines. He was briefly editor of *Punch* magazine, which started life as a radical comic journal, but quickly became more conservative.

Mayhew's enduring legacy is a monumental work called *London Labour and the London Poor*, a series of interviews with London's under-classes, intended as 'a cyclopaedia of the industry, the want, and the vice of the great Metropolis'. He rightly defined it as 'the first attempt to publish the history of a people, from the lips of the people themselves' (Mayhew n.d. – 1862, vol. 1: iii). It had been stimulated by his previous work as London interviewer in a larger, national survey of the poor, sponsored by a newspaper, the *Morning Chronicle* (see Thompson and Yeo 1971). The work provides an extraordinary, vernacular picture of life in the London streets among the poorest of the poor – street sellers, crossing sweepers, rubbish scavengers and rat killers. The late E.P. Thompson hailed Mayhew as the first social survey interviewer. His methodological skill in getting his respondents to talk frankly after short acquaintance supports Simmel's intuition that: 'the stranger often receives the most surprising openness – confidences which sometimes have the character of a confessional and which would be carefully withheld from a more closely [organically] related person' (1950: 404).

But Mayhew's work was not just a compilation of interviews. Like modern social scientists, he attempted to categorize and theorize the data. He divided the people he interviewed into two occupational categories: 'wanderers' and 'fixed'; and within those categories, three more: 'those who will work; can't work; won't work'. From these typologies he organized his massive study into four double-column volumes, and then added an extra volume on London prison life – a total of over two million words that exceeded the length of the Bible (Hughes 1969: 526).

Mayhew's astonishing literary achievement was greatly assisted by an associate whose contribution has been less acclaimed than his. This was a photographer called Beard, who took striking daguerreotype photographs of the London poor. At that time, individual portrait photography was rapidly developing, but there was no way of mass-reproducing the photographs in books. The problem was overcome by taking Beard's immensely realistic portraits and then engraving them on to wooden blocks, which could then be reproduced in quantity.

Little is known of Mayhew's later life after his work on *London Labour*, but he is now recognized as the first and greatest slum journalist to give an authentic voice to groups commonly excluded from written records (Hughes 1969; Razzell and Wainright 1973; Humphreys 1977; Mayhew 1985).

George Augustus Sala – low life, bon viveur

If Engels and Mayhew represent the committed, socio-scientific wing of literary slumming, George Augustus Sala typifies the more tawdry aspects of the entertainer who knows a good story when he sees one. The child of a theatrical family, he spent much of his early life backstage among actors and literary folk, and loafed around London in questionable company, doing not a lot with nobody in particular. He wrote:

> With low life I was perhaps more conversant than I should have been: in fact, as I have elsewhere hinted, it would have been difficult to have found in London town a more outrageous Mohawk than I had been in the last five years.
>
> (Sala 1896a: 10)

Yet despite, or perhaps because of, this peripatetic lifestyle, Sala became a sharp-eyed observer of many social scenes. He also developed multi-tasking skills as a dramatist, reporter, travel writer, society novelist and author of pulp fiction (in those days called 'penny dreadfuls') – and, it is said, as an anonymous pornographer. He was also a comic artist who, despite an eye condition that worsened with age, drew panoramas, designed stage sets and decorated restaurants (Straus 1942).

His first London article was an account of returning home in the early hours after some unspecified jaunt and, finding he had no key, wandering the streets all night. He sent an unsolicited account of this to a magazine that was published as 'The key of the street'. Thereafter, he became a regular chronicler of London life, high and low, for more than thirty years (Sala 1860a and 1896a). A Londoner who knew upper-class Whitehall as well as working-class

Whitechapel, he was one of the earliest to write up the East End, twenty years before it achieved mythic status in the 1880s. He was proud of his slumming expertise:

> There are not half a dozen persons of my acquaintance who can tell me where Bethnal Green is. As to Ratcliffe Highway, Shadwell, Poplar, Limehouse, and Rotherhithe, they are entirely terrae incognitae to shoals of born-and-bred Londoners.
>
> (Sala 1860a: 254)

His most successful book, *Twice Round the Clock* (Sala 1860b) was suggested to him by Dickens. It was a rerun of one published a century before that provided an hour-by-hour account of a London day and night. It was copied 100 years later by Stephen Graham (1933).

Percy Cruikshank and the service workers

Percy Cruikshank is a little-known figure who produced one fascinating low-life text, *Sunday Scenes in London and the Suburbs* (1854; see Figure 2.1). It is not about emiserated industrial labourers or street urchins, but two less conspicuously oppressed groups – domestic servants and shop assistants. Cruikshank believed there were 100,000 retail workers in London, who, he said, 'pass from twelve to fourteen, and even sixteen, hours on their feet, in close atmosphere, contaminated with human breath, thickened with dust, poisoned with gas!' (ibid.: 5).

Sunday was the one free day workers had for leisure from their long hours of retail and domestic drudgery. Yet these brief pleasures were under threat from the Lord's Day Observance Society, an evangelical lobby whose aim was to ban commercial entertainments on the Sabbath. It had recently invoked an ancient law to get workers excluded from a popular Sunday pastime – walking in the parks and gardens of the Crystal Palace and its Conservatory. Cruikshank took up the cudgel against the Society in the same way that his namesake, the great caricaturist George Cruikshank, had opposed similar Sabbath observance lobbies a generation before (Cruikshank 1833). He described and illustrated with large, fold-out lithographs some of the harmless activities and cheap haunts of shop assistants that were threatened by the Lord's Day Observers. They included the Sunday morning market in New Cut, Lambeth, river trips by steamer down the Thames to Gravesend, rides on swings and roundabouts in the pub gardens of Chalk Farm and fortune-telling in Cremorne Gardens. All were popular recreations, rarely celebrated in word or image. In contrast with the crowds enjoying these leisure scenes, Cruikshank pointedly included a pull-out plate of a church, near empty, 'St Peter Le Poor, in Old Broad St.', in the City of London. He ironically dedicated the work to the Lord's Day Observance Society 'without permission' (ibid.).

Figure 2.1 Percy Cruikshank's 'Sunday Scenes in London', 1853–1854

James Greenwood – the doss house reporter

In the last three decades of the nineteenth century, James Greenwood achieved journalistic notoriety as a kind of special correspondent and literary tour guide to an exoticized other world of low life in London and parts of provincial England, which was to be repeated in the early careers of later slum narrators such as Jack London (1903) and George Orwell (1933).

The younger brother of a successful London editor, Greenwood made his literary debut in 1866 with a three-part series of articles on life among the down-and-outs of London, based on spending a night in a workhouse. The article, 'A night in a casual ward', helped to establish his brother's monthly magazine, the *Pall Mall Gazette*, and on the strength of this success he adopted the nickname of the 'Amateur Casual', a kind of branded identity promising vicarious excursions into the world of the outcast. He wrote scores of articles for the London daily press that were collected into illustrated books, with titles that suggested travels into localities of feral otherness: *The Seven Curses of London* (1869), *Unsentimental Journeys Through London or the Byways of Modern Babylon* (1867, 1870), *In Strange Company* (1874), *The Wilds of London* (1874), *Low-life Deeps* (1881), *Mysteries of Modern London* (1883), *Odd People in Odd Places* (1883) and *Toilers in London* (1883). Once again, though the titles were sensational, their impact had value, as Keating noted: 'At best these reports combine astute observation, an inexhaustible curiosity, and strong humanitarian feeling, making his low-life studies valuable documents' (1971: 38).

G.R. Sims – sentimental balladeer and social realist

George Sims, like Mayhew and Sala (both of whom he knew), was a writer with an intimate knowledge of London that he turned to commercial effect in work that was partly melodramatic showmanship and partly pro-social investigative journalism.

He first wrote for comic magazines and the theatre, but made his name with a series of tear-jerking performance poems, the *Dagonet Ballads*, and other works that told low-life tales of motherless orphans, drunken fathers and desperate wives. Two of them – 'Christmas day in the workhouse' and 'Nellie's prayer' – became popular music-hall numbers. On the strength of his poetical concern with the poor, he was approached by a School Board officer in Southwark, one of the poorest parts of London, to visit the area and write prose, rather than ballads, about what he saw. Accompanied by Fred Barnard, a successful artist, he travelled for a month through a borough that, in his words, offered 'the vilest and most insanitary conditions in the capital of the British Empire', mixing with the destitute, the diseased and the dying, as well as pickpockets, thieves and burglars. The result was a series of illustrated articles in the *Pictorial World*, called 'How the poor live', which created a sensation and made slumming fashionable for a time (Sims 1906a; see Figures 2.2 and 2.3). He quickly published a follow-up book that was more crime-oriented

Figure 2.2 G.R. Sims' 'How the poor live', 1883: Sleeping rough

Figure 2.3 G.R. Sims' 'How the poor live', 1883: Street fight between women

(Sims 1906b). He also edited a remarkable, three-volume survey of Edwardian London that was a social and occupational gazetteer of what went on, where and by whom, and was profusely illustrated with photographs (Sims 1906c).

Sims's heyday lasted until the 1880s, when a new generation of Fleet Street editors pioneered the 'new journalism' that professionalized routine low-life coverage and investigative journalism at a more institutional level (Baylen 1972).

Myths of London and Paris

Cities are not just physical and social entities. They acquire symbolic meanings that lend them a mythic character that is partly caught in the notion of 'place image'. The symbolic meanings are established through representation – oral, literary and visual narratives. The effect of the intense illustrative and literary output of texts about London and Paris in the nineteenth century was a proliferation of mythic conceptions about each city.

London

The works that contributed to London's image were not just the slumming texts appraised earlier. They included multi-volume histories (e.g. Knight 1851; Thornbury *c.*1870; Sims 1906c), substantial handbooks for visitors (Cunningham 1849; Knight 1851; Weale 1851) and street directories in the days before London had been divided into postal districts (Elmes 1831). But it was mass-circulation newspapers, weekly illustrated magazines, such as the *Illustrated London News* and *Graphic*, and literary slumming works that had greatest impact upon the perceived images of poverty and crime in nineteenth-century London and Paris.

The myths came in two forms – totalizing and differentiated. The former were myths, sometimes found in book titles, which presumed to summarize the city in a phrase. London was variously described as: 'The infernal Wen' (by the journalist William Cobbett (Sheppard 1971: 83)); 'Babylon the Great' (by Robert Mudie (Anon. 1828)); and the 'Great Metropolis' (by another journalist, James Grant (1836)). It was also regularly characterized in images of night and darkness. *The Night Side of London* was the title of two books published over a fifty-year period (Ritchie 1858 and Machray 1902), and the Salvation Army regularly referred to 'Darkest London' (Law 1889; Booth 1890), as did Jay (1891).

A frequent trope in the constructed imaginary of London was the myth of London as two worlds. In the same way that writers such as Carlyle, Gaskell and Disraeli in the 1840s envisaged England as 'Two Nations' – the industrial poor in the North and those in South – so London was seen as a city divided into two worlds, of wealth and want, in which one half of the city did not know how the other half lived (e.g. Garwood 1853). The radical *Punch* editor, Douglas Jerrold, put names to locations in this binary divide in an eponymous story, 'St Giles and St James', the former signifying grinding poverty, and St James the leisured and pleasured world of 'society' (Jerrold 1851).

The mythology of London went beyond bipolar differentiation. Specific districts and even individual streets were accorded mythic notoriety at various times, making London appear as many micro-geographies within one geography (Steinbrink 2012). In the eighteenth century, the London of Ned Ward and Tom Brown (1715) comprised names such as Grub Street, Tyburn and the Fleet Ditch, locations symbolizing squalor, poverty and criminality (Rogers 1972 , 1980). In the following century their equivalents were, at different times, Monmouth Street, Seven Dials, Ratcliffe Highway, Salisbury Court and the Rookeries off Oxford Street.

But this differentiation declined in the last decades of the nineteenth century, as the mythology of one constructed locality came to stand above all others as an omnibus signifier for disease, delinquency and deprivation in the capital – the East End (Sinclair 1950: 240–77). The exoticized alteriority of its teeming slums and picturesque squalor were cumulatively imagined in pictures and words: in the illustrations of Gustave Doré, in a book with the religious title of *London: A Pilgrimage* (Doré and Jerrold 1872); in exhaustive statistical studies by the philanthropist, Charles Booth (Booth 1892; Fishman 1988); and in the endless retelling of the 'Jack the Ripper' murders after their sensational occurrence in 1888.

Paris

In France, slums and slumming were concentrated in Paris, since France did not have the industrial manufacturing districts in the North that Engels and Mayhew saw in England. Moreover, the texts that emerged and the myths they created about Paris were less heavily polarized in grinding contrasts between the poor and the rich because the contrasts were less visible or remarkable, which is why French visitors to England were often shocked by the extent of conspicuous destitution they saw in London. There was no equivalent in illustrated journalism to the works of Doré, Mayhew, Sims or Cruikshank. French literary liberals, though deploring Parisian poverty and sometimes active in political campaigning for social reforms, manifested a broader, sociological fascination with recording the multiplication of social types and occupational groups developing in the city. As botanists and zoologists studied animate and inanimate nature, illustrators and writers set out to classify the different kinds of people who lived and worked in the city in 'social zoologies' of human life. These were either multi-volume, word-and-picture sketches of different social types, or slim, small-format books describing a single type. The first large-scale social zoology was *Les Français peints par eux-mêmes*, a seven-volume, illustrated dossier on French national types (Anon. 1842–4). It seems to have been the model for a comparable work on Paris, *Le diable à Paris*, published by Pierre-Jules Hetzel, a republican and political activist in 1845–6 (Sheon 1984: 140; M.M. 1845–6). This was a work whose title came from a fantasy scenario depicted on the first page of the Devil coming down to Paris on an observational trip (see Figure 2.4). Its two volumes then became an epic gazetteer of what he saw of the city – its history and geography, and the occupational and social life of its inhabitants.

The work included a statistical account of the city, and sketches in words and pictures of social types and situations. The texts for each were by a galaxy of writers, among them Honoré de Balzac, George Sand, Gérard de Nerval and Alfred de Musset. The illustrations were mainly by Gavarni, an artist who had made his name by engraving illustrations of the counter-cultural and carnival world of Parisian student life, society intrigues and the fashionable pleasures of the 'bal masque' and carnival. His later work reflected the darker side of urban poverty and vice, particularly after visiting London. He contributed 208 drawings, collectively called *Les gens de Paris*, which were distributed in twenty sections throughout *Le diable* (see Figure 2.5). Abridged and translated versions of some of Gavarni's work were published in England (see Janin *et al.* 1840), and he came to London in 1848 and produced a sequence of portraits of London types (Smith 1849). The English also had their own versions of social zoologies, the best known being *Heads of the People*

Figure 2.4 Gavarni's 'Le diable à Paris', 1845

Du tripot à Bicêtre.

Figure 2.5 Gavarni's 'Le diable à Paris', 1845: The tramp

by Kenny Meadows (1840), but none had the same combination of social sweep and sociological ambition as the French.

Two of the most important myths to come out of Paris were those of 'Bohemia' and the 'flâneur'. 'Bohemia' was an imagined demotic fairyland where writers and artists congregated. It was made famous by a struggling writer called Henri Murger in *Scènes de la vie de Bohème*, a serialized book that was turned into a successful play. It described a love affair between a struggling artist living in garret-like poverty and a consumptive working girl or 'grisette', which ended with her death. In the story, Bohemia was a figurative world of cheap lodgings in mean but vibrant streets, where students, artists and writers lived and loved in impoverished equality with poor workers, in conditions of romantic unconventionality and freedom. Though Murger was not the first to use the term 'Bohemian', it was his work that popularized its mythology (Richardson 1969: 101–12). His work had great influence in France and England. Bohemia was widely adopted as a form of self-definition by artistic types affecting expressive poses as free spirits, and flouting bourgeois respectability by adopting eccentric dress, 'advanced' attitudes and sexual freedom. The myth was promoted in words, pictures and drama, and later in music in Puccini's opera *La Bohème* and Balfe's *The Bohemian Girl*.

Talented Bohemians moved out of Bohemia into high society once they became successful. Murger himself had no desire to continue as a struggling nobody after his name was made. But Bohemianism was often nominally or nostalgically adopted by journalists with no great claims to artistic genius. Sims, for example, called his autobiography *Sixty Years' Recollections of Bohemian London*.

Bohemia proved an enduring cultural concept. In Paris, the mythology of Bohemia and its counterpart, the 'Latin Quarter' – a place where, throughout the 1920s and 1930s, classes and races mixed in jazz clubs, theatrical parties, studios and other louche settings – were celebrated in print, film and other forms of popular culture (Morrow and Cucuel 1900; d'Auvergne n.d.; Bayard 1926; Nevill 1927; Huddleston 1928).

After the Second World War, Bohemia was updated and rebranded under different names by other artistic groups and youth subcultures with unconventional and flamboyant life styles: the Beats in the US and the UK in the 1950s, followed by the 'Underground', Hippy 'dropouts', and many rock and pop subcultural groupings (Mods, Rockers, Punks, Goths, Grungies, Crusties, Hip-hop rappers), all playing and acting out their own urban variations of *Bohemian Rhapsody* (see Bradshaw 1978 for a Radio London DJ's popular history of Bohemia).

A related mythic type that came out of Parisian culture and influenced slumming was the 'flâneur'. This was a literary persona exemplified by the poet, Baudelaire, and novelists such as Flaubert and Husymans, whose cultural significance had been theorized by Walter Benjamin (1973: 35–66; 1999: 262–7). The 'flâneur' was the man-about-town, a pedestrian stroller who knew the city intimately – its work and play, its classes and groups, its styles and fashions, its gossip, virtues and corruptions – accepting them with detached, ironical, even amused tolerance. It was a role sometimes accompanied by a Dandyish fastidiousness in manner and dress, removed from the romantic flamboyance and disordered expressiveness of the Bohemian. Like the Bohemian, the flâneur understood the life of the streets, but without necessarily living on those streets among the poor. The flâneur affected a 'cool' distance from events as an ironical observer, blasé and unmoved, like the immaculate, long-coated, satanic figure poring over a map of Paris in the frontispiece to *Le diable à Paris*. Neither the Bohemian nor the flâneur had philanthropic or reforming intentions, and both flouted bourgeois constraints by their passages through low life. Both implicitly suggested that existential authenticity and authority in the city depended on traffic and familiarity with communities on the edge of the mainstream.

There were frequent cultural exchanges between the two capitals in the nineteenth century by novelists, journalists and artists. So London came to have its *soi-disant* flâneurs and Bohemians, and French graphic cartoonists and caricaturists such as Gavarni, Cham and Doré came to London and drew its low life/high life contrasts.

Slumming in the twentieth century

Until late in the nineteenth century, slumming was a small-scale form of independent travel and social exploration, undertaken by writers, artists and, later, by paid or volunteer workers for philanthropic and governmental agencies. The activities of all of them were stimulated, disseminated and reproduced by the printed word and visual image. For three centuries literary slumming affected slumming practices and images of its locations.

At the end of the nineteenth century this situation changed. Instead of remaining a small-scale practice, pursued independently by individuals or small groups, slumming became collectivized and commodified as packaged tourism by commercial companies. It happened first in New York where, between the 1880s and 1920s, unprecedented immigration levels resulted in geographical concentrations of different nationalities (e.g. Irish, Italian, Chinese, Jewish) in different parts of the city, with many living in conditions of poverty and distress. These ghettos attracted charitable agencies, religious groups, journalists and the police. The conditions they encountered were publicized in a sensational, epic volume of more than 700 pages and more than 200 engraved illustrations, called *Darkness and Daylight* (Campbell 1893). The ghettos became sightseeing attractions for visitors curious about their cultural diversity. This led commercial companies to launch package tours, and these have been seen as the prototypes of globalized, modern slum tourism (see Steinbrink 2012).

But small-scale, independent slumming did not go away. It diversified throughout the twentieth century in several forms. In Paris, New York and London slumming survived as a 'smart' social habit in the 1920s and 1940s among upper classes acting out literary and hedonistic Bohemianism and flâneurism in Harlem jazz clubs (Anderson 1982), Soho night spots and Parisian Left Bank cafés and restaurants (Seigel 1986). There was some sexual adventurism in this that resulted in cross-class and cross-ethnic liaisons. These included socialite Nancy Cunard's affairs with black musicians in literary London (Chisholm 1979), and the quest by the English writers, Auden and Isherwood, for 'rough trade' among working-class young men in an interwar Berlin that had become a radical arts melting pot through the work of people such as Bertolt Brecht and George Grosz.

Another strand of literary slumming in the twentieth century was hobo and tramp culture, which offered two alterior forms of escape from the everyday world – one rural, the other urban. Rural tramping attracted writers who rejected the alienation and regimentation of city life by taking to the open road, and living rough among Nature. Their attitudes were highly influenced by previous Romantic literary figures: Rousseau, Wordsworth, Borrow and Thoreau. Exponents included Stephen Grahame, Jim Phelan (an ex-IRA officer who had served time in gaol) and, most famously, the poet W.H. Davies, who lost a leg on a railway line while 'on the tramp'. One account of tramping was written by a patrician liberal whose address was Shipton Manor, Oxford, and who travelled, disguised as a tramp, to get information for a well-researched, sociological study (Gray 1931; see Figure 2.6).

The urban variant of hobo life involved abandoning well-charted urban or suburban areas for more exoticized corners of the city, where the poor, the culturally diverse and the criminal lived lives 'on the edge'. This mythology of life in urban 'sink' areas as existential authenticity was apotheosized in the hagiographic championing by the philosopher, Jean Paul Sartre, of Jean Genet, a small-time thief and homosexual prostitute in Paris. Genet was duly feted as a literary icon (Sartre 1964). Etonian George Orwell's low-life adventures in *Down and Out in London and Paris* were a paler version of skid-row chic (Orwell 1933). In America in the late 1940s and early 1950s, the 'Beat Generation' – artists, musicians and writers celebrated by Jack Kerouac – adopted both tramping forms, slumming in the jazz and poetry haunts of urban New York, but jumping trains and stealing cars for madcap adventures 'on the road' across rural America. The early Bob Dylan shared the same urban and rural orientation with a habitus in the jazz clubs of Greenwich Village and a romantic identification with dust-bowl hobo and down-and-out musician Woody Guthrie. All lent auratic endorsement to low-life encounters, the authenticity of the streets and the freedom of the 'open road' that are inscribed in modern ideas of 'cool', including hip-hop and graffiti culture and backpacking rituals for gap-year adventurers.

THE AUTHOR AS A TRAMP—A ROADSIDE REST

Figure 2.6 The author as a tramp: a roadside rest

In the mid-twentieth century, slumming started to go respectable and entered academia. Social scientists working in Sociology and Anthropology recognized the research possibilities of 'street corner societies' (Whyte 1943) and the social order of slums (Suttles 1968). The result has been an exponential increase over the last half century in research studies of subordinate, marginalized and popular cultures associated with the international urban poor.

Conclusion

This chapter began with three different accounts of the origins of urban slumming: as low-life travel by hack journalists in Elizabethan and Stuart London; as city perambulations by 'Grub Street'; and then as knockabout pleasure trips by young gentlemen through London described by Regency authors.

From the 1830s onwards slumming changed, emerging as a philanthropic activity conducted to identify, understand and relieve urban distress created by industrial development and rapid population growth, and the geographical segregation that followed. Attempts to cope with the problems of the growing urban poor by governmental and philanthropic bodies led to increasing cross-class contacts, as part of investigative and reforming initiatives that included the earliest use of personal interviewing and social surveys.

A related but different impetus to slumming was the growth of a mass press that generated public interest in, and demand for, news of urban pathologies. Slumming became a journalistic commodity with its own reporters journeying into the 'lower depths' of the city, thus pioneering the role of the investigative journalist.

In Paris, there were similar developments in city size, social problems and press development. But urban exploration by journalists was less focused on polarities between rich and poor, than on inventorying the overall social geography of the city in words and pictures, classifying and typifying people by occupation, status, age, gender and district. Literary Paris created the mythic personae of the Bohemian and flâneur, the latter being the quintessential specialist in urban social observation.[2]

Literary influences have made slumming part of a modern quest for identity in the city. It has evolved among the leisure classes as a form of cultural investment, signifying not just escape from the quotidian constraints and routines of 'normal' middle-class life, but a kind of existential rite of passage, an accreditation of the individual's authoritative grasp on modernity and the 'real world'. I have been slumming; therefore, I have seen and know real life is the subtext. Slumming may be seen as a metempsychotic, repeated journey of identity enactment in which the traveller implicitly follows in literary footsteps to gain a small slice of the mythic glamour of the Bohemian, the flâneur, the investigative journalist, the charity worker and other cultural role models whose practices have valorized slumming (Seaton 2001, 2002).[3]

Williams (2008) has distinguished between 'slumming' and 'literary slumming', the one being practice, the other being narrative. The distinction may be too absolute. What this chapter has tried to suggest is that practice has been formed historically, and inherently, by ideologies represented and disseminated in literary narratives. These ideologies are embedded in modern packaged slumming, whose practices may be viewed as a metempsychotic rehearsal of culturally determined roles of the traveller as social explorer, urban anthropologist or philanthropic missionary. The rich Americans who spend an afternoon on rubbish dumps with poor Mexican scavengers, as reported by Evelyn Dürr (2012), have observable antecedents in Mayhew's encounters with London street scavengers of the 1840s.

Slumming, as Koven has argued, was, and is, never entirely altruistic (Koven 2004). Though charitable visits among the global poor may be well meaning, they represent cultural capital that can be cashed in on social occasions with peers and employers: as student union narratives for the returning backpacker; or as dinner party anecdotes for the liberal back from the favelas of Rio de Janeiro or the townships of Soweto.

Historically, slum trips have been brief encounters: a 'fact-finding' visit by a magistrate to a house of correction in the eighteenth century; a visit to a morgue for the poor in Paris in the 1820s; a gaslit shopping expedition into the New Cut in the 1850s (Sala 1860c); an excursion into Harlem to jazz clubs in the 1920s by 'bright young things' (Anderson 1982); or a 'Jack the Ripper' tour of the East End in the 1980s. Not many lasted more than a few hours, a day or two at most. People in comfortable circumstances rarely spent prolonged periods slumming unless they were priests, philanthropic workers or literary and artistic figures such as Charles Baudelaire, Jack London and George Orwell – people with literary material to gather, a point to prove to the bourgeoisie or a disinclination to assimilate with their own class.

Modern slum packages may be seen as modest but temporary experiments with identity, forms of social exchange between rich and poor through which, ideally, the latter get material assistance, while the former gain in authenticity and self-esteem by metempsychotic replication of travels into social otherness. Slumming is thus a transaction in which the poor enable the richer to 'get real'. And behind it all lie several centuries of sedimented acculturation, induced mainly by literary texts.

Notes

1   I refer here to the 1995 hit 'Common People' by the Britpop band Pulp, a humorous reflection on the encounter between the band's front man, Jarvis Cocker, and a Greek millionaire's daughter that Cocker explicitly placed in the context of slumming.
2   The flâneur's expertise in urban classification and typification has now been partially, though not completely, appropriated in socio-demographic analysis and profiling by sociologists, and postcode targeting by marketers.

3 Metempsychosis, metensomatosis and 'eternal return' as conceptual elements in tourism motivation are beyond full discussion within the spatial limits of this chapter. For a full account, see the papers cited: Seaton (2001, 2002).

Bibliography

Anderson, J. (1982) *Harlem: The Great Black Way*, London: Orbis.

Anon. (Robert Mudie) (1828) *Babylon the Great: Or Men and Things in the British Capital*, London: Henry Colburn.

Anon. (1842–4) *Les Francais peints par eux-mêmes*, 9 vols, Paris: Curmer.

—— (1848) *Sinks of London Laid Open: A Pocket Companion for the Uninitiated*, London: J. Duncombe.

Aydelotte, F. (1913) 'Elizabethan rogues and vagabonds', *Oxford History and Literary Studies*, vol. 1, Oxford: Clarendon Press.

Bayard, J.E. (1926) *The Latin Quarter Past and Present*, London: T. Fisher Unwin.

Baylen, J.O. (1972) 'The "new journalism" in late Victorian Britain', *Australian Journal of Politics and History*, XVIII: 367–85.

Benjamin, W. (1973) 'The flâneur', in W. Benjamin, *Charles Baudelaire: A Lyric Poet in the Era of High Capitalism*, London: N.L.3.

—— (1999) 'The return of the flâneur', in W. Benjamin, *Selected Writings*, vol. 2, Cambridge, MA: Belknap Press/Harvard University Press.

'Blackmantle, B.' (pseudonym of Thomas Malloy Westmacott) (1826) *The English Spy*, London: Sherwood, Gilbert, Piper.

Booth, C. (1892) *Life and Labour of the People of London*, vol. 1, London.

Booth, W. (1890) *In Darkest England and the Way Out*, London.

Bradshaw, S. (1978) *Café Society: Bohemian Life from Swift to Bob Dylan*, London: Weidenfeld and Nicholson.

Brown, T. (1715) *The Works of Mr Thomas Brown, Serious and Comical in Prose and Verse*, 4 vols, London: Sam Briscoe.

Campbell, H. (1893) *Darkness and Daylight; Lights and Shadows of New York Life: A Woman's Story of Gospel, Temperance, Mission and Rescue Work*, Hartford, CT: Worthington.

Checkland, S.G. and Checkland, E.O.A. (1974) *The Poor Law Report of 1834*, London: Penguin.

Chisholm, A. (1979) *Nancy Cunard*, London: Sidgwick and Jackson.

Cruikshank, G. (1833) *Sunday in London*, London: Effingham Wilson.

Cruikshank, P. (1854) *Sunday Scenes in London and the Suburbs*, London: Kent.

Cunningham, P. (1849) *Hand-book of London: Past and Present*, London: John Murray.

d'Auvergne, E. (n.d.) *The Night Side of Paris*, London: T. Werner Laurie.

Delgado, G. (1972) *Cony Catchers and Bawdy-baskets: An Anthology of Elizabethan Low Life*, London: Penguin.

—— (1992) *The Elizabethan Underworld*, Stroud: Alan Sutton.

Doré, G. and Jerrold, B. (1872) *London: A Pilgrimage*, London: Grant.

Dürr, E. (2012) 'Encounters over garbage: tourists and lifestyle migrants at a Mexican dump', *Tourism Geographies*, 14(2): forthcoming.

Dyos, H.J. and Wolf, M. (eds) (1973) *The Victorian City: Images and Realities*, 2 vols, London: Routledge and Kegan Paul.

Elmes, J. (1831) *A Topographical Dictionary of London and its Environs*, London: Whittaker, Treacher and Arnot.

Engels, F. (1844/1928) *The Condition of the Working Class in England*, ed. W.O. Henderson and W.H. Chaloner, Oxford: Blackwell.

Fishman, W.J. (1988) *East End 1888*, London: Duckworth.

Fox, C. (1977) 'The development of social reportage in English periodical illustration during the 1840s and early 1850s', *Past and Present*, 74(1): 90–111.

Garwood, J. (1853) *The Million-peopled City; Or One-half of London Made Known to the Other Half*, London: Wertheim and Macintosh.

Godwin, G. (1859; reprinted 1972) Town Swamps and Social Bridges, Leicester: Leicester University Press.

Graham, S. (1933) *Twice Round the Clock*, London: Ernest Benn.

Grant, J. (1836) *The Great Metropolis*, London: Saunders and Otley.

Gray, F. (1931) *The Tramp: His Meaning and Being*, London: J.M. Dent.

Hindley, C. (n.d.) *The True History of Tom and Jerry*, London: Charles Hindley.

Howat, I. and Nicholls, J. (2003) *Streets Paved with Gold: The Story of the London City Mission*, Fearn, Scotland: Christian Focus Publications.

Huddleston, S. (1928) *Bohemian Literary and Social Life in Paris: Salons, Cafés, Studios*, London: George G. Harrap.

Hughes, J.R.T. (1969) 'Henry Mayhew's London', *Journal of Economic History*, 29: 526–36.

Humphreys, A. (1977) *Travels into the Poor Man's Country: The Work of Henry Mayhew*, Athens, GA: University of Georgia Press.

Janin, J. and Others (1840) *Pictures of the French*, London: William S. Orr.

Jay, A.O. (1891) *Life in Darkest London*, London.

Jerrold, D. (1851) *St Giles and St James*, London: Bradbury and Evans.

Judges, A.V. (1930) *The Elizabethan Underworld*, London: Routledge.

Keating, P. J. (1971) *The Working Classes in Victorian Fiction*, Henley: Kegan Paul.

Knight, C. (1851) *London*, 2nd edn, London: Henry J. Bohn.

Koven, S. (2004) *Slumming: Sexual and Social Politics in Victorian London*, Princeton, NJ: Princeton University Press.

Law, J. (pseudonym of Margaret Harkness) (1889) *In Darkest London: Captain Lobo Salvation Army*, London.

London, J. (1903) *People of the Abyss*, London.

Low, D.A. (1999) *The Regency Underworld*, Stroud: Sutton.

Machray, R. (1902) *The Night Side of London*, London: John Macqueen.

Marcus, S. (1973) 'Reading the illegible', in H.J. Dyos and Michael Wolf (eds) *The Victorian City: Images and Realities*, vol. 2, London: Routledge and Kegan Paul.

Mayhew, H. (n.d –1862) *London Labour and the London Poor*, 4 vols, London: Griffin and Farran.

—— (1985) *London Labour and the London Poor*, ed. V. Neuberg, London: Penguin.

Meadows, K. (1840) *Heads of the People*, London: Robert Tyas.

Merriam-Webste r (1976) *Merrian-Webster's Collegiate Dictionary*, Springfield, MA: Merrian-Webster.

Meschkank, J. (2011) 'Investigations into slum tourism in Mumbai: poverty tourism and the tensions between different constructions of reality', *Geographical Journal*, 76(1): 47–62.

M.M. (1845–6) *Le diable à Paris: Paris et les Parisiens*, 2 vols, Paris: J. Hetzel.

Morrow, W.C. and Cucuel, E. (1900) *Bohemian Paris of To-day*, London: J.B. Lippincott.

Nevill, R. (1927) *Days and Nights in Montmartre and the Latin Quarter*, London: Herbert Jenkins.

Olsen, D.J. (1973) 'House upon house', in H.J. Dyos and M. Wolf (eds) *The Victorian City: Images and Realities*, London: Routledge and Kegan Paul.

—— (1974) 'Victorian London: specialization, segregation and privacy', *Victorian Studies*, March: 264–78.

Orwell, G. (1933) *Down and Out in London and Paris*, London: Victor Gollancz.

Razzell, P.E. and Wainright, R.W. (1973) *The Victorian Working Class: Selections from the Morning Chronicle*, London: Frank Cass.

Reid, J.C. (1971) *Bucks and Bruisers: Pierce Egan and Regency England*, London: Routledge and Kegan Paul.

Richardson, J. (1969) *The Bohemians: La vie de Bohème in Paris, 1830–1914*, London: Macmillan.

Ritchie, J.E. (1858) *The Night Side of London*, London: William Tweedie.

Rogers, P. (1972) *Grub Street: Studies in a Subculture*, London: Methuen.

—— (1980) *Hacks and Dunces: Pope, Swift and Grub Street*, London: Methuen.

Rolfes, M., Steinbrink, M. and Uhl, C. (2009) *Townships as Attraction: An Empirical Study on Township Tourism in Cape Town*, Potsdam: Universitätsverlag.

Sala, G.A. (1860a) *Gaslight and Daylight*, London: Chapman and Hall.

—— (1860b) *Twice Round the Clock; or the Hours of the Day and Night in London*, London: Houlston and Wright.

—— (1896a) *London Up To Date*, vol. 1, London: Adam and Charles Black.

—— (1896b) *The Life and Adventures of George Augustus Sala Written by Himself*, London: Cassell.

Sartre, J.P. (1964) *Saint Genet*, London: W.H. Allen.

Seaton, A.V. (2001) 'In the footsteps of Acerbi: metempsychosis and the repeated journey', in E. Jarva, M. Makivuoti and T. Sironen (eds) *Tutkimusmatkalla Pohjoisseen, Acta Universitatis Ouliensis*, Oulu, Finland: Oulu University Press.

—— (2002) 'Tourism as metempsychosis and metensomatosis: the personae of eternal recurrence', in G. Dann (ed.) *The Tourist as a Metaphor of the Social World*, Wallingford: CAB International.

Seigel, J. (1986) *Bohemian Paris: Culture, Politics, and the Boundaries of Bourgeois Life, 1830–1930*, New York: Viking.

Sheon, A. (1984) 'Parisian social statistics: Gavarni, 'Le diable à Paris' and early realism', *The Art Journal*, summer: 139–48.

Sheppard, F. (1971) *London 1808–1870: The Infernal Wen*, London: Secker and Warburg.

Simmel, G. (1950) *The Sociology of George Simmel*, ed. K.H. Wolff, Glencoe, IL: Free Press.

Sims, G.R. (1906a) *How the Poor Live*, London: Chatto and Windus.

—— (1906b) *The Mysteries of Modern London*, London: Arthur Pearson.

—— (1906c) *Living London. Its Work and Play. Its Humour and Pathos. Its Sights and Scenes*, London: Cassell.

Sinclair, R. (1950) *East London*, London: Robert Hale.

Smith, A. (ed.) (1849) *Gavarni in London*, London: David Bogue.

Smith, C.M. (1853) *Curiosities of London Life: Phases, Physiological and Social*, London: William and Frederick G. Cash.

Stedman-Jones, G. (1971) *Outcast London*, Oxford: Oxford University Press.

Steinbrink, M. (2012) 'We did the slum! Urban poverty tourism in historical perspective', *Tourism Geographies*, 14(2): forthcoming.

Straus, R. (ed.) (1927) *Tricks of the Town: Being Reprints of Three Eighteenth-century Tracts*, London: Chapman and Hall.

—— (1942) *Sala: Portrait of an Eminent Victorian*, London: Constable.

Suttles, G. (1968) *The Social Order of the Slum: Ethnicity and Territory in the Inner City*, Chicago, IL: University of Chicago Press.

Taine, H. (1957) *Notes on England*, trans. and ed. Edward Hyams, London: Thames and Hudson.

Thomas, D. (1998) *The Victorian Underworld*, London: John Murray.

Thompson, E.P. and Yeo, E. (1971) *The Unknown Mayhew*, London: Merlin Press.

Thornbury, W. (*c*. 1870) *Old and New London*, London: Cassell.

—— (1865) *Haunted London*, London: Hurst and Blackett.

Troyer, H.W. (1946) *Ned Ward of Grub Street: A Study of Sub-literary London in the Eighteenth Century*, Cambridge, MA: Harvard University Press.

Weale, J. (1851) *London Exhibited in 1851*, London: Weale.

Weylland, J.M. (*c*.1875) *Round the Tower: The Story of the London City Mission*, London: S.W. Partridge.

Whyte, W.F. (1943) *Street Corner Society*, Chicago, IL: University of Chicago Press.

Williams, C. (2008) 'Ghetto-tourism and voyeurism: forays into literary and non-literary slumming', *Favela Bulletin of Latin American Research*, 27(4): 400–40.

3 Beyond 'Othering'

The political roots of slum tourism

Fabian Frenzel

Introduction

Slum tourism is a growing phenomenon in global tourism. It describes organized tours to deprived areas. Having a long history (Koven 2004; Steinbrink 2012; Seaton in this volume), contemporary slum tourism in the Global South first occurred in post-apartheid South Africa in the form of so-called 'township tours', and shortly after in Brazil as favela tourism in Rio de Janeiro (Freire-Medeiros 2009; Rolfes 2009). Although slum tourism has recently developed in many more places, it is important to note that it does not occur in every poor area of the world. Often, the development seems to be triggered by certain events and specific socio-cultural contexts. One of the central issues for slum tourism research is to better understand these specific conditions – for example, by highlighting commonalities between specific cases. A commonality I would like to focus on in this chapter is the role of politically motivated travellers, or those who have been called 'political tourists' (Babb 2004; Brin 2006; Henderson 2007; Moynagh 2008; Frenzel 2009) or 'justice tourists' (Scheyvens 2002; Pezzullo 2007). While there is no set definition of the term 'political tourist', it broadly describes people who travel for political purposes or out of political interests. This includes globally mobile political activists with high levels of involvement either with the politics of visited countries or with transnational political alliances. It also includes globally mobile volunteers and non-interventionist, politically interested tourists. Forms of political tourism have occurred for some time, and have often involved visits of better-off travellers to people living in poverty. Among other things, these visits have been motivated by solidarity with the poor and were intended to build political alliances across national borders and class boundaries. Today, people travelling to take part in events of the global justice movement, such as the World Social Forum (WSF) or international summit protests, demand higher global social equality or wish to 'make poverty history' (Gumbel 2005).

This chapter focuses on the role travelling activists have played in the genesis of three particular slum tourism destinations: two highly developed cases in South Africa and Brazil and one in the less-developed destination of the Kibera slum in Nairobi, Kenya. Reflecting on the differences and overlaps between these three cases, this chapter argues that the development of slum tourism between them follows a certain pattern. This result prompts the question whether this pattern might be applicable to other cases.

In a second, related argument I reflect further on the apparent link between the travels of political tourists and slum tourism. If there is a connection between the two, how can it be interpreted? Can slum tourism be understood as a commercialization of activist travel? Do political intentions remain relevant in the case of slum tourism even after commercialization? In addressing these questions, I seek to contribute to the debate on the ethics of slum tourism. More than other forms of tourism, slum tourism is highly controversial. Slum tourists are often accused of voyeurism, even though the slum tourism literature has not yet clearly determined what this might mean (Selinger and Outterson 2009). While unethical practices are reported in various case studies (Freire-Medeiros 2009; Rolfes *et al.* 2009), the central ethical problem of slum tourism seems to be based on the assumption of radical power differences between the tourists and the visited poor. As tourists gaze upon the poor, Urry's (2002) critique of the post-colonial character of tourism seems to be fundamentally confirmed. But is it really always problematic to look at poverty, and do such criticisms also apply to international activists, who also visit poverty-stricken areas when they travel to slums to intervene and 'make poverty history'?

The chapter is divided into two parts. In the first section I present three empirical cases, in which the development of recent slum tourism can be traced back to forms of political tourism. Highlighting overlaps and differences between the three cases, I propose a developmental model of the genesis of slum tourism. In the second section I discuss the implications of the model for the discussion of the ethics of slum tourism. I chart the ethical controversies over slum tourism, focusing on two moral concerns: voyeurism and the visitors' interventions. This is followed by a discussion of the different ways in which these concerns are addressed when international visitors visit slums. On the basis of this reflection I conclude by answering the initial question: does slum tourism have a political core?

South Africa: from 'struggle junkies' to township tourists

The first case presented here is the development of township tourism in South Africa. Already under the apartheid regime, township tours were offered as an official tourist attraction by the state. This served political purposes, as these visits were meant to portray a picture of untroubled race relations in the apartheid regime. Dondolo (2002) reports that they developed from tours organized by state agencies for local government officials in order to portray the benevolent character of townships, displaying them as 'ethnic villages in the city'. Apart from the 'official' tours, critical NGOs and political groups organized tours for 'local whites, international funders and struggle junkies'

(Pirie 2007: 235). 'Struggle junkies' is a curious term, originally used by Dondolo (2002). It contains a significant value judgement. It indicates the somewhat dubious role of international political activists who come to other countries to join local and national struggles. The notion of 'struggle junkies' seems to indicate that such visitors engage in a rather selfish pursuit, a voyeurism fuelled by interest in the sight of people struggling rather than in the cause of the struggle itself. Such a critical notion is surprising as, arguably, the struggle against apartheid in South Africa has been greatly helped by international solidarity networks (Seidman 2000). Were the unofficial tours of the apartheid period not part and parcel of the intervention of international solidarity activists to support the struggle against apartheid?

With the end of the apartheid regime in 1994, interest in visiting the townships grew. The unofficial tours of the apartheid period became the first township tours of the post-apartheid system. Initially, post-apartheid township tours were explicitly constructed as 'political tourism' (McEachern 2002), highlighting ongoing struggles and injustices in the developing democracy. In the years following, and in the context of a growing tourism industry in South Africa, the township tours increasingly took on the form of heritage tours, reflecting the role of townships in the revolutions leading towards the 1994 regime change. This included visits to Soweto as a place symbolizing oppression and the anti-apartheid struggle, their aim being to see the sites of resistance and the houses in which symbolic figures such as Nelson Mandela and Bishop Desmond Tutu used to live (Steinbrink 2012). In the following years, the historical and political aspects that had initially been the focus shifted to the background, and townships increasingly came to be presented as cultural attractions (Rolfes *et al.* 2009).

Controversies occurred as to whether such displays of 'townships' would not be demeaning (Shepherd and Hall 2007). But such concerns were rebutted in the hope that tourism would provide a form of poverty relief in the new 'Rainbow' nation.

Furthermore, township tours have been highlighted as an indication of non-white entrepreneurship (McEachern 2002). In this vein, township tourism is openly promoted by South African governments on both local and national levels. Although the effectiveness of township tourism to reduce poverty in the townships as a whole may be limited, undoubtedly some have benefitted financially (Rogerson 2004; Koens in this volume). As Rolfes *et al.* (2009) have shown, township tours have become a tourist 'must', certainly in the Cape Region. Township tours are attended by up to 25 per cent of Cape Town visitors, with similar developments in other large South African cities (see also Koens in this volume). Township tours have now become a normal feature of tourism in the country.

The development of township tours followed an interesting route. In the apartheid period, tours were highly politically charged, albeit in different ways: the official tours were part of the political propaganda of the regime and were designed to brush over the conflicts and oppression by highlighting cultural diversity and 'happy', 'black' township life (Dondolo 2002). The unofficial tours were also political, but in the opposite way. They brought international activists into the anti-apartheid struggle. The fact that these visitors were sometimes called 'struggle junkies' shows the problematic nature of their intervention. In the post-apartheid area, tours are less controversial (see Butler in this volume). The focus of many tours has started to include those 'cultural' aspects that were at the core of apartheid township tourism, whereby townships are now increasingly valued as places that display cultural diversity – something positive – rather than poverty and exclusion and the ongoing struggles against them.

Rio de Janeiro: the Earth Summit and the favela tour

The origin of the Rio favela tours is contested and different accounts exist as to who offered these tours first. However, it is uncontested that the development of the phenomenon was started by a specific political event, the Rio summit of 1992 (Freire-Medeiros 2009). The Rio summit is mainly known for bringing forward the sustainability agenda. It is worthwhile to remember that it stood at the beginning of a new wave of transnational politics, enabled by the collapse of the Soviet Bloc. It also marked the beginning of a new form of transnational, grassroots politics, made possible by unprecedented levels of international mobility and communication in the context of globalization. The Rio summit was attended by 178 government delegations, but also by over 30,000 other participants, including NGO workers, activists and the media (Najam and Cleveland 2005). The high number of attendees was probably the most important feature of this new form of international conference. Indeed, the development of event-based political tourism can be dated back to the Rio summit.

During the summit, participants started exploring Rio, either as tourists or to find stories to report about. On their tours to the more conventional tourist sites of Rio, summit participants passed by Rocinha, Rio's largest favela, located between the world-famous beaches and sights like the Corcovado Jesus Statue. The entry points to Rocinha and other favelas in the inner-city areas had an unusually high police presence, arguably to shield the conference from the periodically erupting violence in these favelas. Socially conscious 'political' tourists, however, demanded to know more about the favelas and also inquired whether it was possible to visit them specifically. Tour operators responded to the demand and took the conference participants into Rocinha. Some of these visits are documented in journalist articles written about the favela in the context of the Rio conference (Anon. 1992). To use a term from Freire-Medeiros (2009), the favela 'started travelling', and 'favela' became a concept known globally, far beyond the confines of Brazilian society.

A more immediate effect, however, was the establishment of the first commercial favela tours in Rio. After the end of the Rio summit, the operators were increasingly able to sell their tours among mainstream Rio tourists. The developing business of favela tours initially caused controversy in Rio and the wider Brazilian society. The tours were accused of being voyeuristic and exploitative of the poor living in the favela (Freire-Medeiros 2009). The tour operators were quick to find 'ethical' fixes against these claims of exploitation, mainly by linking their tourism work to charitable engagement in the favela, for which they provided funding from the profits of the tour. It also became increasingly clear that the 'favelados' of Rocinha were puzzled by the visiting tourists, but also generally welcoming. These findings refute the charges of voyeurism (Freire-Medeiros in this volume). In this light it becomes interesting to reflect on the motives behind the initial criticism that the tours provoked. To what extent did such criticism – voiced by local elites – reflect Brazilian class politics? The Brazilian history of the favela is complex; however, one central aspect has been the neglect and stigmatization of people living in the favela (Frisch 2012). The interest of international travellers in the favela pointed at a social problem to which the Brazilian society so far had not managed to find an answer. In this light the initial criticism of favela tourists might bear some similarity to the criticism of township visitors as 'struggle junkies'. As members of a post-colonial society, Brazil's elites rejected the intervention of international tourists into what they might have considered 'their' social question. To dismiss international tourists' motives as voyeuristic was arguably also a way of questioning their right to intervene into Brazilian internal affairs, even if that intervention did not extend much beyond increasing the visibility of the favelas.

The development of favela tours into a tourist 'must-do' in Brazil in the years following the Rio summit has many causes. Crucial were two internationally received films about favelas in Rio, *City of God* (2003) and *Favela Rising* (2005) (Freire-Medeiros 2009). Their popularity among audiences in the US and in Europe extended the phenomenon of the 'travelling favela', with the development of 'favela chic' nightclubs (Freire-Medeiros 2009) and other related phenomena in the West (Linke 2012). Today Rio has several tour operators who offer favela tours. Freire-Medeiros (2009) estimates that the favela of Rocinha receives up to 3,000 tourists per month. Parallel to this development there has been a remarkable change in attitude by Brazilian society towards favela tourism. While scepticism among elites might persist, the political class has started to embrace it. In 2000, the mayor of Rio attempted to create a heritage museum in the favela of Morro da Providência (Menenzes in this volume). As recently as August 2010, the state of Rio has embarked on a specific programme to create favela tourism in a variety of favelas, which was endorsed even by ex-president Lula (MSNBC 2010). These operations have to be seen in the context of a larger favela 'pacification' programme in which a variety of inner-city favelas have been taken over by special police forces in a controversial push for security in advance of international sporting events coming to Rio (Barrionuevo 2010). Despite this broader context of security, favelas are arguably increasingly seen as a cultural asset, while tourism to these areas is affirmed and promoted as a source of development and income in some of the poorer neighbourhoods of Rio (Frisch 2012).

Nairobi: off the beaten track at the World Social Forum

In Nairobi, yet another political event, the World Social Forum (WSF), initiated the rise of slum tourism in the massive slum of Kibera. There is so far limited research about this case of slum tourism, and I base my arguments here largely on my own observations as an attendee of the WSF and slum visitor to Kibera and other Nairobi slums.

In January 2007, Nairobi hosted the WSF, an annual gathering of social movement activists and NGOs designed as a counter event to the World Economic Forum in 2001 (WSF 2006). Like the Rio summit, it can be understood as an event attracting scores of international political tourists. The Nairobi WSF brought together about 20,000 to 30,000 international visitors (Mbugua and Ongwen 2005; Wolfson 2007).

Nairobi is the African headquarters of the United Nations and hosts international summits on a regular basis. The city's infrastructure is prepared for such events, providing guests with world-class hotels and other facilities that stand in blatant contrast to the living conditions of millions of Nairobi's inhabitants who live in slums. The WSF is unique as an international conference because of its grassroots approach, embracing the idea of pursuing democratic political processes on a global level, a 'globalization from below', with maximum inclusivity. Most of the Nairobi WSF took place in the official surroundings of a large football stadium. And many international delegates were indeed housed in first-class hotels in downtown Nairobi. Because of the politics of the WSF, many of the international delegates took issue at the exclusivity of the event and demanded that the WSF connect more with the poor living in Nairobi. Indeed, as poverty featured so strongly as a topic, there was a variety of discussions on how to relate best to the poor. One of the most significant issues concerned the openness of the forum to Nairobi's poor. As the WSF required the purchase of a ticket to cover the organizational costs, and tickets for Kenyans were priced at US$3, most of the urban poor were effectively excluded from the WSF. The WSF itself had strong security (already an omnipresent feature in Nairobi), with heavily armed guards and policemen securing the gates of the event. Licensed caterers provided food and charged international prices unaffordable to the local poor. Local organizers justified the set-up as a result of limited government support for the event. In contrast to Brazil and India, where the WSF had taken place previously, local and central government did not support the WSF in Nairobi financially. Not dissimilar to delegates at the Rio summit in 1992, participants of the WSF contested the exclusion of the poor, and one of the immediate outcomes was the significant drive of many international delegates to move from the locations of the WSF to the poor neighbourhoods. The slum of Kibera, which had gained attention through international documentaries and films such as *The Constant Gardener* (2006), and is often called the biggest slum of Africa, was a principle choice. The visits of delegates to the slum were organized by NGOs that operated locally with projects in Kibera, and offered to take delegates with them to see their projects. The visits to Kibera developed into a 'must-do' at the WSF throughout its duration. As more and more delegates joined the spontaneously organized tours, delegates started to see each other touring Kibera. At the same time, other slums were 'discovered' as new sights. Participants in these visits often praised the fact that these slums were 'off the beaten track' compared to Kibera, and offered a 'more authentic' picture of poverty.

Conflicts about the inclusion of the poor at the WSF persisted to the end of the forum, involving protests of delegates against the local organizing committee (Oloo 2007). The Nairobi WSF is remembered as one of the most controversial events in WSF history. The other legacy of the WSF is the creation of slum tours in Kibera. Mowforth and Munt (2009) have argued that the WSF had created an infrastructure that persisted even after the social forum was over, and that the political event there stands at the beginning of the development of organized slum tourism. Today there is a variety of operators.

Controversies and criticism have focused on the issue of voyeurism (Odede 2010). So far there has been little indication of a particular rejection of slum tours from Kenyan elites. However, there was some clear indication of criticism from Kenyan middle classes towards the burgeoning slum tours during the WSF. The main accusation was that the international visitors romanticized poverty and lacked the ability to understand the specific local configuration of poverty. I have discussed this and other criticisms of western WSF participants' urge to visit and relate to the slums of Nairobi elsewhere (Frenzel *et al.* 2011).

A developmental model of slum tourism locations

As indicated earlier, one of the central questions for slum tourism research is why it occurs in some places and not in others. While it is not possible to answer this question based on the three cases (South Africa, Kenya and Brazil) discussed here, there is a clear indication that politically motivated international tourists play an important role in the development of slum tourism. The destination countries also show some macro-political parallels. In all three cases the political context is one of post-colonialism, involving states that, in different ways, are trying to throw off their colonial past. All three countries display significant levels of inequality among their populations, both economically and in terms of social and political rights. In the last two decades – the period in which slum tourism has developed in these countries – all three countries have democratized significantly. They have also attempted to develop economically, with tourism as a significant factor in their economic development strategy. Their strategies have met with variable success, as poverty has remained a central problem in all three countries.

The frequency and political influence of international political travel in the last two decades is very different, however. While both Kenya and Brazil will have seen some influx of international activists to support their democratic change, their struggle for democracy has never been internationalized to the same extent as in South Africa. Rather than a political revolution in the making, the initial triggers of slum tourism in Nairobi and Rio were events that were less particular to the host cities or countries, but which concerned global issues. Still, in both cases the host cities provided more than a location for the event; they both started functioning as a case study for the global issues under discussion. It is in this way that the slums of both cities were 'discovered' by international political tourists. They became spaces of intervention, of applying the content of the global concern to practical, local conditions much in the same way that the South African struggle offered itself as a space of intervention for international activists.

In all three cases the interventions were contested by local elites. Of course, there is a world between the hostility of the white elite in South Africa against 'struggle junkies', who helped challenge the status quo of the apartheid regime, and the uneasiness that Brazilian and to a lesser extent Kenyan elites display in the face of international visitors who highlight the plight of these countries' poor. The principal ethical question seems to be parallel, however. What conditions justify the intervention of political tourists into domestic issues, or when do 'domestic' issues become a legitimate international, global concern?

Leaving this question open for now, I would like to point out further parallels in the development of organized slum tourism in all three cases. Arguably, they show different stages of parallel development. This concerns not only the initial genesis of slum tourism emerging from political travellers' visits to the slums, but also the fact that there are different levels of controversy over this intervention, often triggered by the scepticism of local elites. It is also significant that, in both the South African and the Brazilian cases, these controversies were overcome to some extent as the tours became more established as tourist 'must-dos'. In particular, it is significant how various local and national policymakers in both countries have started to actively promote tourism in poor neighbourhoods as part of regeneration and poverty alleviation policies targeted at these areas. Both cases also show a shift of discourse in which the tours are promoted. Rather than only promoting the tours as a tool of poverty relief and regeneration, they are also framed in cultural terms. The slums and townships are advertised as places that are culturally different, provide insights into the 'authentic' backstage of the respective cities and add to the diversity of the place. Indeed, this shift in discourse is maybe the most significant difference between the initial slum visits of political activists and the commercialized tours that followed.

This indicates that the development of commercialized slum tourism out of politically motivated travel functions as a mechanism by which the respective local elites cope with the intervention of international political travellers into their politics. Highlighting social and political inequalities and lending visibility and voice to the disenfranchized, political travellers can significantly help challenge the status quo of the societies they visit. Fundamentally, they demand an answer to the inequality they encounter. Political conflicts around the world demonstrate how states react differently to such a challenge. Short of an answer, they may attempt to keep international visitors out. They may attempt to undermine the legitimacy of the intervention of international political tourists by questioning their motives or their position, particularly if the visitors come from former colonial countries.

However, they can also provide an answer in the way the discussed cases indicate. By creating a narrative of development in which slum tourism becomes a crucial part, they successfully justify the inequality that is 'not yet' overcome. Moreover, they may shift a discourse of inequality into one of cultural difference. The slums become 'Other' places in a good sense; they are portrayed as more 'authentic' and hence valuable in the way they are. This entails yet another justification of the state of poverty they are in, and therefore provides answers to the questions that slum visitors pose to countries that have not managed to eradicate slums.

I am not arguing that the development of slum tourism is a deliberate plot to prevent social change by elites in the respective countries. Rather, this is to point towards the mechanism by which to explain the shift towards the appraisal of internationals interested in the 'problems' of a visited society in two of the discussed cases. In the next section I would like to highlight why this discursive shift appeals equally to tourists themselves. For the tourists not only face the ethical challenge of being called voyeurs, they must also justify their intervention, and the fact that they point towards problems abroad, outside their home polities.

Politics and ethics of slum tourism

The ethical controversies concerning slum tourism are often framed as voyeurism, and slum tourists are accused of engaging in 'poverty porn' (see Basu in this volume), transforming the plight of other people into a spectacle. As indicated earlier, the moral concerns of slum visits by political travellers go further. The fundamental question for international activists addressing poverty in countries they visit is: on what grounds can their intervention be justified? In this section I reflect on these two very different moral concerns, starting off by analysing the accusation of voyeurism. At the bottom of this accusation is a phenomenon of tourism that Urry (2002) has theorized as the 'tourist gaze'. Urry takes a cue from Foucault's (1979) notion of the gaze as a tool of surveillance and control, a mechanism of power. Urry provides an application of Foucault's complex philosophical argument, focusing on the ways in which tourists are subject to certain specific and historically predefined 'gazes' on to landscape, nature and people. He differentiates in particular between a romantic and a collective gaze, broadly aligned with the two major British social classes and their pursuit of tourism. While the collective gaze, broadly confined to working-class holidays, casts landscapes of sand, sea and sun where tourists remain happily among themselves, the romantic gaze of the middle classes charts the landscapes of tourism for the romantic encounter of the tourists with the 'Other', be it in nature or people. Ideally, the romantic gaze figures a lonely traveller discovering the 'Other' in search of the true and authentic nature of the self. In evoking and charting the 'Other', the development of the romantic gaze is strongly influenced by the imaginaries of colonialism. The 'Othering' of people encountered in the European conquest of the world and its function in building and identifying the 'West' has been broadly discussed (Said 2001; Pratt 2008). Suffice to say that international tourism is embedded into a post-colonial context in which 'Othering' is combined with radical differences in income, power and mobility between the visitors and the visited. By placing the romantic gaze in the context of power and colonialism, it is important to reflect that 'the Other' is able to gaze back (Hendry 2000). In Freire-Medeiros's observations on Rocinha (in this volume), this 'reverse gaze' is clearly documented. However, the accusation of voyeurism remains based on the idea that tourists cast a powerful gaze upon the less powerful in the pursuit of 'Otherness'. The 'Otherness' is consumed with little or no advantage for the 'Othered' people. Slum tourism arguably mirrors the logic of the romantic gaze in 'Othering' slum dwellers and their lives.

Steinbrink (2012) has taken a closer look at the different ways in which slum tourists have 'Othered' the poor in the history of slum tourism. He determines three periods that he calls 'moral slumming', 'ethnic slumming' and 'global slumming'. All three are linked to particular periods and places and to different ways of 'Othering'. For Steinbrink, the key to understanding the logic of 'Othering' is the dichotomies of attraction/repulsion and fear/desire. The first period, or moralist version, of 'Othering' is linked to Victorian slumming, and displays an understanding of the slum as attractive/repulsive because of its moral ambiguity. The slum is constructed and 'Othered' as a space of dirt, with its double implication of hygienic and moral deviance. In the second period, the American slumming of the early twentieth century, slum dwellers are 'Othered' as 'ethnic' immigrants, reflective of the role that growing communities of new immigrant groups played in cities of the US. The slum is attractive/repulsive in respect of the ethnic difference that is territorialized in it.

Steinbrink places the most recent wave of slum tourism in the South, in the context of globalization. He argues that slum dwellers are construed as 'locals' (opposed to the global traveller), and the slum as a resort of locality, authenticity and uniqueness that makes them special in the eyes of the 'globalized' tourist. It is important to add that there is evidence of the various different forms of 'Othering' in all forms and periods of slum tourism. Indeed, cultural differences played a significant role in London's nineteenth-century slumming discourse, where slum residents were often 'Othered' as Irish or Welsh immigrants (Seaton in this volume). And 'Othering' in the context of Brazilian favelas often takes the form of moral repulsion/attraction when favelas become places of samba, sex and (illicit) substances. These overlaps confirm Steinbrink's argument that 'Othering' is a central mechanism of slum tourism or rather of the way slum tourists view the slums. In regard to the cases discussed above, what forms of 'Othering' can be identified?

The development of more broadly consumed forms of slum tourism, South African township tours and favela tours resulted in a stronger emphasis on the cultural uniqueness of these places. Advertised by tourism agencies and promoted by local government, poor areas are recast as valuable places to visit, not because they provide an insight into the plight of the poorest, but rather because they allow the tourists to appreciate the unique qualities of these places. As Meschkank (in this volume) argues, a semantic transformation takes place in which the slums are redefined in a positive manner. This value can take many semantic forms: it can be seen as 'simple', 'cultural' or 'local'. Crucially, this value can be exchanged, which then enables the seemingly unlikely 'commodification of poverty' (Freire-Medeiros 2009) in slum tourism.

The transformation of the slum into something valuable fulfils another, moral, function for the tourist. If poverty is understood as a problem, gazing at it evokes the necessity to do something about it. Indeed, voyeurism means that poverty is simply consumed for entertainment with no regard for the poor; they are simply 'Othered' as poor. However, if poverty can be seen as something valuable, touring it becomes a 'must-do' just like other valuable sights need to be 'seen'. Arguably, this is what has happened in the most developed slum tourism destinations. 'Othering' is recast in a positive light: the poor are 'Others', but they are good! Concurrently, there is less need to do something about their poverty.

Earlier I described the developmental model of slum tourism in which South African and Brazilian elites have started to embrace slum tourism. One crucial element in this transformation consists of shifting the value of what is being visited. Rather than framing slums as a weakness, they become an asset (for example, as a sign of diversity) of a place. We can now see that this transformation is equally attractive for tourists who are facing the accusation of being voyeurs or of casting a powerful 'Othering' gaze on to the poor. In celebrating the 'Othered' poor as valuable, the tourists may find a route to refute the accusation of voyeurism.

In order to take this argument further, let us turn to the second moral concern, the problem of 'intervention'. This problem seems to be limited to political tourists, assuming that non-political tourists are not interested in the intervention in the first place. Two questions arise. First, how can non-political tourists not be interested in an intervention? What justifies their decision not to intervene, considering what they see is poverty? Second, on what grounds can the intervention of those travellers who do intervene or consider intervening be justified?

The answers to both of these questions are closely related. In order to intervene, political travellers are in need of an ethical discourse or a set of norms that apply equally to them and the countries they visit. The eradication of poverty is widely considered a universal norm, and this is reflected not only in universal norms per se but in most national legal frameworks and policies as well. The problem in invoking the universal norm of poverty eradication as an international visitor, then, is not so much an issue of norm relativity. The problem seems to be rather that, in the act of invoking the problem of poverty in a visited country, the visitor creates a universal political context in which she or he becomes part of the problem. That is, if the problem of poverty is universal, the international visitor is immediately confronted with his or her own privilege – the ability to leisurely travel internationally in the light of poverty. Many tourists who are visiting the slum are very unlikely to intervene, because any criticism of the visited country and its inability to deal with the social problem of poverty will fall back on to the privileged tourist. In order to point to the slums as a social issue that needs addressing, the slum visitor will have to consider income inequality not only within the visited country but also on a global scale.

Looking at the cases I discussed earlier, it is important to point out how they differ in this respect. The intervention of international activists into the South African apartheid regime could be justified by recourse to the universal norms of democracy and human rights and to the extent that South Africa was denying democratic rights to the majority of its population. As visitors considered themselves to be democratic, their inclusion into the normative context in which they judged the South African regime did not question their own position. International visitors who point towards income inequality in the visited country often argue in a similar way, claiming that local elites are failing to address the issue of poverty in their countries. However, it is arguable that such a view is harder to sustain without reflecting on the privileged position the travellers are in. At the very least their appeal for social justice would evoke demands for them to share their wealth. If political travellers want to address poverty in a foreign country they have to fall back on a universal normative discourse from which the visitors' own position cannot easily be excluded.

In the cases of visitors to the Rio summit in 1992 and the WSF in 2007 in Nairobi, political travellers in the slums often resorted to the global economic status quo, as theorized in dependency theory (Wallerstein 2004), as a critique of globalization or neoliberal global capitalism (Hardt and Negri 2000; Kingsnorth 2003; Harvey 2005). Those theories provide powerful narratives that place the poverty that visitors encounter and their own privilege in the same normative discourse. Concurrently, they are often highly critical of the global economic and political status quo. Slums can be understood as evidence supporting this critique of the political and economic status quo. In this context the visits to the slums are justified, as they allow for the collection of evidence and alignment with slum dwellers in their fight against the global status quo.

This is without doubt very similar to the way better-off political activists have attempted to justify visiting slums over the last three centuries. It is, however, markedly different from the logic of justification that reframes poverty as a valued 'Other'. Indeed, in one instance the poor are 'Othered', their difference emphasized and manifested. In another instance the poor are 'Same-d' – integrated into the normative and political context in which the visitors also act. They are not – for better or worse – 'Other'; they are the same.

Looking at the three cases described earlier, how do we explain the transformation of visits of political travellers, arguably interested in addressing poverty as a global issue, into slum tourism, where the slums and slum dwellers are 'Othered' as culturally valuable? Arguably, the distinctly different answers to the ethical problem of visiting slums, namely 'Same-ing' and 'Othering', conflate in the practice of political travellers. The case of Nairobi showed how political activists started debating the authenticity of different slums as tours to Kibera became increasingly popular. Value was placed on the unique 'Otherness' of the alternative slums in so far as few other visitors had yet tainted them. Similar observations can be drawn from other cases of political travels into poverty and slums. Hutnyk (1996) has described and criticized the way in which travellers need to construct Kolkata as a place of poverty in order to justify their charitable engagement. While the 'Othering' here does not give positive value to the slum in the ways described above, it enables an intervention that is not political but charitable. In the same way that slum tourism is often promoted and presented as the solution to poverty, this form of 'Othering' follows a post-colonial logic in which the visitor is not part of the problem, but brings and manifests the solution.

Even cases of literary slumming, which describe the practice of representing slums in literature or film (Williams 2008 and Seaton in this volume), show the trap of 'Othering' that even highly political authors arguably fall into. Davis's broadly received 'planet of slums' (2006) was intended to be a vociferous critique of the current economic status quo. However, it has drawn substantial criticism for a representation of global poverty that evoked imaginaries of hopeless, apocalyptic and fundamental 'Otherness' (Angotti 2006; Harding 2007; Pithouse 2008).

Conclusion

This chapter has presented three contemporary cases of slum tourism. In all three cases the travels of political activists to the slums pre-date and initiate the development of slum tourism. The three cases also show further parallels that point towards a developmental model of slum tourism destinations. At the beginning stands the intervention of international political travellers into foreign countries' political affairs, in particular into their 'social question', the problem of inequality and poverty. Slum tourism infrastructure develops in all three cases in the footsteps of services provided to political travellers who visited slums. With the increasing visibility of slum tourism, controversies occur, triggered mostly by criticism from domestic elites who denounce slum tourists as voyeurs and slum tourism operators as exploiters of the poor. Slum visitors are also questioned on the basis of their positioning: for example, if they originate in former colonizing countries. There are also questions with regard to their own privilege vis-à-vis the poverty. In two of the described cases the initial hostility falters as the destinations mature. Following the development model this would indicate that a similar process should be observable – for example in Nairobi, but also in other developing slum tourism destinations, such as Mumbai or Bangkok.

It furthermore remains to be discussed why the hostility falters. My findings indicate that this has to do with a shift in the discourse of slum tourism, observably taking place parallel to increasing acceptance, in which the political features of the slum tourism give way to cultural ones. This includes the increasing dominance of forms of 'Othering', in which the slums and slum dwellers are portrayed less as a problem and more as an asset of the visited city/country. This shift enables local elites to embrace slum tourism, but it also fulfils important functions for the slum tourists. Indeed, the pressing moral and political questions of global inequality that particularly arise in global tourism can be safely managed in slum tourism. Poverty may be translated into cultural difference that can be valued for what it is. It may also be portrayed as a subject of development in which slum tourists may see themselves as a solution to the problem they observe. In all cases, slum tourism operates as 'Othering' and creates distance and difference between the visited and the visitors.

I have argued that there is a different option for travellers visiting the slums. Indicated by the approach some tourists take when visiting slums, an intervention can also be justified if the slum residents are not 'Othered', but 'Same-d'. This would be based on narratives critical to the global economic order that produces the obscene inequalities we currently live with. It may also involve creating networks of resistance and solidarity with slum dwellers that enable reciprocity in North–South mobility via reverse visits.

Slum tourism seems to have developed out of political travels, and this indicates that political travels are not always successful in solving the moral questions that result from visiting the slums. I have shown that 'Othering' is a fundamental part of the visits of political travellers in literal and literacy slumming. It is therefore without merit to disqualify slum tourism simply on the grounds that it provides false relief for the moral concerns of tourists.

In the eighteenth and nineteenth centuries, the first examples of slum tourism developed parallel to the formation of the 'social question' – the political concern about how to deal with and end poverty, then a national question. There is no space in this chapter to develop the multiple links between the activities of philosophers, social revolutionaries, social entrepreneurs and commercial tour guides in the slums of the developing urban centres throughout this period. Both Seaton (in this volume) and Koven (2004) have done some work on disentangling these connections, indicating the close relation of the development of social and welfare policy in the late nineteenth century and the increasing attention slums received at the time. Further research is needed to address the way that the current forms of 'global slumming' (Steinbrink 2012) might be an indication of the development of a 'global social question'. Slum tourism does not seem to be an appropriate answer, but it arguably shows that there is a growing interest in responding.

Bibliography

Angotti, T. (2006) 'Apocalyptic anti-urbanism: Mike Davis and his planet of slums', *International Journal of Urban and Regional Research*, 30(4): 961.

Anon. (1992) 'Rio's poor make their point', *New Scientist*, 20 June. Available online at www.newscientist.com/article/mg13418260.600-rios-poor-make-their-point.html (accessed 8 October 2011).

Babb, F. (2004) 'Recycled sandalistas: from revolution to resorts in the new Nicaragua', *American Anthropologist*, 106(3): 541.

Barrionuevo, A. (2010) 'In rough slum, Brazil's police try soft touch', *The New York Times*. Available online at www.nytimes.com/2010/10/11/world/americas/11brazil. html?_r=2/ (accessed 8 October 2011).

Brin, E. (2006) 'Politically-oriented tourism in Jerusalem', *Tourist Studies*, 6(3): 215–43.

Davis, M. (2006) *Planet of Slums*, London: Verso.

Dondolo, L. (2002) *The Construction of Public History and Tourism Destinations in Cape Town's Townships: A Study of Routes, Sites and Heritage*, Cape Town: University of the Western Cape.

Foucault, M. (1979) *Discipline and Punish: The Birth of the Prison*, London: Vintage Books.

Freire-Medeiros, B. (2009) 'The favela and its touristic transits', *Geoforum*, 40(4): 580–8.

Frenzel, F. (2009) 'Politics in motion: the mobilities of political tourists', unpublished thesis, Leeds Metropolitan University.

Frenzel, F., Boehm, S., Quinton, P., Sullivan, S., Spicer, A. and Quinton, P. (2011) 'Comparing alternative media in North and South: the cases of IFIWatchnet and Indymedia in Africa', *Environment and Planning A*, 43(5): 1173–89.

Frisch, T. (2012) 'Glimpses of another world: the favela and its transformation from a "social exclusion area" into a touristic attraction', *Tourism Geographies*, 14(2): forthcoming.

Gumbel, N. (ed.) (2005) *Make Poverty History*, London: Alpha International.

Harding, J. (2007) 'Planet of slums', *The London Review of Books*, 29(5): 25.

Hardt, M. and Negri, A. (2000) *Empire*, Cambridge, MA: Harvard University Press.

Harvey, D. (2005) *A Brief History of Neoliberalism*, Oxford: Oxford University Press.

Henderson, J. (2007) 'Hosting major meetings and accompanying protestors: Singapore 2006', *Current Issues in Tourism*, 10(6): 543–57.

Hendry, J. (2000) *The Orient Strikes Back: A Global View of Cultural Display*, Oxford: Berg.

Hutnyk, J. (1996) *The Rumour of Calcutta: Tourism, Charity, and the Poverty of Representation*, London: Zed Books.

Kingsnorth, P. (2003) *One No, Many Yeses: A Journey to the Heart of the Global Resistance Movement*, Montreal: Free Press.

Koven, S. (2004) *Slumming: Sexual and Social Politics in Victorian London*, Princeton, NJ: Princeton University Press.

Linke, U. (2012) 'Mobile imaginaries, portable signs: the global consumption of iconic representations of slum life', *Tourism Geographies*, 14(2): forthcoming.

Mbugua, B. and Ongwen, O. (2005) 'Nairobi to host global civil society forum'. Available online at www.eastandard.net/archives/cl/print/news.php?articleid=25274 (accessed 15 March 2007).

McEachern, C. (2002) *Narratives of Nation: Media, Memory and Representation in the Making of the New South Africa*, Cape Town: Nova.

Mowforth, M. and Munt, I. (2009) *Tourism and Sustainability: Development, Globalisation and New Tourism in the Third World*, 3rd edn, Abingdon: Routledge.

Moynagh, M. (2008) *Political Tourism and Its Texts*, Toronto: University of Toronto Press.

MSNBC (2010) 'Brazil wants tourists to visit Rio slums', *South America Travel*. Available online at www.msnbc.msn.com/id/38922800/ns/travel-destination_travel/t/brazil-wants-tourists-visit-rio-slums/#.TpB1nU8Y5wc (accessed 8 October 2011).

Najam, A. and Cleveland, C.J. (2005) 'Energy and sustainable development at global environmental summits: an evolving agenda', in L. Hens and B. Nath (eds) *The World Summit on Sustainable Development: The Johannesburg Conference*, New York: Springer Science and Business.

Odede, K. (2010) 'Slumdog tourism', *The New York Times*. Available online at www.nytimes.com/2010/08/10/opinion/10odede.html (accessed 8 October 2011).

Oloo, O. (2007) 'OpenSpaceForum: critical reflections on WSF Nairobi 2007', *Open Space Forum*. Available online at www.openspaceforum.net/twiki/tiki-read_article.php?articleId=392> (accessed 8 October 2011).

Pezzullo, P. (2007) *Toxic Tourism: Rhetorics of Pollution, Travel, and Environmental Justice*, Tuscaloosa, AL: University of Alabama Press.

Pirie, G. (2007) 'Urban tourism in Cape Town', in C.M. Rogerson and G. Visser (eds) *Urban Tourism in the Developing World: The South African Experience*, Cape Town: Transaction.

Pithouse, R. (2008) 'Mike Davis, Planet of Slums', *Journal of Asian and African Studies*, 43(5): 567.

Pratt, M.L. (2008) *Imperial Eyes: Travel Writing and Transculturation*, London: Taylor and Francis.

Rogerson, C.M. (2004) 'Urban tourism and small tourism enterprise development in Johannesburg: the case of township tourism', *GeoJournal*, 60(1): 249–57.

Rolfes, M. (2009) 'Poverty tourism: theoretical reflections and empirical findings regarding an extraordinary form of tourism', *GeoJournal*, 75(5): 421–42.

——, Steinbrink, M. and Uhl, C. (2009) *Townships as Attraction: An Empirical Study of Township Tourism in Cape Town*, Potsdam: Universitätsverlag.

Said, E. (2001) *Orientalism: Western Conceptions of the Orient*, 5th edn, London: Penguin.

Scheyvens, R. (2002) *Tourism for Development: Empowering Communities*, Upper Saddle River, NJ: Prentice Hall.

Seidman, G.W. (2000) 'Adjusting the lens: what do globalizations, transnationalisms, and the anti-apartheid movement mean for social movement theory?', in J.A. Guidry, M.D. Kennedy and M.N. Zald (eds) *Globalizations and Social Movements: Culture, Power, and the Transnational Public Sphere*, Ann Arbor, MI: University of Michigan Press.

Selinger, E. and Outterson, K. (2009) 'The ethics of poverty tourism', *Boston School of Law Working Papers*. Available online at www.bu.edu/law/faculty/scholarship/ workingpapers/documents/SelingerEOuttersonK06–02–09.pdf (accessed 27 October 2011).

Shepherd, N. and Hall, M. (eds) (2007) *Desire Lines: Space, Memory and Identity in the Post-Apartheid City*, Abingdon: Routledge.

Steinbrink, M. (2012) 'We did the slum! Urban poverty tourism in historical perspective', *Tourism Geographies*, 14(2): forthcoming.

Urry, J. (2002) *The Tourist Gaze*, 2nd edn, Thousand Oaks, CA: Sage.

Wallerstein, I.M. (2004) *World-Systems Analysis: An Introduction*, Durham, NC: Duke University Press.

Williams, C. (2008) 'Ghettourism and voyeurism, or challenging stereotypes and raising consciousness? Literary and non-literary forays into the favelas of Rio de Janeiro', *Bulletin of Latin American Research*, 27(4): 483–500.

Wolfson, C. (2007) 'Kenyans unite with foreign allies at WSF', *rabble.ca*. Available online at www.rabble.ca/news/kenyans-unite-foreign-allies-wsf> (accessed 29 January 2009).

WSF (World Social Forum) (2006) 'Fórum Social Mundial', *History of WSF*. Available online at www.forumsocialmundial.org.br/main.php?id_menu=2&cd_language=2> (accessed 8 October 2011).

4 Slum tourism: for the poor, by the poor

Kanika Basu

Introduction

Slums may reflect abject human misery, but at the same time they obviously fascinate, incite, excite and inspire people from all walks of life. They have been visited, revisited, researched and reported ever since their first appearance (see Steinbrink 2012 and Seaton in this volume).

Slums are an integral part of India's urban landscape. The total slum population, as per the Census 2001, was reported to be 52.4 million, in 1,743 cities/towns across 26 states in India (NBO 2010). Mumbai, the financial capital of India, has the highest number of slum dwellers, reported to be 6.5 million, followed by the national capital, Delhi, which has 1.8 million (Census 2001). The figures reflect the geographical spread and magnitude of the problem that faces the policy planners and development professionals in India. However, in spite of the strong efforts on the part of the government of India to reverse the trend of increasing slums in Indian cities, success has eluded successive central and state governments. However, although this leads to much frustration for policy planners and implementation agencies, slums have inspired people from different walks of life. For example, the slums of Mumbai – or 'chawls' as they are locally known – have been used as a backdrop and at times the central theme for 'Bollywood' movies. As elsewhere, slums in India have been visited, investigated, researched and reported, and concern and curiosity about life in the slums continues.

The genesis of slum tourism in India may be attributed to this undeterred interest. It started in Mumbai in 2005, followed by Delhi, and has been in operation ever since. Although slum tourism has not proliferated in other major cities, such as Kolkata, Chennai, Hyderabad and Bangalore, it has consolidated and prospered in both these cities. Slum tourism in India may be limited in geographic spread, but it is gaining ground as the number of tourists increases every year, much to the annoyance of the authorities. The phenomenon has created an outcry about its ethics and efficacy among officials as well as development experts in India.

In this chapter I argue that, if 'tourism' in other impoverished areas can be accepted and endorsed as a potential engine of development, there is little and inept logic in discarding slum tourism on ethical grounds. Disregarding slum tourism without a comprehensive impact assessment that incorporates the hosts' perspective and the guests' experiential learning is an unjustifiable intellectual orthodoxy. I need to clarify that I do not attempt a comprehensive impact assessment of slum tourism in this chapter. Instead, I use my experiences of visiting numerous slums as an urban development professional to propound that outright rejection of slum tourism is unwise. If a participatory approach to its design and execution is undertaken, it may potentially benefit both hosts and guests.

Slum tourism: demystifying the excuse of ethics

Marcelo Armstrong introduced favela tourism in 1992 (Loftus 2009); its genesis is often linked to the Earth Summit on Environment and Sustainable Development in Rio, which brought numerous visitors to the city (Freire-Medeiros 2009). Township tours emerged as a niche market in South Africa in the early 1990s (Rolfes *et al.* 2009; Butler 2010). The slum tour of Dharavi, Mumbai, was initiated by Reality Tours and Travel in 2005, and so is a very recent phenomenon (Meschkank 2011). It has continued to thrive and is reported to be 'red hot' after the success of the film *Slumdog Millionaire* (Weiner 2009; Ganguli 2010). While guided tours of slums organized by tour operators, where tourists are required to pay a fee, may be a recent phenomenon in India, 'slumming', or to 'spend time at a lower social level than one's own through curiosity or for charitable purposes' (OED 2011) – to see and report how the other half lives – is not unheard of in India. Slumming has inspired literary works as well as many movies. In an indulgent sense of the term, 'slumming' is also mandatory for academic pursuits in various social science disciplines in India. In other words, the slum as a phenomenon and as an issue has been in the public domain for consumption in various forms. Though not systematically documented, there are anecdotes to suggest that the role of 'slumming' cannot be discounted in the rise of socio-political awareness and demand for justice and equality in India. As such, it may be argued that, as elsewhere, poverty tourism in India is much older than critics acknowledge (Selinger and Outterson 2009).

However, the introduction of slum tourism in its current form, of organized visits of groups of tourists by tour operators, has invited sharp criticism from the authorities. Critics argue that slum tourism turns people's lives and miseries into a spectacle, and is therefore exploitative. It trivializes complex socio-political and economic issues and compromises the dignity of slum dwellers. Expressing concern about who conducts such tours and how, tourism officials in India have opined that slum tourism 'should not to be encouraged since it is neither good for India nor for the people living there [i.e. the slum?]' (Ward 2010). Criticism of slum tourism in India has not stopped there. Government officials have recommended that it should be stopped altogether and that slum tourism tour operators should be punished. A tourism official has even described the organizers of the Dharavi slum tours in Mumbai as 'parasites who need to be investigated and put behind bars' on an Indian television channel (Lefevre 2010).

This articulated response from the officials and authorities of tourism in India is not based on vigorous studies using a comprehensive theoretical framework. Their reaction requires an understanding of handling the slum as a problem by successive governments and various state governments in India. There has been a plethora of policies, programmes and schemes for slum improvement, starting in the very first 'Five Year Plan' in India (1951–6). Most of the cities even instigated specialized institutions, such as the Slum Clearance Board or the Slum Redevelopment Authority, or departments within the Urban Local Body (e.g. the Jhuggi Jhopri department of the Municipal Corporation of Delhi (MCD)). However, as mentioned earlier, the success of these institutions has been elusive vis-à-vis their stated objectives, as is evident from all the relevant and reported statistics regarding slums in India. At best, their performance can be described as mixed, wherein the number of slums and the slum population have increased over the years, but the prevailing conditions in slums, in terms of basic services such as water and sanitation, have improved over time (NSSO 2010).

The reasons for the creation of slums, their rapid proliferation in developing nations and the role of planners in their mitigation are the sources of a raging debate in the development arena (Verma 2002; Davis 2006). This is beyond the scope of this chapter, but its impact is important for the debate on slum tourism. In a globalized world, where cities compete for international capital, the presence or lack of slums is interpreted as an important indicator of the health of the city, and slums are an understandable irritant for city managers. Slums and their proliferation are seen as a blot on India's success story of development and emergence as an economic and political power in the international scenario. Consequently, while launching policies and programmes for slum improvement has remained undiminished, the culture of denial of slums is irrefutable.

This is best understood by having a look at the very system of reporting slums in Indian cities. Slums are essentially of two types: 'notified' and 'unnotified'. The latter category is not recognized, remains unreported and in most cases is not eligible to be covered under most of the government initiatives. The recently launched central government scheme 'Rajiv Awas Yojana', named after the ex-Prime Minister of India, the late Shri Rajiv Gandhi, is an exception and categorically situates both notified and non-notified slums in its scope. The Census of India 2001, the first census to systematically enumerate the slums in Indian cities, reported only notified slums, and experts opine that it is a gross underestimation of the scale of the problem. This culture of denial of slums – or poverty as one may call it – is confirmed by the strange act of the authorities in the recently concluded Commonwealth Games 2010 in Delhi, when the slums that could not be relocated were cordoned off with glamorous bamboo screen view-cutters. To conclude, one may say that the official response to slum tourism is more about slums and the associated stigma (which compromises the image of the city as an investment destination) and less about the ethics of tourism. The decision of the Indian government to lodge a complaint against a BBC documentary on the Mumbai slums by Kevin McCloud, entitled *Grand Designs on Dharavi Slums in Mumbai*, on the grounds that it was poverty-porn and expected to compromise the image of India and negatively affect the tourism industry in India (*Indian Express* 2010), reconfirms the validity of the observation.

Such a strong response from the government, besides being an expression of the associated stigma regarding slums and poverty, can also be partly attributed to the fact that these tours are increasingly described and marketed as 'reality tours' and 'authentic tours'. Slums and poverty are no doubt a reality in India, as in many other developing countries, but describing tours as 'reality' and 'authentic' – even if not consciously, but by implication – disregards one part of the 'whole' reality. The tagging of such tours as 'cultural or ethnic tourism' (Ramchander 2004) or educational tourism (Rolfes *et al.* 2007) has been seen as an appropriate label for slum tourism, but only occupies a modest place in the tour operator's glossary. It is undeniable that the phrase 'reality tourism', associated with slum tours conducted by the tour operator Reality Tours and Travel in Dharavi, irks people in general and officials in particular. Even if not by intention, but by approach, it undermines the other realities, such as the built heritage (e.g. the Taj Mahal), the exotic natural heritage of the beaches of Goa and Kerala, the Himalayan ranges, the rich tribal culture of central India and even the factory that manufactures NANO, the cheapest car in the world. All are as real and appealing as Dharavi. Sensitivity in choice of words for describing as well as marketing slum tourism can allay scepticism to a large extent (if not completely) and improve its acceptability for tourist consumption.

Slum tourism has met with similarly strong criticism from a section of academics who argue that gazing at the poor is not tourism at all, but voyeurism, and therefore should not have any place in the ethical traveller's itinerary (Weiner 2008). Analysing the literary representations of favelas in Rio de Janeiro, Claire Williams (2008) notes that the growth in favela tourism is indicative of a voyeuristic interest in poverty and argues that it is impossible not to be a voyeur when writing about an alien environment, no matter how integrated one becomes or how generous one's intensions are. The moral issues and ethical concerns in slum tourism are extremely relevant, but its outright rejection on moral and ethical grounds is difficult to comprehend, even more so because there are hardly any systematic studies or empirical findings that qualify the claim that slum tourism is an invasion of privacy and cause for irritation of the slum dwellers. The empirical forays into understanding slum tourism by Rolfes *et al.* (2009) are largely restricted to the analysis of the perspective of tour operators, tour guides and tourists. Similarly, the primary research question addressed by Meschkank (2011), while analysing the construction of reality in slum tourism, is: 'how do the different actors in slum tourism – the participating tourists as well as the tour providers – observe slums?' While the motivation and perception of these actors are important considerations in analysing the moral and exploitation concerns, the perceptions of the residents, whose work, homes and lives are on display, are an issue of equal if not greater consideration. An empirical analysis of the people's (i.e. residents of Dharavi) perspective on the tour and tourists when analysing and evaluating the ethicality of the tours – though not 'comprehensive enough to draw conclusions' – is offered by Ma (2010: 30; see also Freire-Medeiros in this volume).

One of the strongest criticisms of slum tourism from the academic world has come from Professor David Fennell. He crisply summarized the ethical issue by asking: 'Would you want people stopping outside of your front door every day, or maybe twice a day, snapping a few pictures of you and making some observations about your lifestyle?'(cited in Weiner 2008: 1). There is no denying that the issue of ethics is quite pertinent. Recent years have seen a renewed and rising interest in ethics in various academic disciplines, such as economics, environmental and urban planning and anthropology, to the extent that it is impossible to separate ethics from the question of development in general and tourism development in particular (Smith and Duffy 2003).

Few, if any, would disagree that tourism is not all about satisfying those with the ability to pay, but ethics have a definite role to play in tourism development. However, while recognizing the importance of ethics, it is equally important to acknowledge that ethics or ethical disputes are not culture-neutral concepts, but are conditional upon the different stages of development, social expectations and aspirations. It may be argued that it is on these grounds that Fennell's criticism falls short, by disregarding the local culture and aspirations and, to some extent, imposing western values while raising ethical concerns. The claim that residents of slum communities would feel distressed by people visiting and interacting with them merely because authors may feel the same is a conjecture, and therefore should not be grounds for outright and total rejection of slum tourism. Such extreme recommendations should be supported by convincing and compelling logic.

I also question the validity of rejecting slum tourism on ethical grounds while endorsing tourism as a tool for economic development and poverty alleviation. How different is slum tourism from tourism per se? Tourism has long been defined as a path to economic development precisely because it places a value on objects, landscapes and even people that were previously deemed economically 'worthless' – that is, they may have held a moral, aesthetic or even spiritual but not monetary value (Smith and Duffy 2003). Tourism represents an insidious form of consumptive activity (McKercher 1993). In other words, commodification is obvious in tourism, be it landscape, art, culture, people or poverty. There is abounding literature that endorses tourism as the world's foremost economic engine (Fennell 2006).

Another popular theme of research related to tourism is the cost–benefit analysis, which, while tabulating the economic benefits, also quantifies the cost of socio-economic, ecological and cultural fall-outs that are intrinsic to tourism. One example, as set out by Fennell (ibid.), showcases all the possible ill effects of tourism, ranging from infrastructure, ecology, health, sex abuse and drugs to the displacement of local people; Fennell finds that scarcely 10 per cent of Goans are found to have benefitted from tourism. The case study upholds the observation of Rothman and Britton (cited in Ioannides 2003: 43) that: 'it [i.e. tourism] may or may not rescue economies', and 'only a few locals, including a handful of major landowners and developers, benefit from the industry's growth'.

As such it would seem that tourism can be best described as an economic activity that produces a range of positive and negative impacts, and the social, cultural and environmental impacts associated with tourism development appear to be inevitable regardless of the type of tourism activity (McKercher 1993, 2003). In fact, criticism of tourism is not new and has been around as long as people have travelled for leisure (Butcher 2003). This led to the development of the 'alternative tourism and sustainable tourism' paradigm that aims to minimize the negative impacts and maximize the benefits of tourism. However, development of locally rooted, equitable and environmentally responsive forms of tourism has been agonizingly slow. Understanding the reasons for this and overcoming obstacles to change still remain fundamental challenges (Mowforth and Munt 2009). In spite of the challenges put up by the tourism industry on sustainability issues, tourism has not been disregarded as a tool of economic development but has, rather, been endorsed by the United Nations (UN) for fulfilling its Millennium Development Goals (WTO 2005).

On these observations I base my argument that, if tourism in impoverished areas may be accepted and endorsed elsewhere, why then should slum tourism, which suffers from similar dilemmas and moral concerns, be rejected outright? Concern for the poor and safeguarding of their interests and privacy are laudable aims, but even the harshest critics agree that slum tourism can have some trickle-down benefits for the slum communities. Is the rejection of slum tourism an ethical response, then? It can even be argued that there is little logic and morality in denying the right to tour slums to one section of people (i.e. tourists), when similar activities are undertaken by development professionals, sociologists, journalists and artists, often with no tangible, immediate and direct benefit to the community.

Slum tourism: a learning experience

While critics reject slum tourism on the basis of ethics and morality and the invasion of people's privacy, its defenders mostly base their arguments on describing it as a learning experience – 'a valuable window into the lives of the poorest of the poor' that also 'funnels tourist dollar into the slums' (Weiner 2009: 1). The idea that slum tours are not just about showcasing poverty but more about learning is articulated by Chris Way, the founder of Reality Tours:

We're trying to dispel the myth that people there sit around doing nothing, that they're criminals. We show it for what it is – a place where people are working hard, struggling to make a living and doing it in an honest way.

(Lefevre 2010)

Similar sentiments are reflected in the Dharavi Slum tour outline, which says:

On our tours, you will see why Dharavi is the heart of small scale industries in Mumbai (annual turnover is approximately US$665 million). We show you a wide range of these activities – from recycling, [to] the making of clay pots, embroidery, bakery, soap factory, leather tanning, papad (poppadom) making and many others, most of which take place in very small spaces.

We also pass by the residential areas, where you really get a feel of how the people are living and you see the sense of community and spirit that exists in the area . . . The tours are not just about observing. One of our guides, who all speak very good English and have a wide knowledge of the area, will explain the industry and talk about the people including the issues that they face. You are encouraged to ask questions.

(Reality Tours and Travel 2012)

The image of Dharavi that the tour operators promote appears to be one of economic activity that prevails even under difficult living conditions. Other research also discusses how tours in Dharavi expose the high economic energy and extreme industriousness of the slum inhabitants, rather than their abject poverty (Rolfes 2010; Meschkank 2011; see also Meschkank in this volume).

I have visited Dharavi as well as many other slums in India in a professional capacity, with the primary objective to identify problems, issues and constraints and consequently evolve solutions. In order to personally experience the 'learning' and 'educational' motivations often associated with slum tourism, I planned a visit to Dharavi on my own (i.e. not on a conducted tour) as a non-intrusive 'participant', thus distancing myself from my professional identity as a planner as well as a confirmed 'tourist' in order to observe life and people in Dharavi as unobtrusively as possible. The approach was to be distinctly different from my other visits to the slums, wherein the interaction was impersonal but intrusive, mostly through a structured questionnaire. In my description of slum visits I highlight certain positive aspects of slum tourism. I aim to show how a total rejection of slum tourism leads to lost opportunities to understand the situation and dynamics of urban poverty and slums, and more specifically that slums do not necessarily epitomize economic poverty. Critics may point out that such a description of slum visits is biased and romanticizes slums. I admit that I use primarily positive anecdotes, with scant reference to the 'other' view of slum tourism, about how the poor feel 'gawked at' or 'as animals in the zoo'. Romanticization is, however, not my intention, and I fully acknowledge that slum tourism can have negative impacts as well. I do not validate my argument in favour of slum tourism on the logic that slum tourism translates to personal and professional learning and therefore should always be accepted and upscaled. Instead, the narrative is used merely to reconfirm that there is an inherent learning that may or may not translate to tangible or intangible benefits for the community. However, it can never be a counter-argument to disregard and dismiss the people's perception of being demeaned. The extent of economic opportunities for local community members in slum tourism is debatable (Freire-Medeiros 2010), and the derived benefits through inherent, tacit learning are inconclusive. These notions are important and should not be forgotten when reading the following narrative of a visit to the Indian slums.

Anybody visiting Mumbai has little chance of escaping Dharavi. Even if one misses the aerial view during touchdown at Mumbai airport, any taxi driver would in all probability point out Dharavi to 'outsiders', often mentioning that it is the biggest slum in Asia. In one of my recent visits, when I politely corrected my taxi driver, saying that Dharavi is no longer the biggest slum since, officially, that dubious honour now belongs to Orangi in Pakistan, the reaction was one of disbelief and something akin to disappointment. My taxi dropped me off at '90ft Road', and from there I started my journey to Dharavi with a friend (an ex-student of social work from Mumbai University who knows Dharavi like the back of his hand). Very soon we were deep inside the narrow by-lanes of Dharavi. I promised myself to be as invisible and non-intrusive as possible, which, given that there are many people of my regional identity in Dharavi, required little more than a careful choice of clothing.

In no time we were traipsing the narrow lanes. My first thought was that Dharavi had changed. It was not just the high-rise development on the periphery that was not there before, but something else. It was seven in the morning and people were getting ready for the day, cleaning the house, having a bath and washing clothes, just like before, but what was different this time was the ample water that was flowing. I also saw men in uniform sweeping the streets of Dharavi, something unheard of even a few years previously. We walked around the residential area, observing the two-storey dwelling units with iron staircases that would be bound to give shivers to any structural engineer. They definitely looked precarious, but, decorated with lights to celebrate Diwali, they looked like well-cared-for homes rather than dilapidated structures.

Dharavi expresses a seamless land-use pattern. We saw a dwelling that also housed a small unit manufacturing leather belts, just beside a bakery. Embroidery shops stood next to an eatery, and eateries next to a garbage collection point where wastes were being segregated: nothing is a waste in Dharavi. It may seem disconcerting to those advocating compatible land use and zoning, but the efficient use of every available inch of space was impressive. We looked around and found that the potters, embroiderers, bakers, manufacturers of recycled goods, leather workshops and others that define the character of Dharavi were still active. The development efforts (and land grabbers) have not been able to take away Dharavi's soul. Orangi has taken over in matter of size, but Dharavi's capacity for accommodating such a wide variety of activities over such a small area still seems unsurpassed.

We kept walking and stopped twice to ask for the way out after meeting a dead end. We saw breads and huge packets of 'namkeen' (an Indian snack) being carted away for distribution in other parts of the city, huge sacks of leather goods and embroidered garments being put in trucks – obviously to be sold at a premium price in high-end shops in Mumbai – and truckloads of many other packaged goods waiting to be driven away. We really got the impression that Dharavi gives much more to the city than the city gives back. It reflects the hard work people put in during long hours and under trying circumstances. Interestingly, I saw a gym where, even so early in the day, a few youngsters were pumping weights. I could not imagine that the local body responsible for slum improvement had provided this structure. My guess was that it was another example of the poor taking care of themselves and all their needs, and it reminded me of my experiences as a student in a slum in the city of Ahmedabad. Seeing that most of the slum households have televisions and refrigerators, I could not help wonder aloud why they did not build toilets rather than buy such luxury items. One young man answered promptly: 'Because toilet cannot be bought. Constructing a toilet would be useless, till the city authorities allow integration with the city service lines.' I learnt in no uncertain terms that, wherever possible, the poor take care of themselves, and for whatever they depend on the government, they are failed miserably.

Next, I tried to locate a medical college student from Bihar who was staying in Dharavi and who had shared his dreams with me during my last visit, almost eight years before. I somehow located his 'kholi' (apartment), but he was not there. Hopefully, Dharavi had been a stepping stone for him, just like Ashish Chadha, who 'moved into Dharavi one wet monsoon day in September 1996 . . . and left it only to go to Stanford University in 1999' (2009: 1), showing that slum dwelling is not the end of the line for all of its inhabitants.

It was on my way out, feeling thirsty and tired after a gruelling walk in the by-lanes of Dharavi, that I stopped to buy a bottle of water, and then broke the promise I had made to myself that this time I would be absolutely non-intrusive during my visit: I asked one lady for a glass of water. She came back with water and a couple of home-made sweets on a plate, insisting that on the eve of Diwali no guest can be allowed to go without having sweets, since guests are no less than God. She said 'atithi devo bhava' (the guest is God), which I remembered was the official tagline of Indian Tourism. Just before hailing a taxi for the journey back home, I succumbed to my obsession for bags and bought beautiful leather handbags at a bargain price from shops that thrive in Dharavi. I did not even try to figure out whether my spending in Dharavi would lead to any benefit for those workers in the tannery and leather workshops that I had just seen, because, borrowing words from Andrea Gross, I would say, 'deep down I know . . . [they] have changed my life more than I'll ever be able to change theirs' (Gross 2010).

It needs to be reaffirmed that there are serious problems in Dharavi that require intervention. Overcrowding, precarious housing, inadequate infrastructure, pollution and, most importantly, unhealthy living conditions are apparent in the Dharavi landscape. What is also apparent, however, is the resilience of the people, which makes me agree with the observation that 'it's not an abrasion that must be hidden. It is a heritage to be preserved . . . It is not where slumdogs quit to become millionaires. It is where slumdogs thrive and celebrate their doggedness' (Chadha 2009: 1). Irrespective of the intent of the tour operator and tourist, a visit to Dharavi throws up such myriad experiences that 'learning' is inevitable. In fact, in support of his critique of slum tourism, when David Fennell says that slum tourism 'affirms in my mind how lucky I am – or how unlucky they are' (cited in Weiner 2008: 1), he inadvertently conforms to a typical experiential 'learning' whose importance in life should not be undervalued. Thus, based on my experiences, I would argue that a visit to the slums may help in dispelling prejudices that tourists have been found to have about such areas (Steinbrink 2012). I am convinced that, while it may have many names and as many criticisms, it is undeniably educational tourism.

It also made me believe that, if our own citizens would also take part in such tours (as with the initial slum visits in Victorian London), it could help create an awareness and sensitivity that would make people realize that not everything about a slum is evil, and that, in demolishing slums, we are just not demolishing houses but destroying homes. This may lead us to think twice before demanding the eviction of slum dwellers on petty pretexts, and encourage us to create more understanding of their situation among the Indian upper and middle classes, who currently seem insensitive regarding slums, as evidenced in the film *Hamara Sahar* (1985), in which they bluntly express their hatred for slum dwellers and demand evictions and demolitions (Das 1997).

My belief is that one useful impact of slum tours for policy planners and scholars (in contrast to visiting slums as a researcher to identify problems and constraints) would be to unravel the myths and misconceptions that still exist in their own minds and that often have negative effects on their actions. A good example of such existing misconceptions is the recent observation made by professors Vijay Govindarajan and Christian Sarkar (2010: 1) that 'to move beyond charity, the poor must become owners of their homes, responsible for their care and upkeep'. The suitability of their concept for mass adoption is a different debate altogether, but their perception about poverty is erroneous to the extent of being insulting. A few hours spent in a slum would have helped them to realize that the poor in the developing world do not enjoy the welfare benefits from the state that are so common in the western world. They survive because they take care of themselves. Similarly, when Fennel says, 'if you are so concerned just write a cheque' (cited in Weiner 2008: 1), he misses the point: if only money could do it, many cities would have been slum-free by now.

Typically, it is erroneous policies and programmes that have been the cause of perpetuating slums, even when an enormous amount of money has been spent for their alleviation. The distinctive charm of touring slums is that it is not just about learning, it is a complete experience of delearning and relearning ... a deconstruction of the slum image.

Slum tourism: in search of a participatory approach

The only democratic way to avert slum tourism is to have no slums. This remains a cherished dream for all development professionals, but with little chance of realization in the near future. The fundamental question to be addressed is not whether slum tourism should happen or not, but how to conduct it in an ethical way that 'will not only have a positive impact on the tourist – but on the community being toured, as well' (Slater 2010: 1). The question 'how' is central to the sustainability of slum tourism. Not only are slum communities incredibly diverse, but, as Koens points out elsewhere in this volume, even within tourism, actors can have conflicting interests. It is incredibly difficult to ensure a situation in which both local communities and tourists gain, but an insensitive approach and denial of the existence of slum tourism will certainly lead to a lose–lose situation. What, then, is the 'right' way? The answer to this question is not easy and is encased in a myriad of such complex issues that the search may appear futile at the outset. In my consideration, a 'pro-poor approach' to slum tourism is the most critical requirement for ensuring its sustainability, wherein 'pro-poor tourism' is not an end but a means. It basically implies the ways and approaches through which a slum tourism operator chooses to do its business (Goodwin 2005). In the field of tourism, those who speak of sustainable development almost always include the participation of the destination communities as one essential element or principle of sustainability (Mowforth and Munt 2009). The first step in participation, as few would disagree, is incorporating people's perspectives. And so, what is seriously lacking in the currently available literature on slum tourism – scholarly papers and journal articles included – is a comprehensive documentation and analysis of the hosts' perception on the phenomenon (see Freire-Medeiros in this volume).

There are limited empirical studies to accommodate the perspective of community members (who are the most important stakeholders in resolving the ethical concerns in the slum tourism debate) either by critics or defenders. Of the 210 comments received on Eric Weiner's (2008) article in *The New York Times* at the time of writing, only three demanded: 'why not ask the residents?' Selinger and Outterson (2009: 19) point to the necessity of getting approval of the slum community when they say, 'the consent of the community matters greatly, and complaints and suggestions from residents and their leaders should shape poverty tour practices'.

However, all the current recommended methods are rooted in the guests' prescriptive and diverse experiences. Eric Weiner's article is a case in example when he recommends:

- **Small is Beautiful**. There's a big difference between a group of 50 tourists barreling through the slums on a tour bus and a group of five or six on foot. One is an invasion, the other is not.
- **No Photos, Please**. Snapping photos is bound to raise suspicions among the slum inhabitants and, justifiably or not, give credence to charges of voyeurism. Leave the camera at the hotel.
- **Funnel Profits Back Into the Slums**. The good slum-tour companies are already doing this, donating a portion of their profits to help build community centers, clinics and other worthwhile projects. They need to do more.
- **Soft Sell**. Brochures and websites touting slum tours should not bundle them together with adventure tourism, as if the tours were some sort of cultural bungee jumping. The marketing should be low-key and respectful.

(Weiner 2009: 1)

Similar thoughts are reflected on Amanda Kendle's web-page: 'don't take photographs, don't give money or candy away (donate through a suitable charity or organization instead), stay in small groups and so on – and then perhaps poverty tourism really does provide some benefits for the locals' (Kendle 2008). My disagreement with such recommendations is not based on an analysis of their ability to deliver the desired objective of conducting slum tours properly and ethically, but primarily on their approach of prescribing unilateral recommendations. To my understanding this is a reflection of intellectual arrogance, and is best avoided. As an example I would like to debate the issue of taking photographs by quoting Andrea Gross:

One child points to my camera and then to himself. I take a picture, then show it to him, and a grin spreads across his thin face. Other children crowd around. I snap and show as they laugh, begging for more. Good. At least I'm a distraction in a day filled with precious little entertainment.

(2010: 1)

I substantiate this opinion not because of the emotional appeal of Andrea Gross's writing, but because it largely conforms to my own personal experience, wherein taking photographs of children and women (invariably with prior permission and sometimes at their request) had been the 'ice-breaker' for community discussions. Therefore, taking photographs with permission and respecting objections (if any) appears more reasonable to me. I must clarify that I pose this argument within the particular cultural context only, knowing that it is taboo and completely prohibited in certain other cultural contexts. More importantly, this must not be interpreted as a conclusive recommendation for allowing cameras or photography in Dharavi or any other slum tourism sites in India, but emphasizes the necessity of involving people and communities in decision-making on all issues that impact – or are perceived to impact – on their physical and emotional well-being.

Taking it as a foregone conclusion that participatory planning is the most credible approach to making slum tourism sustainable, acceptable and pro-poor, it must be understood that the 'participation' of people should not be limited to participation in the tourism enterprise as providers of services and goods, but should also include the planning and decision-making process (see also Rolfes *et al.* 2009). Unfortunately, the current approach of recruiting local people as guides for these tours, often heralded as reflective of people's participation in slum tourism, only validates that participation as providers of services. To my understanding, it is motivated more by the guests' needs than by the tour operator's conviction about the philosophy of participation. It must be understood that to have a local person as a guide is a fundamental prerequisite for the smooth operation of the tour, as well as enabling the tourists to experience slums.

The current approach has a very restricted, almost non-existent scope for people's participation. Ma's (2010) study of the slum residents in Dharavi shows that slum residents are mostly ambivalent about the tour. They are split between liking, disliking and feeling neutral about the tourists. It also demonstrates that the community is largely ignorant about Reality Tour and Travel's mission. This evidently implies a lack of knowledge and consent of the community in conducting tours in Dharavi, and consequently poses serious doubts about the sensitivity of the tour operator in respecting the sentiments of the people involved.

Tour operators justify their good intentions by contributing part of the profit or running charities in various forms. These efforts are laudable as demonstrating a commitment to social responsibility, but do not fulfil the agency's obligation to involve community and so ensure a pro-poor approach. There is a definite need to increase the scope of community participation in slum tourism, and especially on issues such as the timing of the tours (time of the day and even days of the year), the number of tours and visitors, the length of stay, the use of cameras and even pricing. Tour operators must realize that these important decisions should not be determined only from the business perspective of cost minimization and profit maximization. However, the most critical input is provided by the knowledge and consent of the people, without which slum tourism would be reduced to voyeurism and would soon evoke antagonism from the community. This brings forth the next issue in participation – that of 'consensus' building. Dharavi (and almost all other slums all over the world) is not a homogeneous entity. Slums represent extreme diversity in economic well-being, social background, cultural ethos and regional identities. A homogeneous response from such heterogeneous societies is an absolute impossibility.

Therefore, the expected challenge facing any participatory planning exercise would be to collate an extreme diversity of views and build a consensus. There is no denying that it is an enormous assignment. The challenge is limited not just to collating extremely diverse views but also to interpreting them. And although various techniques of participation and consensus building have been proposed, there is still no comprehensive framework that enjoys absolute acceptability. One of the inherent criticisms of participatory planning principles is that the consensus-building process often degenerates into feeble and ambiguous interpretations of diverse opinions, and is 'interpreted' as participation and consultation without actually being so – that is, wherein the attempt is to 'win the people over' (Freire 1970: 95) without ceding power or control to enable the people to decide for themselves (Turner 1977).

The other criticism of 'participation' is that it is so often hijacked by a comparatively influential component of the community, and that it thus may not represent the larger community perspective; self-interest is therefore pertinent in this context. The execution of any process or technique for participatory planning in slum tourism is bound to be criticized for its imperfections, since it always involves such diverse and extreme opinions. However, it should be appreciated that, as a practice, it would be comparatively more democratic and of greater benefit than the current approach, wherein community members are mere recipients of benefits that do not necessarily feature in their 'wish lists' (Ma 2010). The current ambivalence, apathy and sense of doubt about the intent of the tour operators and western tourists can undermine the social sustainability of slum tourism, since it potentially runs the risk of being converted to social hostility. The main accomplishment of the participatory process, even if rudimentary and riddled with imperfections, would be to dispel the doubt and suspicion (if there are any) from the minds of the people in slums about the intentions of visits made by the tourists, especially western tourists. This, to my understanding, is a crucial input, since even if we accept the 'good intent' of the operators as well as the tourists, it does not necessarily confirm that the poor will not feel demeaned by such visits. We must not forget that it is the feeling of the people or community, and not the intent of the operators and visiting tourists, that is central to the issue of making slum tourism pro-poor (Selinger and Outterson 2009). To my mind, the only way to do this is to involve the community in decision-making. Perfection of the process will happen once we begin practising it.

Conclusion

Slum tourism is controversial since it provokes serious moral and ethical dilemmas. While on the one hand it has been described as educational tourism, on the other it has been labelled as invariably voyeuristic, irrespective of intent. Although the moral issues and ethical concerns, along with economic impact, personal enrichment and learning from slum tours, are widely debated, its rapid growth as a niche form of tourism worldwide indicates that, just like slums, this phenomenon is here to stay. The intent of tourists can be varied, from simple curiosity to the search for authenticity, self-learning or a simple diversion from everyday life, but it consistently puts the work, homes and lives of slum residents on display. The simple fact that it is people, and essentially poor people, who are the centre point of this show means that it is imperative to evolve the right approach that can ensure people's participation, so that community members are partners and not just recipients and mere bystanders.

Bibliography

Butcher, J. (2003) *The Moralisation of Tourism*, Abingdon: Routledge.

Butler, S.R. (2010) 'Should I stay or should I go? Negotiating township tours in post-apartheid South Africa', *Journal of Tourism and Cultural Change*, 8(1–2): 15–29.

Census of India (2001) *Slum Population in Million Plus Cities (Municipal Corporations): Part A*, New Delhi: Office of the Registrar General, Ministry of Home Affairs.

Chadha, A. (2009) 'Dharavi's real slumdog stories', *Hindustan Times*, 18 January. Available online at www.hindustantimes.com/Dharavi-s-real-slumdog-stories/Article1–367851.aspx (accessed 14 October 2010).

Das, P.K. (1997) 'Manifesto of a housing activist', in S. Patel and A. Thorner (eds) *Bombay Metaphor for Modern India*, Delhi: Oxford India Press.

Davis, M. (2006) *Planet of Slums*, London: Verso.

Fennell, A.D. (2006) *Tourism Ethics*, Clevedon: Channel View.

Freire, P. (1970) *Pedagogy of the Oppressed*, New York: Continuum.

Freire-Medeiros, B. (2009) 'The favela and its touristic transits', *Geoforum*, 40(4): 580–8.

—— (2010) 'Gazing at the poor: favela tours and the colonial legacy', *London Debates 2010*, London: School of Advanced Study, University of London. Available online at www.sas.ac.uk/fileadmin/documents/postgraduate/Papers_London_Debates_2010/Freire_Medeiros__Gazing_at_the_poor.pdf (accessed 15 June 2011).

Ganguli, S. (2010) 'Everybody loves a good slum!' Available online at www.dare.co.in/opportunities/idea/everybody-loves-a-good-slum.htm (accessed 15 June 2011).

Goodwin, H. (2005) 'Pro-poor tourism: principles, methodologies and mainstreaming', paper presented at the International Conference on Pro-Poor Tourism, Mechanisms and Mainstreaming, Universiti Teknologi Malaysia, Johor Bahru, 4–6 May.

Govindarajan, V. and Sarkar, C. (2010) 'The $300 house: a hands-on lab for reverse innovation?' Available online at http://blogs.hbr.org/govindarajan/2010/08/the-300-house-a-hands-on-lab-f.html (accessed 7 November 2010).

Gross, A. (2010) 'How slum tourism can change your life'. Available online at www.yourlifeisatrip.com/home/how-slum-tourism-can-change-your-life.html (accessed 10 November 2010).

Indian Express (2010) 'India to complain about BBC's "poverty porn" Mumbai film', *Indian Express*, 25 January. Available online at www.indianexpress.com/news/india-to-complain-about-bbcs-poverty-porn/571514 (accessed 9 June 2011).

Ioannides, D. (2003) 'The economics of tourism in host communities', in T. Singh and R. Dowling (eds) *Tourism in Destination Countries*, Oxford: CABI.

Kendle, A. (2008) 'Poverty tourism: exploring the slums of India, Brazil and South Africa'. Available online at www.vagabondish.com/poverty-tourism-touring-the-slums-of-india-brazil-and-south-africa (accessed 15 November 2010).

Lefevre, N. (2010) 'Slum tours: awareness-raising or voyeurism?' Available online at www.suite101.com/content/slum-tours-awareness-raising-or-voyeurism-a263032 #ixzz14WQVaxZV (accessed 15 October 2010).

Loftus, M. (2009) 'Slum tours: real or tacky?' Available online at http://traveler. nationalgeographic.com/2009/03/feature/slum-tours-text (accessed 10 November 2010).

Ma, B. (2010) 'A trip into the controversy: a study of slum tourism travel motivations', *Undergraduate Humanities Forum 2009–2010: Connections*, Penn Arts & Sciences. Available online at http://repository.upenn.edu/uhf_2010/12 (accessed 16 June 2011).

McKercher, B. (1993) 'Some fundamental truths about tourism: understanding tourism's social and environmental impacts', *Journal of Sustainable Tourism*, 1(1): 6–16.

—— (2003) 'Sustainable tourism development: guiding principles for planning and management', paper presented at the National Seminar on Sustainable Tourism Development, Bishkek, Kyrgystan, 5–9 November.

Meschkank, J. (2011) 'Investigations into slum tourism in Mumbai: poverty tourism and the tensions between different constructions of reality', *GeoJournal*, 76: 47–62.

Mowforth, M. and Munt, I. (2009) *Tourism and Sustainability: Development, Globalisation and New Tourism in the Third World*, Abingdon: Routledge.

National Building Organisation (NBO) (2010) *Report of the Committee on Slum Statistics/Census*, New Delhi: Ministry of Housing and Urban Poverty Alleviation (MoHUPA).

National Sample Survey Office (NSSO) (2010) *Some Characteristics of Urban Slums 2008–2009*, NSS 65th Round, New Delhi: NSSO, Ministry of Statistics and Programme Implementation.

Oxford Dictionaries Online (OED) (2011) Available online at www.oxforddictionaries. com/definition/slum>.(accessed 31 October 2011).

Ramchander, P. (2004) *Towards the Responsible Management of the Socio-cultural Impact of Township Tourism*, Pretoria: University of Pretoria.

Reality Tours and Travel (2012) 'Dharavi slum tours'. Available online at www.realitytoursandtravel.com/slumtours.html (accessed 10 October 2011).

Rolfes, M. (2010) 'Poverty tourism: theoretical reflections and empirical findings regarding an extraordinary form of tourism', *GeoJournal*, 75(5): 421–42.

——, Steinbrink, M. and Uhl, C. (2007) *Township Tours in Cape Town*, Potsdam: Universitätsverlag.

—— (2009) *Townships as Attraction: A Case Study on Township Tourism in Cape Town*, Potsdam: Universitätsverlag.

Selinger, E. and Outterson, K. (2009) 'The ethics of poverty tourism', Working Paper No. 09–29, Boston, MA: Boston University School of Law.

Slater, M. (2010) 'Poverty tourism: immoral or illuminating'. Available online at http://humanrights.change.org/blog/view/poverty_tourism_immoral_or_illuminating (accessed 15 November 2010).

Smith, M. and Duffy, R. (2003) *The Ethics of Tourism Development*, Abingdon: Routledge.

Steinbrink, M. (2012) 'We did the slum! Urban poverty tourism in historical perspective', *Tourism Geographies*, 14(2): forthcoming.

Turner, J.F.C. (1977) *Housing by People*, New York: Parthenon Books.

Verma, G.D. (2002) *Slumming India: A Chronicle of Slums and Their Saviours*, New Delhi: Penguin Books.

Ward, M. (2010) 'Booming trade in "slum tourism" dispels some myths, creates others'. Available online at http://this.org/magazine/2010/01/28/slum-tourism (accessed 10 November 2010).

Weiner, E. (2008) 'Slum visits: tourism or voyeurism'. Available online at www.nytimes.com/2008/03/09/travel/09heads.html?_r=1 (accessed 15 November 2010).

—— (2009) 'Slumming it: can slum tourism be done right?' Available online at www.worldhum.com/features/eric-weiner/slum-tourism-the-responsible-way-20090312 (accessed 15 November 2010).

Williams, C. (2008) 'Ghettourism and voyeurism, or challenging stereotypes and raising consciousness? Literary and non-literary forays into the favelas of Rio de Janeiro', *Bulletin of Latin American Research*, 27(4): 483–500.

World Trade Organization (WTO) (2005) *Declaration: 'Harnessing Tourism for Millennium Development Goals'*, Madrid: WTO.

5 Competition, cooperation and collaboration

Business relations and power in township tourism

Ko Koens

Introduction

Holidaymakers to South Africa increasingly include a visit to the townships on their itinerary, and the townships in the Cape Town region receive an estimated 250,000 to 500,000 international tourists annually (CTRU 2006a, b, c). While there are inherent ethical concerns with tourism to economically deprived areas, township tourism has also been credited with giving pride to people whose local culture has long been ignored, as well as providing an additional source of income to inhabitants (Maliepaard 2010; Rolfes 2010). This latter point is explicitly emphasized by the South African government. More particularly, township tourism is viewed as having the potential to stimulate entrepreneurship and local economic development, while at the same time addressing inequalities in the South African tourism industry (Rogerson 2004a). Notwithstanding the potential benefits of tourism, many authors have pointed out that it is not a panacea, and economic benefits for local communities are not self-evident (e.g. Archer *et al.* 2005; Wall and Mathieson 2006; Koens *et al.* 2009). In recent years, the pro-poor tourism movement has garnered increased interest with regard to using tourism as a development strategy. Its premise is that, if tourism is to provide poverty reduction, small tourism businesses need to be integrated into the (mainstream) tourism industry. In this way tourism is more likely to end up providing net (economic) benefits for 'the poor' (Ashley and Haysom 2006).

One of the most significant problems for small township tourism businesses appears to be a difficulty in gaining market access (Rogerson 2004a, b). This issue is not well understood, as business relations have received only little attention in academic research, particularly in the context of township tourism (Kirsten and Rogerson 2002). Hence, a greater understanding of business relations is required to maximize the potential of township tourism in assisting local economic development. This chapter will contribute to this discussion through an investigation of business relations in the context of township tourism around Cape Town. More specifically, it will investigate how inequalities in power and conflicts of interest between small township tourism businesses influence relations of *competition*, *cooperation* and *collaboration* among (small) businesses in the townships and other actors in the tourism industry.

Most existing research on relations between small tourism businesses and the tourism industry has been 'functionalist' in nature (see Table 5.1). Its primary aim has been to identify factors that contribute and constrain

Table 5.1 Beneficial and constraining factors influencing relationships of small tourism businesses and the wider tourism industry

Demand related factors	Absence of immediate appeal and understanding (Conforti 1996)
	Maturity of tourism industry (Kirsten and Rogerson 2002)
	Concerns about safety and violence and unhealthy circumstances (Rogerson 2004a)
	Seasonality (no full-time work in tourism) (Torres 2003; Maliepaard 2010)
Supply related factors	Quantity, quality, timeliness and reliability of small businesses (Bélisle 1983, 1984; Bah and Goodwin 2003; Kirsten and Rogerson 2002)
	Technological and processing limitations of small tourism businesses (Bélisle 1983, 1984; Kirsten and Rogerson 2002)
	Competition (Torres 2000; Bah and Goodwin 2003)
	Lack of knowledge of mainstream tourism industry and marketing skills (Rogerson 2004a).
Marketing and intermediary factors	Marketing and infrastructure constraints (Rogerson 2004a; Hill and Shaw 1995; Telfer and Wall 1996)
	Small business services not suited to demand (Hill and Shaw 1995; Rogerson 2004a)
	Geographical proximity of small businesses (Hill and Shaw 1995; Conforti 1996)
	Mistrust (Telfer and Wall 1996; Ramchander 2004; Torres and Momsen 2004)
	Middle-men (Freitag 1994; Dahles 1999)
	(Lack of) contact and dialogue (Bah and Goodwin 2003)
Government policy	(Lack of) government support, e.g. marketing, training, skills, technology acquisition (Kirsten and Rogerson 2002)
	Limited training and education (Torres 2003)
	Government bureaucracy and corruption (registration and accreditations) (Freitag 1994; Torres and Momsen 2004)

Source: adapted from Meyer (2007: 570).

cooperative relations. Although leading to useful insights, this kind of research has been criticized: authors such as Long (1997), Fuller and Lewis (2002) and Watkins and Bell (2002) point out that it adopts a deterministic bias and it suggests that certain factors are sufficient to create successful business relations, thus underplaying the importance of the historical, social and political setting (Larson 1992). Furthermore, it often fails to recognize diversity among small businesses and the dynamics and differences in the ways businesses engage with others (Doz 1996). Differing and opposing orientations and interests provide for a complex system of cooperation and competition between small businesses that are interdependent. Such a complex and highly competitive environment inevitably causes turbulence, and suggests the necessity to take issues of power relations into account (Bastakis *et al.* 2004; Go and Pine 1995; Upadhya and Rutten 1997). The importance of power can, for example, be observed in the experiences of small accommodation businesses on remote islands of Greece that are strongly dependent on the few major tour operators that they cooperate with. Tour operators bargain hard and offer low prices. This makes it hard for the small accommodation businesses to survive, and has led to a vicious circle of 'declining quality and depreciated price' (Bastakis *et al.* 2004: 162). While the context is different, it does show how the 'weakness' of small tourism businesses hinders tourism in providing economic benefits.

Rather than looking at potential factors supporting and constraining business relations, the current research takes a process-oriented perspective. A framework developed by Watkins and Bell (2002) is used to distinguish three different types of relations: competition, cooperation and collaboration.

1   'Competition' is defined as simply generating more business for oneself, typically at the cost of others.
2   'Cooperation' entails stimulating custom and profit by engaging in joint activities and sharing information. Normally this happens on a short-term basis and can be through informal (business) networks, business contracts or membership of an industry association.
3   'Collaboration' can be seen as a long-term, formalized arrangement between two or more complementary partners with the aim of securing a longer-term business advantage. Businesses can collaborate for direct personal gain or work together to actively develop a region and in order to achieve personal gains in the long run.

Watkins and Bell (2002) view these different categories as a continuum, with competition at one end and cooperation at the other. It is, however, possible to have multi-faceted relations that change over time. For example, accommodation businesses may compete with each other but, at the same time, cooperate by sharing tourists if they are full.

Methodology

The current research is explorative in nature and investigates tourism in Langa and Imizamo Yethu, two townships around Cape Town. The choice to focus on two specific townships as case-study regions rather than township tourism in general was based on a desire to gain a deeper insight into the interdependencies and mutual relations between businesses in these two townships. An inventory of demographic and business characteristics of small tourism business owners was made (e.g. type of business, date of starting the business) and semi-structured interviews were held with eighty people who were either self-employed or owned a small business in township tourism. In order to get a more nuanced perspective on the relations between tourism businesses inside and outside the townships, ten managers of hotels, B & Bs and (inbound) tour operators that are based in Cape Town's Central Business District were also interviewed. Interviewees were chosen purposefully in order to reflect different possible forms of business relations.

Locating the study

When investigating township tourism, it is impossible to ignore the troubled history of South Africa. The legacy of apartheid is still visible in many aspects of society. Although it is beyond the scope of the current research to discuss the continued influence of apartheid policies extensively, their importance needs to be acknowledged. This concerns, in particular, the way the apartheid regime used 'divide and rule' tactics to maintain its power. Among others it promoted racial and tribal separation, set up and maintained numerous townships and tried to undermine interpersonal trust. As a result, a 'systematic pattern of distrust' towards black individuals continues to exist (Burns 2006: 813; see also Dondolo 2002). After apartheid, the South African government initially aimed for socialist growth redistribution and equality. Yet, by 1996, the country had adopted a more neoliberal course to create wealth and fight poverty (Dierwechter 2006). Its main tourism policy documents reflect this strategy and stress the role of small businesses in local economic development through responsible tourism (RSA 1996, 1998). In a wider policy sense, tourism policy adheres to the wider objective of Broad Based Black Economic Empowerment (BBBEE). Large, white-owned businesses are strongly stimulated to cooperate with businesses owned by formerly disadvantaged individuals (FDI – black, Indian or coloured (mixed race) persons). Alternatively, white-owned businesses can 'merge' with an FDI-owned business and form a 'Black Economic Empowerment Business'. Such businesses are eligible for preferential treatment by the government.

Turning to the townships under investigation, both are primarily inhabited by people from the Xhosa tribe (85 per cent in Imizamo Yethu, 97 per cent in Langa). Despite all policy efforts, unemployment remains high at just under 50 per cent. Furthermore, over 75 per cent of people with a job earn less than

1.600 Rand (£125) per month (City of Cape Town 2003). The high levels of unemployment are accompanied by a great sense of economic insecurity, and tourism is a welcome additional source of income for people in these areas. Langa is the nearest township to the city centre of Cape Town and was one of the earliest to be visited by tourists. In the 1980s, international 'struggle junkies' and local policymakers were already coming to look at the living circumstances of local people (Dondolo 2002; Frenzel in this volume). Currently, Langa has a relatively well-developed tourism infrastructure and receives a great number of visitors. The majority of the estimated 40 to 50 township tour operators that are active in township tourism around Cape Town visit the township (Rolfes *et al.* 2007). Imizamo Yethu is situated further away from Cape Town, near Hout Bay. Tourism to the township did not start until the turn of the century, but since 2003 it has been an official stop on one of the 'hop-on hop-off Red Open Top Tourist Bus' routes (similar to those in many other large cities). This makes it one of the few townships around Cape Town that can easily be visited with only a guide, rather than via a more expensive and time-consuming township tour organized by a tour operator. On the other hand, Imizamo Yethu is much less popular with these tour operators, only one of which visits the township.

Findings

Small businesses' involvement in township tourism

Small businesses are involved in township tourism in a variety of roles. Tour operators provide township tours themselves, but also hire (freelance) tour guides. Some tours make use of so-called 'walking-tour guides' to provide a half-hour walk through the township. Township tours visit 'exotic' businesses that are associated with township life (herbalists, 'shebeens', sheep-head vendors), and in some cases include a dancing, singing or theatrical performance. Outside the realm of the township tours, restaurants offer 'traditional African' (Xhosa) meals, and accommodation businesses provide tourists with the opportunity to stay overnight in the townships. Craft workers are found along the township tourism route, as well as selling at or near popular restaurants. Only a few restaurants and accommodation businesses provide services for the domestic market; the rest are strongly focused on the international market and offer very similar products both to each other and to businesses in townships elsewhere in South Africa. This makes them interchangeable and limits their chances to attract tourists that have already visited another township (Hughes 2007).

Although at first practically all businesses involved in township tourism were managed by FDI (Rogerson 2004b), nowadays large tour operators from outside the townships and BBBEE tour operators have become involved and taken over much of the market. Most of the FDI-owned tour operators are small and economically relatively unsuccessful. Nevertheless, on average, tour operators are still among the most successful small township tourism businesses. Out of the sample (n=80), only 18 interviewees are able to hire employees, 16 use the business to provide (incidental) work for family members, and all others act as sole traders. Furthermore, less than half of the interviewees are able to earn enough with the tourism business to sustain themselves without additional work (even during the summer tourism season). They note difficulties in getting enough custom to work in the business full-time. Instead, they use their tourism activities as additional sources of income in what can best be described as a livelihood strategy of income diversification. In this way they minimize financial risks in a context of social and economic vulnerability. It would seem that, despite the numerical dominance of small township tourism businesses, their lack of market access and small size limits the potential of tourism to reduce poverty.

The recent nature of the phenomenon of township tourism is reflected in the age of township tourism businesses. At the time of the research, the average age of businesses was four years, but 21 businesses had been started in the last two years and 30 more within the last five years. Only eight businesses (in crafts, tour operation and catering) had been active for more than ten years. In general, owners of businesses have the most contact with those people who started at around the same time as them. Contact between owners of older and younger businesses is relatively limited. The majority of the business owners are male (51 male/29 female). The owners of accommodation businesses (primarily women) are the oldest, with an average age of 52 years. Tour guides (most of whom are men) are the youngest with an average age of 35. The mean age for the other business types ranges between 38 and 42. These age differences confirm earlier findings for township tourism (Rogerson 2004a; Nemasetoni 2005).

Owners of township tourism businesses also differ with regard to the length of time they stay in the townships as well as their ethnicity. Thirty-one interviewees were already living in the area during apartheid or were born there. These owners are more likely to manage a business that requires assets such as tour operation, accommodation or catering, but are active with other businesses as well. Others came to the townships more recently from elsewhere in South Africa (27) or from other countries in Africa (14). These interviewees are more likely to work as tour guides or as craft workers. In fact, all interviewees from elsewhere in Africa sell crafts. Six economically successful interviewees are no longer living in the townships. They have been described by other interviewees as disloyal to others in the townships. The majority of interviewees are Xhosa; five people belong to other South African tribes and 14 come from elsewhere in Africa. These differences among the owners of small township tourism businesses with regard to gender, age, migratory status and ethnicity show the diverse composition of the township tourism business community. This diversity is important for understanding both cooperative and competitive aspects of business relations within township tourism.

Competition: gaining at the cost of others

All three types of business relations – competition, cooperation and collaboration – can be observed in the two townships. Most obvious is competition. The great number of (part-time) small businesses, combined with a lack of alternatives and a situation of underemployment, means competition is fierce, something that has apparently increased in recent years due to the FIFA 2010 World Cup:

> I hope to continue with my work. The next year is going to be very difficult as so many small businesses are getting into tourism for 2010. You see it as well with the B & Bs. People are busy building homes to make it into a B & B. This increases competition. More and more people come in and are jumping on the bandwagon. Instead of making more, we are now making less money. We do not know what will come afterwards.
>
> (Craft vendor, Langa township)

Tour operators primarily compete on price and have very small margins. Interviewees accuse the larger tour operators that go into the townships of selling their township tours at less than cost price and paying a higher commission to travel agents in the city centre in order to draw in custom and sell other, more lucrative tours. The large scale of township touring activities among the larger tour operators means that vehicles are nearly always full, allowing them to keep prices very competitive. Since the majority of small tour operators cannot always fill their vehicles with tourists, they either have to operate some tours at a loss or cooperate and share customers among themselves. The 'walking-tour guides' in Langa also rely heavily on price as a differentiator, and their average pay is low. Officially they are paid 30 Rand per tourist, but in reality this is much lower. They give discounts to larger groups of tourists and, as will be discussed later, they are not always paid their full fee when cooperating with a tour operator.

Freelance tour guides receive a more secure payment and compete more by delivering a good service. Accommodation businesses, restaurants and craft workers also try to offer as good a product as possible to ensure further custom. Unfortunately, as mentioned earlier, their products are also very similar. For example, nearly all accommodation businesses are run as B & Bs, and craft workers sell many similar products. Economically successful small-business owners have blamed the lack of innovation on laziness and/or a lack of willingness to invest time and money to come up with something new. Little evidence was found to support this line of thought. Instead, it was found that many entrepreneurs are inexperienced and uncertain about what tourists would like to see and do. Others struggle to survive on the market and have few resources to put towards product innovation. In a way, the high levels of competition actually cause a stifling of innovation: it is always uncertain whether new products will work (particularly if they need bigger investments), and small-business owners can ill afford not to make any money. Thus small-business owners follow the principle of 'risk minimization' in their economic behaviour, which is economically rational and a common observation in situations of insecure livelihood (Steinbrink 2009).

A minority of small-business owners specialize in a niche area of township tourism. One tour operator in particular ('X') concentrates on the backpacker market. He is able to regularly fill his minibuses and dominates this segment of the township tourism market. His success is largely based on his ability to dissuade other tour operators from competing for this market. He does this by sharing his surplus customers with befriended tour operators, as well as by persuading potential competitors that they will not be able to attract this niche market. One interviewee mentions that it is impossible to compete with this successful tour operator since 'X' represents township tourism businesses in several organizations that are lobbying in favour of backpacker tourism. The interviewee reports that 'X' is using this power to corner the backpacker market (although no specifics are shared).

Backpacker hostels in Cape Town city centre are very eager for different township tourism offerings and are frustrated at the lack of new products. There might be a potential market here for others, but market competition means that the tour operator strongly protects his own interests and does not want to risk opening up the market. In this way he constrains the development of a more diversified spectrum of township tours.

Numerous other examples exist where specific small businesses are accused of abusing their power. For example, small-business owners who work for local NGOs or government, or who have a dominant position in townships as local elders (persons who take decisions in a township neighbourhood), can exercise influence over other people's lives and use this to ensure they get more business. One craft vendor takes power from the ownership of a taxi company (which is notorious for taking the law into its own hands) and uses this notoriety to ensure he gets the most prominent place at one of the tourist hotspots in the centre of Langa. Another craft vendor pays local unemployed men a small sum of money to help set up and break down the craft stand. Other craft workers do not dare sell near there for fear of retribution from these young men. Finally, one walking-tour guide uses threats of violence through membership of a criminal youth gang to get more work. In all cases it is not so much the actual use of power that is influencing business decisions – there is typically no direct sanctioning – but the fear of the use of power, which is enough to discourage others from competing with people who are deemed as powerful.

Cooperation: engaging in joint activities and sharing information

Trust in the quality and reliability of service of the partner is a prerequisite for cooperation. Small-business owners refer to this as acting 'professional' and consider it to be the most important thing in business relations. So-called 'chancers' come around on a daily basis to businesses elsewhere in Cape Town and offer their services even when they do not have any kind of business. This has led the owners of businesses in Cape Town to become highly suspicious and distrustful of small-business owners from the townships. The trustworthiness of businesses from the townships is further affected by the fact that they cannot always guarantee availability because of their multiple income strategy (sometimes other work needs to take preference). As a result, they appear unreliable to the full-time businesses in Cape Town. The vast majority of cooperative business relationships are started with people whose credentials are verifiable. An example is tour operators, most of whom started as tour guides and so already had many connections, with travel agents, tourism offices, guesthouses etc., before they started their own businesses as tour operators.

Local business organizations and central government have tried to get small township tourism businesses involved in more formal networking meetings that they organize. However, this does not work well and small-business owners do not often attend such meetings. These are often in the evening somewhere in the city centre, take much time and effort to get to and are not seen as very valuable. Interviewees who start to visit these meetings are acutely aware of their inexperience with the unwritten norms and rules of dealing with people in this setting. Many don't feel comfortable, become frustrated that they cannot get much out of the meetings and so stop going. One of the few small-business owners who has continued to visit these meetings mentions how, for the first two or three times, he only observed and listened and only later felt confident enough to start networking. Given this knowledge, it comes as no surprise that a government programme aimed at creating business relations by sending small township tourism business owners to the international tourism and travel market in Durban (Indaba) has not been very successful. Trust also is key in small-business relations between businesses inside the townships. Most cooperative relations here are based on friendships or family ties:

> I know [owner of other business] more than others. He is living next by from my uncle's place. He's sort of my uncle's neighbour.
>
> (Tour operator, Langa)

The use of informal social networks as the basis for cooperation has several benefits for owners of small township tourism businesses. It is convenient as there are fewer issues with trust, but it is equally a matter of repaying favours and ensuring that others become financially independent. Also, it helps create stronger social bonds between existing friends and family members, which can be of great use in times of crisis and acute insecurity. However, it does mean that cooperative relations are often mitigated by factors such age, gender, migratory status or ethnicity. As a result, certain potentially lucrative forms of cooperation, with people who are not close personally, hardly take place.

As mentioned earlier, strong competition means small, township-based businesses are nearly always in a weak position. Tour operators have particular difficulties in forming a sustainable cooperative relationship with hotels and guesthouses outside the township:

> Today could be you, tomorrow they dump you. They are with them [large tour operators]. That is how guest houses work, that will apply similar to hotels
>
> (tour operator, Langa township).

Tour operators themselves are also accused of abusing their powerful position when dealing with others. For example, employed tour guides are often required to work longer hours for less money than agreed beforehand, or get called up to work at extremely short notice, having to leave whatever they are doing to get to work. Another way in which tour operators abuse their power is by holding back payments. This is exemplified by the story of a beginning tour guide who provided a (series of) tours worth over 2,000 Rand (£160) each, but was never paid. Instead, he was given additional, small, poorly paid guiding jobs. The tour guide has since more-or-less given up on the initial large sum of money and feels abused, yet knows he has no other option but to continue to work for the tour operator because he has no alternative income opportunity.

> What they are doing, they're just giving me other tours. So that I cannot pressurize them. You know? So that I cannot pressurize or come hard to them saying: pay my money! Because they are still giving me some tours.
>
> (Tour guide, Langa township)

Such forms of power abuse in cooperative relations rarely happen with most of the large tour operators; that is why they are most favoured by tour guides. The preference of tour guides to work with the large companies may also be due to reasons of status. One interviewee describes the importance to younger guides of being seen driving the large, modern minibuses of a big tour operator and using their expensive mobile phone headsets. Finally, large tour operators are said to have no hidden agendas, connections or other interests in the townships:

> there's a lot of jealousy in the industry. Especially with the commission [payment] and the amount of work that the guide gets. Yeah, but once you join big companies. At least they try to balance to give their guides equal work.
>
> (Tour guide, Langa township)

The concept of jealousy as it is used here requires some further clarification, as it may help to explain some of the problems with cooperation between businesses in the townships. Xhosa language makes no distinction between 'envy' and 'jealousy' (both are translated as 'umona'). Within the townships a strong fear of causing envy exists. People fear that causing umona (e.g. by insufficiently supporting others) may lead to witchcraft being used against them and/or may lead to different forms of business disruption (violence, theft). 'Umona' can be seen as an indirect means of sanctioning those not willing to share their wealth, and thus contributes to the maintenance of an informal social security system. Unfortunately, the levelling pressure can be a hindrance for people trying to grow a business (Steinbrink 2009). Success can cast a shadow of inferiority on peers and cause envy. Thus people doing well fear they will be 'pulled down' to maintain the status quo. This results in a latent distrust among business people in the townships (Bailey 2003; Ashforth 2005; Steinbrink 2009). A similar principle has been observed with small tourism businesses in other economically insecure livelihood situations. For example, in Turkey community members actively try to ensure no one ever gets beyond a level of approved mediocrity (Mottiar and Tucker 2007). As such, the concept of envy needs to be seen in a wider context of poverty and social vulnerability rather than as a given cultural aspect of Xhosa society. Using 'essentialist' cultural notions as explanatory factors for failed relations would not do justice to the complex reality of small township tourism business owners (Meagher 2004).

With visitor attractions and performance it is tour guides who are blamed for abusing their power in order to get more money themselves. This includes those who complain about being abused by tour operators. One tour guide admits that he discourages tourists to give tips to visitor attractions and has little interest in supporting craft workers. He claims this ensures that he gets a larger tip at the end of the tour. Again, it can be seen that there is very little loyalty between township businesses, and individual interests are put before common interests in this uncertain setting.

In a number of cases, businesses cooperate with the primary intention of excluding others rather than gaining more business. In Imizamo Yethu, tour guides cooperate to try to keep 'drive-by township tours' (in which minibuses simply drive through the township) out of 'their' township. While this can be seen as a positive action to protect the interests of township businesses, at the same time these operators are accused of excluding others from guiding, even though they complain about the great amount of work they have. In Langa there are three competing groups of walking-tour guides that have a several-year history of mutual conflicts. In one case, such a conflict can be translated in ethnic terms; for example, one Zulu tour guide states that he was not given equal chances on the market because he was not part of the dominant Xhosa tribe. Here, ethnicization of cooperative competition can be seen as an effect of the 'divide and rule' politics during the apartheid era.

Collaboration: building towards long-term formalized business arrangements

Collaborations have a longer-term and more enduring perspective than cooperative relations. They are relatively rare in township tourism. Only two small tour operators have managed to get involved in a collaborative relation with large, inbound tour operators (Thompsons and Tourvest) that serve the whole of South Africa. One is owned by a business person of Indian heritage and another is run as a BBBEE business with most of the marketing done by the white co-owner. The owner of Indian heritage explains that BBBEE policies had made a difference for his business in achieving this collaboration. As a result he is very supportive of BBBEE. All other interviewees, however, suggest that BBBEE policies are out of touch with the real needs of small township businesses and only work for businesses that are larger than theirs. They actually feel BBBEE policies have made their situation worse because the BBBEE township touring businesses are now taking a large part of the market due to the white partners' better business contacts. Here, conflicting interests between different small tourism businesses can be observed.

Most collaborations have evolved from informal cooperative relations or were set up with (former) employees. An example is one tour operator who is dominant in the backpackers' market. He already was a trusted tour guide with many of the hostel businesses, and has been able to achieve collaborative relations after several years of cooperation. Owners of businesses other than tour operators have even greater difficulties in building up collaborative relations with large businesses from outside the townships. Successful exceptions are a tour guide in Imizamo Yethu, who is the main contact person for the Red Open Top Bus, and a catering business in Langa that has gained a number of long-term contracts with inbound tour operators after a successful collaboration with one of them.

Some owners blame the difficulty in achieving collaborative relations on continuing (racial) prejudices. Although this may happen (unconsciously) in certain cases (Burns 2006), it is denied by businesses from outside the townships, who mention that small businesses have only been around for a relatively short time and that it is difficult to ascertain their long-term sustainability. This seems particularly important for inbound tour operators. An example is given in the following account in which the business owner of Indian heritage discusses the difficulties in gaining the trust of the inbound tour operator he is now working with:

> I was walking past [name of tour operator]'s stand at Indaba [travel market] when I was there for the fourth or fifth time. Every year I ensured I made eye contact with some people and have a quick chat: 'Hi Fred! First time here's my card, I'm [name] of [name of tour operator]', second year the same, etcetera, etcetera. And the fifth year he said: 'Are you still around?!' I said 'yes' and he invited me in. We chatted and I sent him a pricelist when I came back. He became my customer with a meeting of 1.5 minutes. We are now trading four years, it's a great relationship.
>
> (Tour operator, Langa township)

This collaboration was struck up during the Indaba travel market in Durban. Two other collaborations were also formed at similar, larger-scale travel markets. This explains the appeal of such markets, particularly to (beginning) small-business owners: there may be little chance of striking up a deal, but if one is successful it can be the basis of an enduring collaborative relationship with much financial potential. However, as mentioned earlier, it takes time to understand the unwritten rules of these markets. In all cases it took small-business owners several visits to such markets to clinch a deal, and even then they felt it was partially due to luck.

Little collaboration exists between tour operators and other businesses on the township tours. For example, no long-term relations are established with (essential) businesses such as shebeens, the 'smiley' (sheep-head) vendors or the herbalists. Nearly all of these businesses, as well as the assisting walking-tour guides, are viewed as interchangeable. Only when tour operators have family or friendship relations or have another connection with other business owners (such as belonging to the same church) do they appear willing to get involved in more collaborative relations. A limited number of freelance tour guides have started a collaborative relationship with the tour operator they work for. Although they were formally independent, they feel like being employed and reaping some benefits by being assured work even in winter when there are few tourists around. The gain of the tour operators is that they are assured good-quality guides the following summer.

In 2008, two formal initiatives were started by local and regional governments to stimulate local economic development in Langa and create overarching collaborative relations. It is interesting to discuss them, as they highlight some of the difficulties in setting up collaborations in the context of township tourism, as well as the lack of knowledge among government organizations.

The first initiative was called the 'Langa Walking Tour'. It aimed to get walking-tour guides in Langa to become better organized so that they could get a fixed (higher) price per tourist and could compete more effectively with businesses from outside the townships. Unregistered tour guides had their accreditation course paid for, and four Langa township walking-tour routes were created. However, the organizers of this initiative had taken insufficient note of the existence of different factions among the guides after years of harsh competition. At the time of the research, the Langa Walking Tour was not functioning because, rather than working together, the tour guides had each tried to become the representative person who controlled the other guides. At the same time, tour operators from Langa were unhappy with the development of the Langa Walking Tour. They feared it would provide tour operators from outside the township with a cheaper substitute for existing township tours, resulting in less money ending up in the townships.

The second initiative was the 'Langa Tourism Forum', which was supposed to represent all tourism businesses in this township. It was set up to give businesses a more powerful negotiating position when dealing with businesses outside the townships and beyond the restrictions of government. City and regional government are very much in favour of the creation of a forum, as they believe it would help them to better gauge the needs and desires of township businesses. Also, it is easier to free funds for a group of businesses rather than for individual entrepreneurs. In practice, the Langa Tourism Forum has not worked well. It proved very difficult to get all businesses together. The people who set up the forum were relatively new to tourism, and primarily had contact with only a limited number of other, recently founded businesses. They forgot to invite certain businesses to the initial meeting of the forum. This caused envy, mistrust and grievance, particularly with owners of uninvited older businesses. Another problem was that some of the more successful businesses did not feel the need for such an organization and did not want to participate. The fact that the initiators had cooperated earlier disgruntled other small-business owners who felt they were used to provide legitimacy to a group of befriended businesses. Also, ethnicization came into play again: two of the three involved were Zulu, and this was seen as further evidence that the forum was unrepresentative. The forum finally lost all momentum when it was used as a platform to flyer for the ANC during the hectic presidential elections of 2009. This politicizing led to decreased credibility, which made the organizers give up on it for the time being. Again, this project failed because of underlying frictions (in society), combined with envy, mistrust and a fear of loss of power.

Discussion

Township tourism is seen by the South African government as one possibility to reduce the lily-white complexion of South African tourism (Rogerson 2004a). Although many small township tourism businesses are owned by formerly disadvantaged individuals, they have difficulty in getting market access. Most are currently used in a combined income livelihood strategy and provide essential but limited additional income to their owners.

This lack of access can be understood by acknowledging that small businesses in the townships are not a homogeneous group. Instead, they consist of people and businesses with a wide number of conflicting interests. Van der Duim *et al.* (2006) eloquently discuss similar issues for communities in Kenya and Tanzania and coin the term 'fractured communities' to describe this situation. It would seem that township communities can be regarded as fractured. Networks of reputation, trust and cooperation are disjointed, and most small businesses try to work together only with friends and family. The 'divide and rule' tactic by the apartheid government has created a society in which distrust is rife. This is further emphasized by the high levels of livelihood insecurity and extreme competition in the townships.

'Envy' and 'jealousy' towards other small township tourism businesses are common. Small-business owners put great emphasis on trying to get in a powerful position with regard to other township tourism businesses and deter (potential) competitors. This stifles cooperation between small businesses and greatly increases competition. In a way, this is similar to what Mottiar and Tucker (2007) found in small communities in Turkey. They describe a collaboration of businesses to control the business environment at the cost of others with the term 'webs of power'. Although in the townships these 'webs of power' are less sophisticated, the principle seems the same, with small-business owners preferring to work with businesses from outside the township that are not entwined in township life.

It has been recommended that small tourism businesses focus on a niche such as lower-income travellers (e.g. backpackers) rather than the overcrowded higher-income tourism market (Kirsten and Rogerson 2002). Findings from the current research confirm these findings, albeit with reservations. Having a distinctive offering gives small-business owners a stronger power position when relating to others (Bastakis *et al.* 2004). However, such a strategy is only successful if others do not copy the concept. Preventing others from copying business ideas requires great effort and limits the total income of money flowing towards small tourism businesses.

Initiatives set up by the South African government to encourage business relations are well intended, but turn out to be inappropriate in practice. They take insufficient notice of the complex social, structural and cultural norms that small-business owners' decisions are embedded in. The idea to install overarching bodies to represent township businesses is understandable, but at the moment the communities are so 'fractured' that the creation of such bodies seems impossible. Future initiatives to develop broader, township-wide representation need to be very much aware of the local context if they are not to be appropriated by certain groups and so actually create or reproduce divisions in society that negatively influence business relations.

The current research has been one of the first to really focus on business relations within township tourism. Further research is required to better understand these relations, as well as the ways in which historical and social configurations influence business relations. It may only be a first step, but a recognition of conflicting interests between small businesses that are involved in township tourism, as well as the importance of power and the structural, historical and social setting, are important for understanding the difficulties in starting and maintaining business relations. At the moment these issues limit the effectiveness of using township tourism as a local economic development strategy, despite having a positive influence on some people's individual livelihoods.

Bibliography

Archer, B., Cooper, C. and Ruhanen, L. (2005) 'The positive and negative impacts of tourism', in W.F. Theobald (ed.) *Global Tourism*, 3rd edn, Amsterdam: Elsevier Butterworth-Heinemann.

Ashforth, A. (2005) *Witchcraft, Violence, and Democracy in South Africa*, Chicago, IL: University of Chicago Press.

Ashley, C. and Haysom, G. (2006) 'From philanthropy to a different way of doing business: strategies and challenges in integrating pro-poor approaches into tourism business', *Development Southern Africa*, 23: 265–79.

Bah, A. and Goodwin, H. (2003) *Improving Access for the Informal Sector to Tourism in the Gambia*, London: Pro-Poor Tourism.

Bailey, B. (2003) *The Plays of Miracle & Wonder: Bewitching Visions and Primal High-jinx from the South African Stage*, Cape Town: Double Storey Books.

Bastakis, C., Buhalis, D. and Butler, R. (2004) 'The perception of small and medium sized tourism accommodation providers on the impacts of the tour operators' power in Eastern Mediterranean', *Tourism Management*, 25(2): 151–70.

Bélisle, F.J. (1983) 'Tourism and food production in the Caribbean', *Annals of Tourism Research*, 10: 497–513.

—— (1984) 'Tourism and food imports: the case of Jamaica', *Economic Development and Cultural Change*, 32: 819–42.

Besteman, C. (2008). *Transforming Cape Town*. Berkeley: University of California.

Burns, J. (2006) 'Racial stereotypes, stigma and trust in post-apartheid South Africa', *Economic Modelling*, 23(5): 805–21.

City of Cape Town (2003) *2001 Census Ward Profiles*. Available online at www.capetown.gov.za/en/stats/2001census/Pages/Profiles.aspx (accessed 4 October 2011).

Conforti, J.M. (1996) 'Ghettos as tourism attractions', *Annals of Tourism Research*, 23(4): 830–42.

CTRU (Cape Town Routes Unlimited) (2006a) *Research Programme to Track Visitor Patterns and Trends for Cape Town and Western Cape: Report from the June/July 2006 Survey*. Available online at www.tourismcapetown.co.za/ctru/action/media/downloadFile?media_fileid=12550 (accessed 4 October 2011).

—— (2006b) *Research Programme to Track Visitor Patterns and Trends for Cape Town and Western Cape: Report from the May/June 2006 Survey*. Available online at www.tourismcapetown.co.za/ctru/action/media/downloadFile?media_fileid=12549 (accessed 4 October 2011).

—— (2006c) *Research Programme to Track Visitor Patterns and Trends for Cape Town and Western Cape: Report from the Spring Survey September/October 2006*. Available online at www.tourismcapetown.co.za/ctru/action/media/download File?media_fileid=12552 (accessed 4 October 2011).

Dahles, H. (1999) 'Small businesses in the Indonesian tourism industry: entrepreneurship or employment?', in H. Dahles and K. Bras (eds) *Tourism and Small Entrepreneurs: Development, National Policy, and Entrepreneurial Culture: Indonesian Cases*, New York: Cognizant Communication Corporation.

Dierwechter, Y. (2006) 'Geographical limitations of neo-liberalism: urban planning and the occluded territoriality of informal survival in African Cape Town', *Space and Polity*, 10: 243–62.

Dondolo, L. (2002) *The Construction of Public History and Tourism Destinations in Cape Town's Townships: A Study of Routes, Sites and Heritage*, Cape Town: University of the Western Cape.

Doz, Y.L. (1996) 'The evolution of cooperation in strategic alliances: initial conditions or learning processes?', *Strategic Management Journal*, 17(S1): 55–83.

Freitag, T.G. (1994) 'Enclave tourism development: for whom the benefits roll?', *Annals of Tourism Research*, 21: 538–54.

Fuller, T. and Lewis, J. (2002) '"Relationships mean everything"; a typology of small-business relationship strategies in a reflexive context', *British Journal of Management*, 13(4): 317–36.

Go, F.M. and Pine, R. (1995) *Globalization Strategy in the Hotel Industry*, London: Routledge.

Hill, T. and Shaw, R.N. (1995) 'Co-marketing tourism internationally: bases for strategic alliances', *Journal of Travel Research*, 34(1): 25–32.

Hughes, H. (2007) 'Rainbow, renaissance, tribes and townships: tourism and heritage in South Africa since 1994', in S. Buhlungu, J. Daniel, R. Southal and J. Hutchman (eds) *State of the Nation: South Africa 2007*, Cape Town: HSRC Press.

Kirsten, M. and Rogerson, C.M. (2002) 'Tourism, business linkages and small enterprise development in South Africa', *Development Southern Africa*, 19: 29–60.

Koens, J.F., Miranda, M.A. and Dieperink, C. (2009) 'Ecotourism as a development strategy: experiences from Costa Rica', *Environment, Development and Sustainability*, 11(6): 1225–37.

Larson, A. (1992) 'Network dyads in entrepreneurial settings: a study of the governance of exchange relationships', *Administrative Science Quarterly*, 37(1): 76–104.

Long, P.E. (1997) 'Researching tourism partnership organizations: from practice to theory to methodology', in P.E. Murphy (ed.) *Quality Management in Urban Tourism*, New York: John Wiley and Sons.

Maliepaard, C.F. (2010) *Township Tourism: A Responsible Tourism Approach?*, Bochum: Ruhr University.

Meagher, K. (2004) *Identity Economics: Informal Manufacturing and Social Networks in South-eastern Nigeria*, Oxford: University of Oxford Press.

Meyer, D. (2007) 'Pro-poor tourism: from leakages to linkages. A conceptual framework for creating linkages between the accommodation sector and "poor" neighbouring communities', *Current Issues in Tourism*, 10: 558–83.

Mottiar, Z. and Tucker, H. (2007) 'Webs of power: multiple ownership in tourism destinations', *Current Issues in Tourism*, 10(4): 279–95.

Nemasetoni, I. (2005) *Contribution of Tourism Towards the Development of Black-owned Small, Medium and Micro Enterprises (SMMEs) in Post-apartheid South Africa: An Evaluation of Tour Operators*, Johannesburg: University of Witwatersrand.

Ramchander, P. (2004) *Towards the Responsible Management of the Socio-Cultural Impact of Township Tourism*, Pretoria: University of Pretoria.

Rogerson, C.M. (2004a) 'Transforming the South African tourism industry: the emerging black-owned bed and breakfast economy', *Geojournal*, 60(3): 273–81.

—— (2004b) 'Urban tourism and small tourism enterprise development in Johannesburg: the case of township tourism', *Geojournal*, 60(3): 249–57.

Rolfes, M. (2010) 'Poverty tourism: theoretical reflections and empirical findings regarding an extraordinary form of tourism', *GeoJournal*, 75(5): 421–42.

——, Steinbrink, M. and Uhl, C. (2007) *Research Group Township Tourism*, Potsdam: Universitätsverlag.

Republic of South Africa (RSA) (1996) *White Paper on the Development and Promotion of Tourism in South Africa*, Pretoria: Department of Environmental Affairs and Tourism.

—— (1998) *Tourism in GEAR: Tourism Development Strategy 1998–2000*, Pretoria: Department of Environmental Affairs and Tourism.

Steinbrink, M. (2009) *Leben zwischen Land und Stadt: Migration, Translokalität und Verwundbarkeit in Südafrika*, Osnabrück: VS Verlag.

Telfer, D.J. and Wall, G. (1996) 'Linkages between tourism and food production', *Annals of Tourism Research*, 23: 635–53.

Torres, R. (2000) *Linkage Between Tourism and Agriculture in Quintana Roo, Mexico*, Oakland, CA: University of California Press.

—— (2003) 'Linkages between tourism and agriculture in Mexico', *Annals of Tourism Research*, 30: 546–66.

—— and Momsen, J.H. (2004) 'Challenges and potential for linking tourism and agriculture to achieve pro-poor tourism objectives', *Progress in Development Studies*, 4: 294–318.

Upadhya, C. and Rutten, M. (1997) 'In search of a comparative framework: small-scale entrepreneurs in Asia and Europe', in M. Rutten and C. Upadhya (eds) *Small Business Entrepreneurs in Asia and Europe: Towards a Comparative Perspective*, New York: Sage.

Van der Duim, R., Peters, K. and Akama, J. (2006) 'Cultural tourism in African communities: a comparison between cultural Manyattas in Kenya and the cultural tourism project in Tanzania', in M.K. Smith and M. Robinson (eds) *Cultural Tourism in a Changing World: Politics, Participation and (Re) Presentation*, Clevedon: Channel View.

Wall, G. and Mathieson, A. (2006) *Tourism: Change, Impacts, and Opportunities*, Harlow: Pearson Education.

Watkins, M. and Bell, B. (2002) 'The experience of forming business relationships in tourism', *International Journal of Tourism Research*, 4(1): 15–28.

Part II

Representation of poverty

6 A forgotten place to remember

Reflections on the attempt to turn a favela into a museum

Palloma Menezes

Introduction

Much of the recent research on heritage suggests (according to Appadurai and Breckenridge 2007) that the appropriation of the past by actors situated in the present is subject to a variety of dynamics. These range from:

> problems associated to ethnicity and local identity, nostalgia, and the search for a 'mummified' authenticity, to the tension between the State's interest in establishing local identities and the pressures exerted by the localities when they seek to transform these identities.
>
> (Ibid.: 13)

In this context, one of the main roles of the academic literature on this topic is to remind us that 'heritage is increasingly a profoundly political issue in which localities and nation-states are in frequent disagreement, and the museums are in the middle of this specific storm' (ibid.: 14).

By approaching the definition and establishment of heritage as politics, or, as it is commonly called, the politics of heritage, we must not forget that we are dealing with history, memory and identity, interrelated concepts whose contents are continuously defined and modified through time. With this in mind, this chapter seeks to analyse the failed attempt to transform the Morro da Providência, a favela in Rio de Janeiro, into heritage: an open-air museum and a tourist site. I seek to explain the failure of this project, resulting in a forgotten museum, employing a critical analysis of the Mayor's Office initiative to do so.

The open-air museum in the Morro da Providência is a particular case – not absolutely unique, nor a mere generic coincidence – based upon which it is possible to reflect on the following issues: What changes have public policies for favelas undergone in the last few years? In what ways are these changes linked (if they are linked at all) to a progressive expansion of the semantic range of the favela – which in the last few years has been treated by the state not only as a 'problem' for the city, but also as its 'heritage' and therefore worthy of preservation and being visited? (See also Meschkank in this volume.)

Throughout this chapter I will seek to question if, in the case of the Providência Museum, we are facing an attempt to 'folklorize' the favela as a marketing element of the city, a sophisticated orientation towards the 'demarginalization' of the favela in social representation, or both. Many authors, based on different empirical cases, suggest that 'heritage' as a category is beginning to incorporate new meanings and is itself being incorporated into 'revitalization' policies or citizenship 'expansion' programmes among sectors of society hitherto considered excluded from the right to memory (Abreu *et al.* 2007; Gonçalves 2007; Grynszpan and Pandolfi 2007; Oliveira 2008). But can the rhetoric of revitalization be just another marketing strategy (in which the valorization of memory plays an important role) to transform the city into a marketable product? This chapter reflects upon the shift (or extension) of the conflict between the rejection and (symbolic) incorporation of the favela.

Several authors have been using the concept of the 'city as a commodity' as one of the analysis tools of 'new urban planning'. As pointed out by Sánchez:

> the transformation of cities into commodities comes to indicate that the process of spatial commoditization has reached a new level, the product of the development of the world of commodities, the realization of capital-ism and of globalization in its present stage. The recent phenomenon of the existence of a market of cities demonstrates the increasing importance of space in capitalism – the strategic positioning for the conquering of space, which now affects entire cities now circulating in a global market, is evidence of the globalized production of social space.
>
> (2003: 33)

The hypothesis I am advancing in this chapter is that the Rio de Janeiro Municipality attempted to transform the favela into an official attraction of the 'city as a commodity' when the open-air museum in the Morro da Providência was created. Ultimately, the intent of this chapter is to show how the juncture of new meanings of heritage, tourism and public policy plays out and unfolds in the case of the Morro da Providência open-air museum, pointing out the potentialities and limits of this project and its implementation.

Open-air museum and the discussion on the new museology

There are more than a few reports, both academic and journalistic, that attribute to the Morro da Providência, located in the Port Zone, the title of Rio de Janeiro's first favela. Its history supposedly began with the returning soldiers of the Canudos War, who settled there awaiting compensation from the government. There are no official records proving that the Morro da Providência is in fact the first favela in Rio, but, as Valladares states:

It is the Morro da Favela, already existing with the name Morro da Providência, which became part of history due to its connection to the Canudos Wars whose former combatants went there to live . . . The Morro da Favela, little by little, began to spread its denomination to any group of agglomerated shacks without paved streets or access to public services, on public property or on invasions in private property.

(2005: 26)

The Morro da Providência, with around ten thousand residents today, represents, therefore, 'from the historical and urban point of view, the characteristic type of disorganized occupation of the city's slopes and hillside all over the city' (Social Communication Division, Mayor's Office of Rio de Janeiro 2003: 42). Believing that the location holds both general attributes (the Providência as an 'original generic' of the other favelas) and distinguishing ones (the visual contrast the favela establishes with the pavement) simultaneously, in the early 2000s the Rio de Janeiro Mayor's Office came up with the idea to convert the Providência into a museum and tourist attraction.

The planning for the Providência Museum took place within the Favela-Bairro programme and the revitalization of the Port Zone, which, besides the museum, also houses the Cidade do Samba (Samba City) and the Gamboa Olympic Village. The Favela-Bairro programme invested R\$14.3 million in the construction of water and sewer lines, public spaces and a day-care centre, just as in other favelas, but also turned it into a 'tourist site', making the location part of the city's patrimony. The intention of the project creator, the architect and urban planner, Maria Lúcia Peterson, was not to make a conventional building and label it a 'favela museum', but to turn the favela itself into a museum. Unlike other museums in favelas – such as the Maré Museum, for example, which, according to Freire-Medeiros (2006: 20) can be understood as an 'inward museum' or, in other words, a museum conceived for the very residents of the favela – the Providência Museum was planned as a 'outward museum', designed for outside tourists in order to 'inoculate the favela into the city'.

The open-air museums are part of a trend called 'new museology' – a movement that seeks to stretch the limits of traditional museums, which, according to Aquino (2007: 11), were ridden with power games and designed to establish a determined identity as the 'prevalent and absolute identity', necessarily excluding any differences. Taking advantage of the opportunity that arose with the new museology to create museums about anything, politicians, businessmen, NGOs and social movements have suggested and, in some cases, sponsored the creation of museums that explore the memory of diverse social groups, which until recently seemed forgotten – or deliberately ignored – in discussions concerning Brazilian heritage.

One of the greatest challenges that researchers face 'may be the careful consideration of the discrepancies between the interests of the creators of these museums, the desires of those who are represented, and the demands of the general public' (Chagas 1994: 19). Another challenge is trying to understand the struggles for negotiating what will be considered patrimony and so transformed into a museum. This happens, according to Gonçalves, because:

> patrimonies are strategies through which social groups and individuals narrate their memory and identity, trying to find for them a public space of acknowledgement, and at the same time transforming them into patrimony. Transforming objects, architectural structures, urban structures into cultural patrimony means attributing to them a 'representation' function that establishes a cornerstone for memory and identity. The dialogues and struggles to define what is true patrimony are struggles to guard the frontiers of what can or cannot be named 'patrimony'.
>
> (2007: 155)

Currently, it is possible to notice that marginalized areas and populations in the city are becoming subject to 'heritage' and to having their collective narratives raised to the status of 'memory'. One example of this process is the emergence of social projects dedicated to the subject of memory in favela areas. These are projects that defend the idea that the favela has a memory; that the favela is not only part of the city, but a part of it that is historically relevant to the urban cityscape (Freire-Medeiros 2006).

Grynszpan and Pandolfi (2002) suggest that, starting in the 1990s, this memory recovery, preservation and dissemination movement started to gain strength in Rio de Janeiro. According to the authors, besides the significant rise in projects dealing with the memories of favelas, there was also, in the last few years, the diversification of the agents that are directly or indirectly involved. Today, there are countless social projects especially dedicated to the theme of memory in favela areas (see Table 6.1).

It is increasingly easy to notice in the city of Rio de Janeiro actions that can be identified as manifestations of a desire for memory, a desire for patrimony and a desire for museums expressed by different social groups. These are projects that, endogenously promoted or not, defend the idea that the favela has a memory, and stress that the favela is not only part of the city, but a historically relevant part of the city's urban area. The projects also invest in the 'promotion of the self-esteem of the favela populations' and in the valorization of favelas as a patrimony of the city.

In the case of the Providência favela discussed in this chapter, these ideas took the shape of an open-air museum instead of a more traditional museum. When we asked Lu Petersen, the creator of the Providência Museum, if she had based her project on an existing experience, she said she had no idea whether there were other open museums and that 'in reality I wanted to create a favela museum, I thought the favela deserved a museum'. We asked why she had not conceived of it in a more formal museum format. She responded with excitement:

Table 6.1 Projects dedicated to the memory of the favela

Projects	Created by
Center for History and Memory of Rocinha	The project was created by NGO 'Rocinha Comunidade XXI', with the goal to construct a history of Rocinha based on the testimonies of its inhabitants, with an emphasis on the cultural diversity of the favela.
Cultural Center *Casarão dos Prazeres*	The project was sponsored by the Municipal Secretariat of Education to recover the history of the favela based on testimonies.
Website www.favelatemmemoria.com.br	The site was created by NGO Viva Rio with the goal to build the memory of the slums in Rio de Janeiro, value the memories of older residents, rescue collective experiences of religious participation, political or associative, and circulate stories of the past to strengthen ties and identities.
Heart of the Favela: Stories of Mangueira	A book compiled by Sueli de Lima.
Maré: Life in the Favela	A book written by Drauzio Varella, Paola Berenstein Jacques and Ivaldo Bertazzo.
Salgueiro, 50 Years of Glory	A book written by Haroldo Costa.
Stories of the Favelas of Grande Tijuca Told by Those Who Are Part of Them: Project Conductors of Memory	A book compiled by Neiva Vieira da Cunha and pubished by IBASE.
Memory Network of Maré	A project created by the Center of Studies and Solidarity of Maré – CEASM. CEASM's initiatives culminated in the Maré Museum, inagurated in May 2006, which fights for the title of the 'first open-air favela museum in Brazil' with the open-air museum of Providência.

Because I think it is ridiculous! . . . If I am going to make a building and say: 'look, this is the favela, you can't!' We place that museum in Providência and it is alive, it is not open-air because it is not static, it is a living museum, because there is no way the visitor is not going to interact with the people, the history, everything is automatic there. That is like a kind of information in which the past is shown, the present is there, and it will have in the next few years some mechanisms of change, it will evolve or it becomes unviable.

(Lu Petersen, interview, 29 March 2006)

Heritage building and the construction of the favela as an attraction in the 'city as a commodity'

According to Gonçalves (2007), the understanding of the nature of 'heritage' is important for overseeing the social and symbolic social processes of reclassification that elevate certain assets to the condition of patrimonies. Following the author's suggestion, I sought to monitor the reclassification processes of some locations of the Morro da Providência that elevated them to the status of permanent components of the museum. My analysis was based on visiting the site of the open-air museum project as well as reflections of the creator published in the book *From Relocations to the Urban Cell: Social-urban Evolution of Rio de Janeiro's Favelas* (Petersen 2003). I also conducted interviews with the architect.

The 'reclassification' processes of those sites in Providência that are now considered heritage involved the reform or restoration of constructions that the Mayor's Office considered to have some 'historical value' for the favela. These include a stairway, which had historical value because it was built by slaves; a church built before 1860; and a chapel (see Figures 6.2 and 6.3).

These three buildings were very badly preserved and seemed to be in a constant state of deterioration. Also restored was an abandoned water reservoir, built in 1913. This small construction, built in the shape of an octagon, was being used to raise chickens at the time the reconstruction began. It is supposed that it once served as an important meeting place for favela residents (see Figure 6.4).

Jeudy (2005: 87) emphasizes that any 'restoration inverts the direction of the intrinsic movement of the destiny' of a monument that survives its own transformation through time. Therefore, the 'fidelity' to the original authenticity of constructions, like the water reservoir of Morro da Providência, would be a 'purely moralist illusion', since according to the author:

> it is a matter of pretending that restoring a construction is preserving it as it was before, when in reality, what is being done is the opposite, that is, denaturing it by idealizing its temporal immutability.

> (Ibid.)

The Mayor's Office, on the other hand, responded by stating that the project's idea was not only to restore a building, but also to transform it into a 'memory bank'. A visual-acoustic installation was supposed to enable the visitor to hear testimonies from old inhabitants telling of their experiences and remembering facts. The idea was to verbally reconstruct the spatial and social image of the past of Rio's favelas. Therefore, the Mayor's Office aimed to preserve not only the 'material good' that is the historical value of the reservoir building, but also the valuable 'immaterial' or 'intangible' good: the memories of the older inhabitants.[1]

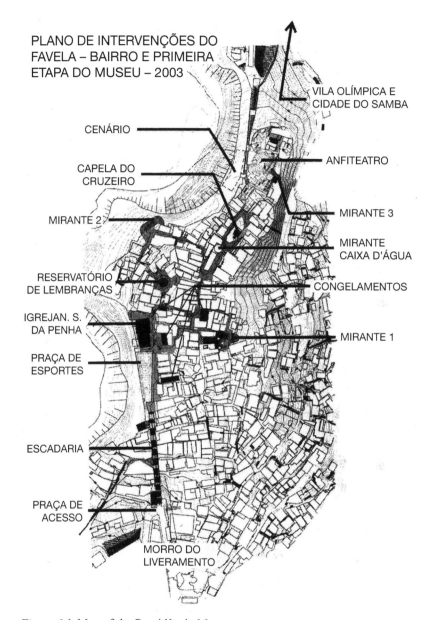

PLANO DE INTERVENÇÕES DO
FAVELA – BAIRRO E PRIMEIRA
ETAPA DO MUSEU – 2003

VILA OLÍMPICA E
CIDADE DO SAMBA

CENÁRIO

ANFITEATRO

CAPELA DO
CRUZEIRO

MIRANTE 3

MIRANTE 2

MIRANTE
CAIXA D'ÁGUA

RESERVATÓRIO
DE LEMBRANÇAS

CONGELAMENTOS

IGREJAN. S.
DA PENHA

MIRANTE 1

PRAÇA DE
ESPORTES

ESCADARIA

PRAÇA DE
ACESSO

MORRO DO
LIVERAMENTO

Figure 6.1 Map of the Providência Museum
Source: Petersen (2003).

Figure 6.2 The Nossa Senhora da Penha Church in the background
Source: photo by Palloma Menezes.

Figure 6.3 The Cruzeiro Chapel in the background
Source: photo by Palloma Menezes.

Figure 6.4 Water reservoir that Mayor's Office planned to turn 'bank memory'
Source: photo by Palloma Menezes.

A further site to be lifted to the status of patrimony was the house of Dodô da Portela. It was transformed into a carnival museum named after its former owner. According to Petersen:

> besides being a carnival icon and being 85 years old, she has a real patrimony of carnival in her house. She has the costumes she paraded in, she has the first flag Portela used when it won the first official samba school parade of Rio de Janeiro in 1937.
>
> (Lu Petersen, interview, 29 March 2006)

Other ideas for reclassifying spaces in the favela were put into practice. One of these ideas was to 'freeze' some houses, alleys and small streets (Figure 6.5). According to Petersen (2003: 48), 'this means that the visitor can walk in these houses and have a clear notion of how the inhabitants of the favela live'. To Jeudy, this kind of proposal is a little complicated, since:

> if we freeze a monument, trying to maintain it in its present state, interrupting as much as possible the advancement of its degradation, what

Figure 6.5 House 'frozen' by the Mayor's Office
Source: photo by Palloma Menezes.

we are actually preserving is nothing more than a group of buildings that were restored. Being an endless process, restoration preserves only what has already been restored.

(2005: 87)

In Petersen's project, the interior space of 'frozen' houses was to accurately reproduce in its interior the furniture, decor and family possessions. Each family would be compensated for their house and the right to use its image in works of art, photography and video. Also, there was a plan to rebuild, based on photographic and video archives of the time, 'the wood shacks built on the quarry slope by the freed slaves, soldiers, and women who were returning from the Canudos War' (Petersen 2003: 48).

In addition to all these already completed renovations and restorations, and with some projects still in blueprint, the process of 'inventing' an open-air museum also involved the creation of tourist sites, the beautification of certain areas and the placing of markers indicating the tourist itinerary of the Morro Providência. Three outlooks were created in the Morro da Providência, intended to become tourist sites of the museum. Wooden decks were built to create vantage points for privileged views of the city and its postcard landmarks – the Sugarloaf, the Corcovado Mountain, the Guanabara Bay – and other not so famous ones such as the Central Station, the Sambódrome, the Port Zone, the Rio-Niterói Bridge and the Maracanã Stadium (Figure 6.6).

Figure 6.6 Outlook with view of Port Zone
Source: photo by Palloma Menezes.

The creation of these tourist spaces required the removal of several houses. According to museum supporters, the creation of such vistas was important, not only to give tourists access to views of the city, but also to 'increase air circulation' and improve ventilation.

In the Mayor's Office's original plans, two telescopes and a 360-degree map would give visitors a comparative perspective of urban growth in different areas of the city, especially the Port Zone and the favelas located on the hillsides of central Rio. However, due to problems related to violence this idea was not put into practice.

At the third outlook, a bar, Beto's Bar, was renovated in order to offer tourists, as stated by Petersen, 'food and beverages in a hygienic environment, and on top of that a magnificent sunset over the Guanabara Bay'. The owner of the bar was filled with enthusiasm for the renovation, sponsored by the Mayor's Office (Figure 6.7).

In addition to tourist infrastructure works, identification signs were placed in visitor locations (Figure 6.8). The city government also placed special markings on the ground indicating the itinerary to be followed by visitors (Figure 6.9). The museum's new landscape, created by Favela-Bairro constructions, according to Petersen, 'replaces what would be the galleries in a traditional museum'. As pointed out by Freire-Medeiros:

> visibility strategies organizing the presentation of buildings and artifacts to be targeted by the tourist's gaze continue in place. Alternating thin strips

Figure 6.7 Bar renovated by the city government with outlook in background
Source: photo by Palloma Menezes.

Figure 6.8 Sign indicating the Capela do Cruzeiro
Source: photo by Palloma Menezes.

Figure 6.9 Tracks indicating the open-air corridors of the museum
Source: photo by Palloma Menezes.

of metal and then small pieces of black marble form, along with cement blocks on the ground, a sort of track which indicates the itinerary. It frames the empirical plurality of the favela and guides the tourist's gaze to that which has been previously selected as 'attractive.' In this process, a new local hierarchy is established: the supposedly more relevant constructions are 'tagged' with a signpost placed by the city government; older houses aren't tagged but are 'presented' to tourists by guides; other constructions, whose touristic potential is apparently null, are ignored and left to mingle with the garbage and untreated waste.

(2006: 21)

Michael Pretes (1995) emphasizes that the marker confers importance on the touristic object. The creation of signs signifies a touristification of the favela. The signs, moreover, structure the tourist's gaze, transforming localities into perceived objects, whereby decisions are made about what is rendered visible and invisible.

Discussion: urban development and favela tourism

It is important to try to situate the Providência Museum within the context of the urban development of the Port Zone and in the larger context of the city's urban planning strategy. The project of the museum involved first and foremost the spatial reproduction of the favela, that is to say, the transformation of part of the favela's space into a commodity. Works were conducted to ensure that 'public spaces start functioning in interaction with the museum's equipment producing a hitherto inexistent symbiosis', as pointed out by Petersen (2003: 49).

It does not seem an exaggeration to say that, in cases such as the Morro da Providência Museum, the political mobilization for the restructuring of space and the city's image as a whole is the result of actions both in the symbolic field and in material action. In projects such as this one it is evident that political power can be mobilized and exerted by both physical and symbolic urban modernization.

Sánchez (2003) has argued that the production of a material object in the city, such as a square, a monument or a building, goes hand in hand with its form of consumption through ideological practices that reproduce the object as a discourse or image. The production of commodity-spaces necessarily involves the production of attendant representations. And these spaces are conceived partly by means of the production of signs that 'seem to realize desires and consumption fantasies shaped by the values of "worldliness"' (Sánchez 2003: 48). Often, commodity-spaces are constituted as a result of advice from, or partnerships with, international institutions.

The signs produced in the process of spatial commoditization are usually signs disseminated through photography, promotional videos and television advertising, for example. These materials can be read as texts that communicate complex meanings, since they are at once the image and the means used to express its meaning. In this sense, Freire-Medeiros analyses the promotional DVD made for the Providência Museum:

> A production of Cara de Cão Filmes made at the request of Rio de Janeiro's Mayor's Office, the DVD opens with aerial views of the Corcovado to the sound of a discrete samba beat and follows with a historical contextualization made by César Maia [the mayor at the time] in his office. Employing a didactic tone, he stresses the museum's insertion within the context of the Favela-Bairro project and the urban renovation of the Port Zone. There are also testimonies provided by three residents and by Lu Petersen in the urbanization of the Morro da Providência, but little of the actual favela is shown. There are interesting visual takes of Dodô da Portela in his House-Museum, but the church, the chapel and the reservoir are shown quickly. The emphasis is not so much on the elements of the museum but rather on what can be seen from it: the postcard view of the city as it is lays [sic] before the tourist's feet.
>
> (2006: 23)

This analysis demonstrates why public authorities made an effort to endow the museum with the function of creating 'integration' with the rest of the city. This effort has a 'double existence, real and imaginary' (Lefebvre 1998: 99). First, it was built upon physical landmarks, such as the outlook built in the favela, with its metallic structure, which, according to Petersen, functions as a 'balcony' that valorizes and integrates the favela and the view surrounding the morro. It was built, second, as a symbolic investment that is evinced, for example, in the discourse formed by image sequences and the verbal commentary provided by the DVD.

It is interesting to note that the spatial production of the museum involves the 'selective edition of history', which places a greater value on and idealizes certain swathes of the path while others are erased. The history of the city, in cases such as the Providência Musuem, according to Sánchez, is re-edited by the city government for tourism and future generations by the selection, reduction and recombination of cultural references. Hence, new spaces are created, and they are:

> completed by synthesis-images of the history of each group, reinterpreted from an official prism, and offered to tourists and citizens as a simplified version, a distilled experience, which replaces the undisciplined complexities of the city with the elaboration of the existent order. The production of these spaces offers an 'improved version' of complex reality.
>
> (Sánchez 2003: 535)

It is worth remembering that public authorities capitalize on the success of the touristic favela in a way that is different from private initiatives[2] – which basically hope to make a financial profit from this kind of activity. The hypothesis I am advancing in this text is that the César Maia administration made an attempt to transform the favela into an official attraction of the 'city as a commodity' when the open-air museum in the Morro da Providência was created. We can point out several reasons behind this initiative – to generate local development, to democratize the right to memory, to raise the 'self-esteem' of favela residents – but, as the Mayor's Office itself states, the main objective was to create a 'definite landmark, proving that favelas are part of the contours of Rio de Janeiro' (Secretaria Especial 2003: 42).

I believe it is possible to liken the idea of creating 'a definitive landmark' to the 'synthesis-image', which 'conforms values and beliefs, providing elements to those involved with marketing and technological means of information and communication, to try to articulate consensual elements of the discourse of the city with social and economic activities' (Sánchez 2003: 109). If this approximation truly makes any sense, it would then be possible to claim that the Mayor's Office created the Providência Museum as a synthesis-image of 'social harmony' it wants to pitch in order to add value to the city as a commodity. In so doing, the Mayor's Office was, in a certain way, using 'the marketing and promotion of the city' as a tool to 'demarginzalize' the favela and integrate it into the image of the 'marvellous city'.

However, as much as public authorities might try to create a better representation of the city, there is always space for actions that do not obey the official logic. Sánchez reminds us that 'collective subject constituting processes express life styles and reappropriations of the city distinct from the forecasts of urban order promoted by official images' (2003: 123). This becomes clear in this example given by Freire-Medeiros:

> when talking to us of their experiences as 'guides' some residents of the Morro da Providência exposed the tensions and disputes already being caused by the museum: if, on one hand, the Mayor's Office seeks to capitalize on the positive image of itself through the implementation of a museum that is 'inclusive and democratic', on the other one, residents want to benefit from the presence of tourists precisely to 'show the world that public authorities don't care about them'.
>
> (2006: 15)

This kind of thinking, shared by some favela residents, indicates the existence of a gap between the symbolic appropriation of 'modernized spaces' and the effective appropriation of the 'products of modernization'. As part of the process of spatial production, urban renovation projects that are mediated by city marketing, such as the museum, can always engender 'contradiction and forms of resistance that, in certain circumstances, hardly acquire social visibility but in others emerge and signal the long distance between life in a place and the official image' (Sánchez 2003: 34).

Lack of 'resonance', security and the forgetting of the museum

Duncan Light (2007: 63) states that the 'State is an important actor in the cultural policy of tourism'. This cultural policy involves choices concerning the forms of tourism considered appropriate and how, where and with which target they should be promoted. As Light summarizes, 'the representation of local culture is a political act, just as the choice of the places that will be encouraged or celebrated as part of the identity of a territory' (ibid.).

The political act of turning a place into an asset and of making investment so as to transform it into a tourist attraction does not always find 'resonance' among the local population – which, theoretically, is being 'benefitted' by public authorities. In the case of Providência, although the museum 'construction' ended in 2005, years later several residents were still making statements such as: 'The mayor promised to build the Providência Museum, but so far it's still in blueprint' (a man who lives in the favela). I consider such statements rather meaningful and relevant since they suggest that, although the museum has already been completed, it is not perceived by residents as such for at least three reasons.

The first reason is probably connected to the fact that the museum is a new conception. As the exhibition's ordering of its content and its spatial organization departs from conventional conceptions – the traditional museum comprising a building that houses a collection of objects most people are familiar with – the project can easily be misunderstood. As Petersen remarks, in some cases even visitors had a hard time understanding the concept of an open-air museum:

> The funniest thing happened when we took one of the architects [for a visit of the favela] . . . and when the visit ended the urban planning and architect professor asked: 'And how about the museum? Where is it?' And this despite the translator, another professor who speaks English and Duca [the person who was guiding the visit] who also speaks English!
>
> (Lu Petersen, interview, 29 March 2006)

This example makes it clear that misunderstanding the concept of the museum cannot simply be labelled as 'ignorance' on the part of the favela residents. I suppose this lack of understanding also happens because people do not experience the museum according to the premises and intentions of the Mayor's Office. As stated by Gonçalves:

> There are situations in which certain cultural assets, classified by a certain State agency as patrimony . . . are not supported or acknowledged by certain sectors of the population. What this experience of rejection seems to bring into focus is less the relativity of the conception of patrimony in modern societies (an aspect which has been excessively stressed already) and more the fact that a given patrimony does not solely depend on will and political decisions taken by a government agency or by market initiatives, although they are closely connected to them. It does not depend exclusively on the conscious and deliberate activity of individuals or groups. The objects that compose a patrimony need to find 'resonance' within its public audience.
>
> (2007: 33)

Interestingly, 'the effort of constructing collective identities and memories is not evidently bound to succeed. It can, in many ways, not be accomplished' (ibid.: 37).

A second reason for the failure of the open-air museum of Morro Providência might have been the lack of 'resonance' among those who were supposedly represented by the patrimony and/or those who should be the target audience of the project. Often patrimony does not gain 'resonance' as a result of not being considered legitimate. The museum project was discussed on no occasion with the residents' association of the Providência – as Petersen expressed in our interview, 'because the association there is a null factor, non-existent' –

or with the residents in general – 'because there is no level of organization in Providência'. Regardless of the factors that led the Mayor's Office to decide not to call upon the favela population to participate in decision-making procedures related to the museum, this lack of participation may certainly have contributed towards the lack of 'resonance' among residents.

The residents do not visit the museum or participate effectively in the tours made by tourists. Moreover, people do not talk about the existence of the museum in their everyday conversations. Thus, the museum has become a stage where everything is an aesthetic and contemplative (and not participative) object of consumption. In fact, 'participation' occurs by its negation, by unawareness of the museum's existence, by forgetting, or by the destruction of the equipment installed. This may also explain why the museum was merely conceived as 'outward looking,' a tourist attraction, a favela museum tailored for gringos and not to be experienced by residents.

Hence, the Providência Museum could not escape one of the greatest temptations faced by projects that combine the transformation of a site into a patrimony and its promotion as a tourist destination: 'that of reducing heritage sites to "stages" for the cultural industry and the entertainment industry, disconnecting the enjoyment of cultural assets from social and historical memory' (Funari and Pelegrini 2006: 111).

An important third reason for the failure of this project is the atmosphere of insecurity[3] – generated by constant conflicts in the favela between drug-dealers and the police. The Mayor's Office was not able to suppress violence in order to open the possibility of constant and regular visits to the Morro da Providência. Thus, the museum was not consolidated as a tourist attraction recognized by visitors and endorsed by the promoters of tourism in Rio de Janeiro.

To summarize, there were three main reasons that led to the museum being forgotten: (1) the museum did not find 'resonance' among those who were supposedly being represented by the patrimony (favela residents) and those who should be the target audience of the project (tourists); (2) the lack of participation of residents in the museum project may certainly have contributed towards the lack of 'resonance' among residents; and (3) due to an atmosphere of insecurity there are no regular tours through the museum.

As a result, frustration concerning the potential reach of the open-air Morro da Providência Museum is twofold: the museum is not remembered as a heritage site either by residents of the favela or by tourists as a tourist destination. Thus, instead of becoming a dense place in the realm of sociability, it became merely a space 'in which social ties seem fragile and social interaction lost its meaning and potential' (Leite 2008: 141).

Final remarks

The existence of the open-air Morro da Providência Museum seems to have been forgotten even by government official representatives, who recently publicized the construction of a new museum in the favela as if it was breaking news. The idea emerged after Providência received in May 2010 the seventh UPP[4] unit in Rio de Janeiro.

Coincidence or not, the police occupation of the Morro da Providência started the same week the Social Urban Forum was taking place in the Port Zone. The police occupation was followed by the announcement of a project that will 'revitalize the region'. The municipal Housing Secretary, Jorge Bittar, announced that around 800 of the 2,000 families in the favela would be 'relocated' in areas close to the favela. According to Bittar, the new urbanization plan would include the building of two cable cars. One small cable car would connect Providência to the City of Samba and, at the other end, to the Central do Brasil (train station). The other larger cable car would connect Avenida Francisco Bicalho and three other favelas in the Port Zone: Morro do Pinto, Livramento and Conceição:

> the installation of the Providência UPP is extremely welcome and guarantees the continuation of the reurbanization project. It is important to remember that the community went through interventions by the Favela-Bairro program, but the problems continued ... The Providência reurbanization is fundamental for the revitalizaiton of the Port Zone.
>
> (Jorge Bittar, cited in *O Globo*, 29 March 2010)

An article published on the first page of the *O Globo* newspaper on 29 March 2010 – with half a page dedicated to the model that shows how the favela would look after the new urbanization – pointed out that the Nossa Senhora da Penha church and the Cruzeiro Chapel would be renovated. The article also mentioned that the project included building colonial-style houses with a double function: commercial and residential. According to the architect Fernanda Salles, responsible for the urbanization project, 'there is a deactivated and deteriorating water reservoir. It will be replaced by a museum, with the proposal to preserve the history of the Morro da Providência'. The announcement of the idea to build a museum in a favela was not accompanied by any reminder of the existence of an open-air museum in the Morro da Providência.

At the same time, a new project, called Rio Top Tour, was created by the government with the goal to create a tourism structure within the pacified favelas. Launched on Monday, 30 August 2010, by President Luiz Inácio Lula da Silva, Rio Top Tour was initiated in May by the State Secretary of Tourism, Sport and Leisure and TurisRio with the aim of improving favela tourism by giving residents the training and tools to show off their neighbourhood and offering the tourist a more meaningful insight into the culture and life of the community. Following Santa Marta (one of the first and most publicized communities pacified by the UPPs), Rio Top Tour will eventually be initiated in other pacified communities, with the next one to receive the project being Providência in the centre of Rio.

So, once more there seems to exist a project for the favela that associates community policing – previously the GPAE and now the UPP – with urbanization projects linked to the revitalization of the Port Zone; César Maia's old project for the region has been renamed the Porto Maravilha Project.[5] It remains to be seen whether this story will have a different ending, or if another museum will be built in Providência only to be, paradoxically, forgotten.

Notes

1   Despite the fact that the reservoir building was renovated, the installation has not yet been set up inside it due to 'lack of security' on the site.

2   With regard to the subject of favela tourism, the paradigm case is no doubt the Rocinha favela, which currently receives 3,000 visitors every month, taken by seven different agencies – in addition to individual guides and taxi drivers who regularly carry out tours. However, Rocinha is not the only favela that has been promoted as a tourist destination in the city. In recent years, the number of favelas in which strategies and partnerships have been traced with the intent of capitalizing on their 'tourist potential' is on the rise: Babilônia, Prazeres, Vidigal, Vila Canoas, Pereira da Silva and Tavares Bastos are examples of a few localities where there are (or have been) attempts to organize a routine of visitors and/or housing tourists. Among the many favelas that have been promoted as tourist attractions, the case of the Morro da Providência is different because, in contrast to Rocinha and most of the favelas mentioned above, public authorities, and not private capital, are the driving force behind tourism there.

3   The conflicts between dealers and the police in the favela escalated after a GPAE base was established in a six-storey house – formerly abandoned and then occupied by a drug-trafficking gang – which later became the base for the CRAS Dodô da Portela social-assistance centre. Created by a partnership between the Secretariat of Public Security, NGOs and the Catholic Church, the Grupamento de Policiamento em Áreas Especiais – GPAE (Special Area Police Group) – comprised military policemen who had experience in a pilot project implemented in the Pavão/Pavãozinho and Cantagalo communities in the year 2000. According to the military police's website, the three basic principles of the GPAE were: 'the GPAE does not tolerate weapons; the GPAE does not tolerate the recruitment of minors for illegal activities and the GPAE does not tolerate police abuse' (www. policiamilitar.rj.gov.br/antigo/ac_gpae.htm (accessed 8 December 2007)).

4   The Pacifiying Police Units (Unidades de Polícia Pacificadora – UPPs) are community policing projects idealized during the Sergio Cabral administration in the state of Rio de Janeiro, which began in December 2008, in the Santa Marta favela. In the course of 2009, 2010 and 2011, other favelas also received units. The occupation of all these favelas was supported by the Special Operations Unit (Batalhão de Operações Especiais – BOPE) and the shock troops that ran operations in order to 'prepare' for the arrival of new police units. After the UPPs were implemented, 'fresh' police academy graduates – who received training in community policing and approach tactics used by BOPE – started permanently operating in these territories.

5   In 2001 the Recovery and Revitalization Plan of the Port Zone of Rio de Janeiro was launched by César Maia. Also known as the Porto do Rio Project, the plan was divided into six areas: urbanism, transportation, housing, economic development, special projects and urban management. The project made possible works such as the 'Cidade do Samba' and the 'Vila Olimpica' of Gamboa, both

inaugurated in 2005. The project 'Porto Maravilha' was officially launched on 23 June 2009 as a result of a partnership between the municipal (Eduardo Paes administration), state (Sergio Cabral administration) and federal (Lula's second administration) agencies, intensifying once more the discussion agenda surrounding the Port Zone.

Bibliography

Abreu, M. de Almeida (1994) 'Reconstruindo uma história esquecida: origem e expansão inicial das favelas do Rio', *Espaço e Debates*, 14(37): 34–46.

Abreu, R. and Chagas, M. (eds) (2003) *Memória e Patrimônio: Ensaios Contemporâneos*, vol. 1, Rio de Janeiro: DP&A Editora.

—— and Sepúlveda, M. (2007) *Museus, Coleções e Patrimônios: Narrativas Polifônicas*, Rio de Janeiro: Garamond Universitária.

Appadurai, A. and Breckenridge, C. (2007) 'Museus são bons para pensar: o patrimônio em cana na Índia', *MUSAS – Revista Brasileira de Museus e Museologia*, 3: 10–26.

Aquino, R. (2007) 'Museu do bispo do rosário arte contemporânea: da coleção à criação', *MUSAS – Revista Brasileira de Museus e Museologia*, 3.

Arantes, O.B.F. (1999) 'Uma estratégia fatal: a cultura nas novas gestões urbanas', in C.B. Vainer, E. Maricato, O. Arantes (eds) *A Cidade do Pensamento Único, Desmanchando Consensos*, Petrópolis: Editora Vozes.

Carlos, A., Lemos, F. and Geraiges, A.I. (2005) *Dilemas Urbanos: Novas Abordagens Sobre a Cidade*, São Paulo: Contexto.

Chagas, M. de Souza (1994) *Novos Rumos da Museologia*. Available online at www.cadernosociomuseologia.ulusofona.pt (accessed 30 October 2011).

Freire-Medeiros, B. (2006) 'Favela como patrimônio da cidade? reflexões e polêmicas acerca de dois museus', *Estudos Históricos*, 38: 49–66.

—— (2007) 'A favela que se vê e que se vende: reflexões e polêmicas em torno de um destino turístico', *Revista Brasileira de Ciências Sociais*, 22: 61–72.

—— (2009) *Gringo na Laje: Produção, Circulação e Consumo da Favela Turística*, Rio de Janeiro: FGV.

——, Freire, A. and Cavalcanti, M. (2009) *Lu Petersen: Militância, Favela e Urbanismo. Depoimentos ao CPDOC*, Rio de Janeiro: FGV.

Funari, P. and Pelegrini, S. (2006) *Patrimônio Histórico e Cultural*, Rio de Janeiro: Jorge Zahar.

Gonçalves, J.R.S. (2005) 'Ressonância, materialidade e subjetividade: as culturas como patrimônios', *Horizontes Antropológicos*, 11(23): 15–36.

—— (2007) 'Os limites do patrimônio', in M.F.L. Filho, C. Eckert and J. Beltrao (eds) *Antropologia e Patrimonio Cultural: Dialogos e Desafios Contemporaneos*, Blumenau: Nova Letra.

Grynszpan, M. and Pandolfi, D. (2002) 'Poder público e favelas: uma relação delicada', in L.L. Oliveira (ed.) *Cidade: História e Desafios*, Rio de Janeiro: FGV.

Jeudy, H.-P. (2005) *Espelho das Cidades*, Rio de Janeiro: Casa da Palavra.

Lefebvre, H. (1998) *The Production of Space*, London: Blackwell.

Leite, M. (2008) 'Entre o individualismo e a solidariedade: dilemas da política e da cidadania no Rio de Janeiro', *Revista Brasileira de Ciências Sociais*, 15(44): 73–90.

Light, D. (2007) 'Dracula tourism in Romania: cultural identity and the state', *Annals of Tourism Research*, 34: 746–65.

Oliveira, L.L. (2008) *Cultura é patrimônio: um guia*, Rio de Janeiro: FGV.

Petersen, L. (2003) *Das Remoções à Célula Urbana: Evolução Urbano-social das Favelas do Rio de Janeiro*, Rio de Janeiro: Cadernos de Comunicação da Prefeitura do Rio de Janeiro.

—— (2006) *Depoimentos ao CPDOC/FGV*, Rio de Janeiro: FGV.

Pretes, M. (1995) 'Postmodern tourism: the Santa Claus industry', *Annals of Tourism Research*, 22(1): 1–15.

Sánchez, F. (2003) *A Reinvenção das Cidades para um Mercado Mundial*, Chapecó: Argos.

Secretaria Especial de Comunicaçao Social da Prefeitura do Rio de Janeiro (2003) *Das Remoções à Célula Urbana: Evolução Urbana-social das Favelas*, Rio de Janeiro: Prefeitura Rio.

Urry, J. (1990) *O Olhar do Turista: Lazer e Viagens nas Sociedades Contemporâneas*, São Paulo: Nobel.

Valladares, L. (2005) *A Invenção da Favela: Do Mito de Origem a Favela.com*, Rio de Janeiro: FGV.

Zylberberg, S. (1992) *Morro da Providência: Memórias da Favela*, Rio de Janeiro: Secretaria Municipal da Cultura.

7 Tourism of poverty

The value of being poor in the non-governmental order

João Afonso Baptista

Introduction

This chapter is about a problem, but it is also about a solution. More precisely, this is an analysis of the constitution of a ('South'-wide) problem and its solution, as well as the ways in which those who 'fall into' the problem appropriate and reproduce it in attempting to achieve their own solution. In particular, the problem is poverty – the 'slums', the 'local communities' and in the 'South' – and the solution is tourism.

Concerns about poverty and the poor have long been at the core of conceptualizations of society. Still, it was only in the latter part of the Industrial Revolution that poverty became firmly placed and interpreted as a serious social problem. More recently, as addressed by Arturo Escobar:

> One of the main changes that occurred in the early post-World War II period was the 'discovery' of mass poverty in Asia, Africa, and Latin America . . . [which provided] the anchor for an important restructuring of global culture and political economy.
>
> (1995: 21)

Since then, ideas of poverty have evolved and techniques of measurement have become the prime effect in characterizing it (Hagenaars 1991). Poverty became a global statistical process of knowledge that appears to require a solution via expert intervention.

Nevertheless, destitution is far from being unequivocally defined; indeed, poverty is a controversial construct, entangled in social, political, economic and historical struggles, which unsurprisingly originates new imageries, identifications and values. The modernized category of poverty thus surpasses mere communicative practice. It encompasses powerful ideological systems, shaping perceptions, producing workable subjects and making a 'reality'. Can poverty be a value for those categorized as poor? And if so, what do these developments tell us?

My objective is to approach the globalizing and globalized effects of poverty as a socially constructed category within which, and according to which, some peoples strategize their lives. As we will see, the incorporation of developmental problems and solutions in particular settings in the 'developing world' is fostering new performing spaces and fields of agency. The globalization of normative ideas of socio-economic order and progress, in which a perception of poverty and its solution are an inherent constituent of this order, reproduces local performances of neediness as a market opportunity. In this process, the 'peripheral', 'slummy' and 'underdeveloped South' is being progressively incorporated in the neoliberal economy as a product and producer of a (poverty) problem that matches 'western' cultural imagery; and, thus, is seeking a solution that is morally assigned to 'western' non-governmental expertise.

This is not to say, however, that there is a uniform entity (the 'West') unilaterally inducing other powerless ones (the 'Rest'). Neoliberal and non-governmental regimes might elicit new capacities and statuses to individuals. More than being simply absorbents, the globalization of the imaginary of poverty also provides historically subjugated peoples with new opportunities, stimulating the emergence of new fields of creative agency. The very category of 'slum' and the word compounding that it generates (e.g. 'slum dwellers') represent a good example. 'Slums' are by nature linked to poverty, places where development is necessary in the social moral imaginaries (Taylor 2002), particularly in 'northern' societies. This irresistible association with poverty and the 'will to improve' (Li 2007) generates opportunities for the 'slum dwellers' themselves: 'slum tourism' is one response. How do those categorized as poor react to the developmentalization and touristification of poverty?

This chapter shows that poverty can indeed be apprehended as a value for some of those categorized as poor. The arguments come from a specific approach: the global diffusion of representations of poverty as a problem in 'developing countries' and the social implications of this for those categorized as poor, explored through the lens of tourism. However, to understand the value of poverty or the poor in tourism, one must look at the large-scale ideologies and economic systems in which it is embedded. Therefore, this chapter is about questioning and analysing the processes that make it possible to ascribe value to poverty for the supposed subjugated peoples in the 'South', turning it into touristic capital.

Canhane: a developing case

I began to reflect on the complexities intrinsic to conceptions and manifestations of poverty while conducting fieldwork in the village of Canhane,[1] in the south of Mozambique. According to data from 2006 provided by the community leader, Canhane then had a population of 1,105 residents. Due to the predominance of informal emigration to South Africa, particularly to work in the mines, it is hard to ascertain a precise number of people living in the village. Nevertheless, my estimate is that no more than 650 people currently live in Canhane. The residents speak Shangane, and only a few are fluent in Portuguese, the national language of Mozambique.

Canhane has developed the first 'community-based tourism' project in Mozambique. As a corollary of an initiative of the Swiss NGO Helvetas, the 'community' of Canhane embraced the construction of a lodge located about 7 kilometres away from the village. The tourism project was mainly established by Helvetas with funds coming from the United States Agency for International Development (USAID). However, as part of the 'community-based' scheme, the infrastructure of the lodge and the tourism business are owned by the 'community'. The lodge opened its doors to tourists in May 2004. Since then the words 'tourist' ('turista'), 'community' ('comunidade'), 'development' ('desenvolvimento') and 'poverty' ('pobreza') became part of residents' common vocabulary.

There is a prevalent ordered way for tourists to encounter the residents and visit Canhane: the 'village walk'. The village walk is basically a tourist product that can be purchased at the lodge. As a staff member of Helvetas said:

> That tour represents what we really want for tourism there: tourists who are interested in the community. The five-star tourists who used to go to coastal areas, and who don't want to know about local cultures, are not our aim.
>
> (6 October 2008)

As the main form of encounter between tourists and the residents of Canhane, the village walk is an inherent component of the 'front side' (Goffman 1959) of the 'community' and supports the social constitution of tourist sights. It institutionalizes ordinary places, materials and people as tourist attractions. However, the touristification of specificities in the village was not random. They were chosen as tourist sights because of their potential to represent the logic behind the implementation of the 'community-based tourism' project: that is, poverty eradication via tourism. Let me illustrate this with a short example.

One of the spots most visited by tourists in Canhane is the shallow well, which is a hole dug in the centre of the village to allow access to water. At the shallow well, the visual impact of shortage is strong and authenticates (a) poverty. Tourists experience there what many call 'real tourism' in the sense of their 'notion of a genuine local experience' (Smith and Duffy 2003: 114). They experience 'real people' and 'real situations' in a circumstance that is often shocking, but also part of a recognizable imaginary for them – it is a poverty show. On one occasion, a 41-year-old British woman remained immobile for two minutes, seated on a rock, under strong sunlight, looking at the setting of the place. I asked her: 'Are you okay?' 'When I see these same situations on TV or on the computer screen', she said, 'I'm not close enough, so it's easy to turn off feelings. But now that I'm here . . . It's impossible to ignore it' (29 January 2008). She confirmed what some authors have suggested: 'There has always been a nagging inadequacy around the assertion that one cannot sell poverty, but one can sell paradise. Today, the tourist industry does sell poverty' (Salazar 2009: 92). Canhane is an example of that.

But Canhane is also an example of self-entrepreneurship initiatives and of social progress, and also encompasses non-poverty settings. Nonetheless, tourists are not led to such sites. The only manifestations of betterment that tourists have access to in the village are those that have had, precisely, tourists' direct contribution. That is, they see sites/sights of 'community development' that were endowed by the profits of tourism, thus suggesting (and confirming) to tourists that local poverty solutions are possible and being implemented because of tourism. In the tourism arena, the crucial indicators of well-being or destitution informed by the Canhaners' own social mores – cattle, agricultural fields, family relatives – are kept separate from the exhibition of themselves. Specifically, the tourists visit mostly two sites/sights embodying developmental solutions: the primary school and the water tank. Both display a way of 'developing' the community in which the revenues of the tourists are morally justified. The cartography of signifiers of poverty – the problem – and the potentialities to solve it through tourism predetermine the physical and psychological itinerary to be toured in the village. Yet the narrative of poverty and its (tourism) solution in Canhane are constructed in conjunction with other narratives about Mozambique and Africa where the same problem and solution are placed.

Nonetheless, and perhaps even more effectively, Canhane can be acknowledged and realized by its non-poverty attributes in many other places and circumstances. For example, I met a man who implemented a system close to his house that allows other residents to watch South African football matches. He acquired a generator that provides energy to a television that is inside a hut with a parabolic antenna outside. Confronting the dire material conditions in the village, the technological attribute of the hut obtains the significance of social progress; or, more concretely, it has the potential to embody, in contrast with most of the sites/sights visited by the tourists, non-poverty characteristics. However, no tourist had ever visited the hut where the television is located. The question that therefore arises is: why are the tourists persistently led to the shallow well and not to the hut where Canhaners watch television? I believe the answer to this simple question gives evidence about the broader context of the recent emergence of many other 'community-based tourism' settings in the 'developing world'.

Although understanding the very category of poverty is empirically problematic, my intention here is to approach the making of poverty as a discursive and imaginative object that spans the 'developing countries'. The subject of poverty will be thus referred to in terms of how it orders, classifies and constitutes social units (e.g. 'slums', 'local communities'), leading to the institution of global regimes of meaning. Moreover, this chapter intends to analyse how such an imaginary of poverty is apprehended and appropriated by some of those categorized as poor in the same social units. Geographically speaking, I extend the space of problematization further than the empirical case brought by my fieldwork in Mozambique. This approach bears upon an understanding of anthropology that may be gained from a critical analysis of an array of multi-local angles, together with an assessment of the global forces at work.

The recovering of a hope in developing: the tourist

Academic approaches to tourism began during the 1960s. They were described largely in terms of economic development, and were seen almost entirely in a positive light (Crick 1989). However, 'despite the early hopes, tourism as a "passport" to macroeconomic development did not pan out quite as planned' (de Kadt 1979, in Stronza 2001: 268), and the pessimism about tourism became common in academia. Rather than alleviating poverty, tourism was declared as one of the causes.

More recently, though, societies all over the world have been presented with an ideology shift, and the harmful character of tourism has progressively been replaced by one more benign. Alarmist insights and general antipathy towards tourism have led to contemporary calls for ethical tourism and for the incorporation of development, pro-poor principles by the tourism sector. As addressed by Mowforth and Munt, 'the start of the twenty-first century has seen efforts to stimulate development through tourism', and the overriding goal of poverty alleviation has generated 'a long line of terms and types to attract attention, funding and energy' in the tourism industry (2009: 335). While ethical tourism initiatives tried to minimize harm, tourism activity was now integrated into the solution mechanisms in poverty contexts. Tourism became inscribed in the global discourse of good governance in the developing world. What this has caused in practice is the beginning of new types of tourism, commonly called 'new tourisms' (Mowforth and Munt 2009). The 'community-based tourism' in Canhane is one of them.

Although the term emerged during the 1990s and has been widely used since then, there is no single and unanimous definition of 'community-based tourism'. Its definition has been blurred by commonplace ideas of promoting welfare for so-called rural, poor and economically marginalized popula-tions. For example, according to a 'toolkit' published by the Netherlands Development Organization (SNV), 'Community-based tourism [CBT] is a type of sustainable tourism that promotes pro-poor strategies in a community setting. CBT initiatives aim . . . [at] alleviating poverty' (2007: 7). In a report involving a legion of researchers and consultants on *Sustainable Tourism and Poverty Elimination*, produced for the UK Department for International Development (DFID), 'community-based tourism' is acknowledged, among other things, as 'creating a supportive policy framework and planning context that addresses needs of poor producers and residents within tourism' (Deloitte & Touche *et al.* 1999: 14). To Patullo *et al.* (2009, in Tourism Concern 2009: 7), '[c]ommunity-based tourism is where visitors stay in local homes, have a glimpse into traditional life, and most importantly, where management and benefits remain with the community'. While to NGO Planeterra, 'community-based tourism [brings] . . . the financial benefits of tourism to the local economy' (Planetterra.org 2012). In sum, 'community-based tourism is a hope to fight poverty' (Suriya 2010).

Despite the variety of perspectives and meanings of 'community-based tourism', there is a single aspect we can attribute to it, and that is the nature of the concept, which arose from non-governmental ideology as a means of poverty reduction through tourism. Consequently, international aid agencies have increasingly encouraged and financed NGOs engaged in it (Butcher 2003). As the director of the Mozambican NGO working in Canhane's tourism business once said, after he attended a three-day local workshop, 'now everybody wants community-based tourism: it seems that it's the new fashion!' (27 October 2008). Indeed, one thing is certain at the present: 'CBT, undoubtedly, remains the option of choice for most NGOs and governmental agencies that include tourism in their developmental [solution] portfolio' (Weaver 2010: 206). The corollary of the developmental significance attached to 'community-based tourism' is that a myriad of travel agencies have embarked on such representations and have moralized their tourism business. Following the communication approach of many others, Asia Adventures, for example, says that it 'is proud to be supporting community based tourism in South East Asia, helping those less fortunate help themselves, and [thus] alleviate poverty' (Asia Adventures 2012).

Regardless of the desirability of poverty eradication, what seems to be at the heart of this model of coalition between 'hosts and guests' (Smith 1989) is meaningful participation; more concretely, the sale, production and consumption of meaningful participation. This participation, however, can take many forms, and the subject of poverty can serve as the moral motivation for it. Consider the example of Canhane.

Two years after the lodge opened to tourists, the residents of Canhane started building and organizing a water supply system. 'Water is the biggest priority to solve our poverty', said a middle-aged resident at the early stage of the water planning (6 September 2006). Poverty and the water effort were implicitly linked to a moral matter that appeals for tourists' empathy and, therefore, their participation in 'community development'. The materials used for the constructions, which were powerfully aestheticized as part of the tourist experience, were purchased with the incomes of the lodge. This means that it was the money the tourists spent and donated that was being directed towards the social betterment of the 'community'. The allocation of tourists' spends and donations was prominently announced at the reception and in the rooms of the lodge. The tourists were informed from the start about their meaningful participation in 'community development' and poverty eradication, which in this case took the form of consumption.

However, behind the physical apparatus of the water efforts, there is another version to be told. Due to local ways of ordering the social structure, the implementation of the water supply system was doomed to failure even before it was established. After the system was operational, it was used only a few times by the residents, becoming a controversial issue in the village. The placement of the new source of water had to respect technical requisites, which led to the positioning of the water tank out of the purview of the community leader. In practice, however, this challenged the customary practices of control over the commonalty, thereby fostering social upheaval in Canhane. Yet, this version was missing from the touristic experience. In the end, Canhaners continue to resort to the communal shallow well or the Elephants River, around five kilometres from Canhane, to access water (for an ethnographic description and analysis of this case, see Baptista 2010).

Poverty and the attraction of the 'slum'

The subject of poverty and the model of coalition are not a privileged theme restricted to 'community-based tourism': 'slum tourism' also carries with it the potentialities of the discourse of poverty and the participatory model through which the tourists relate to the subjects they visit. Perhaps more than 'communities' in the 'South', 'slums' are defined in public discourses almost solely by poverty and precariousness. Such discourses channel them as 'different'. Fundamentally, the notion of 'slums' is embedded in the sense of governmental unwillingness to improve local socio-economic conditions. This, in turn, facilitates the emergence of a new cartography of power and intervention: 'slums' as non-governmental arenas.

One of the most influential theses of Foucault (e.g. 2008) is that the mechanisms of power cannot function unless knowledge is formed, organized and put into circulation (made visible). Tourism is a privileged field in which to test such a theory. Taking Foucault's thesis into consideration helps us comprehend why, as in 'community-based tourism', the subject of poverty is not the only subject on display in 'slum tourism': charitable and development projects are popular destinations for 'slum' tours. Referring to the politics of 'township tourism' in Cape Town, for example, Rolfes says: 'the tour operators intentionally present the poverty and developmental potentials of the townships at the same time' (2010: 430). Many authors have indeed noted that the negative preconceptions associated with 'slum', 'township', 'favela' or 'ghetto' are challenged and nuanced by the tourists when they visit the local developments taking place (e.g. Freire-Medeiros 2007; Meschkank 2011). Such developments are normally run by NGOs using tourism incomes to support their activities. As in 'community-based tourism', poverty in these cases is converted into an incentive for tourists' meaningful participation in 'developing', which can take the form of donations or consumption; and therefore 'slum tours' gain the aura of non-governmental solidarity, and tourism becomes a catalyst for 'local development'. Clear examples of this, which can be multiplied endlessly, are the NGOs 'Reality Gives', created by Reality Tours and Travel in Mumbai with the purpose of canalizing part of the profits from 'slum tourism' into charitable work; or the non-profit 'Salaam

Baalak Trust', which uses the revenues coming from 'slum tours' to fund medical care and schooling projects in India.

The aestheticization of urban poverty has become fashionable even beyond the realm of tourism. The experience and imaginary of urban precariousness, adversity and marginality are inspiring many artists, originating what has been widely called 'slum chic'. Lorraine Leu, for example, has noted that the imaginary of the 'favela' and its peculiar 'culture' is being used internationally, in advertising campaigns for various products (Freire-Medeiros 2007: 64). Why, it seems reasonable to question, has such a contemporary symbol of poverty become so valued? One possible explanation is that the enchantment of neglected spaces and peoples mirrors the desire of the wealthy 'West' for the unmapped, different, illegal and disordered. Such a trend, particularly evident in tourism, seems to lie less in the pleasant experience of (a) poverty per se than in the 'inversion' (Graburn 1983) that it offers to its consumers. Graburn (ibid.: 11) argues that tourism 'is one of those necessary breaks from ordinary life that characterizes all human societies', meaning a privileged space for what he calls the 'ritual inversion' from everyday life. This perspective throws light on to tourist attractions as reproducing (the sensation of) difference for the visitor. For this reason, situations of social, spatial and economic disadvantage, such as the 'slum life' in urban contexts or the 'community life' in the countryside of the 'South', become competitive tourism markets for the different experience available to the tourist. Put in this way, more than the fields of exoticism, pleasure, authenticity, liberty, responsibility, education or awareness, the contemporary 'new tourisms' mentioned by Mowforth and Munt (2009) are arenas of consumption and production of difference. This perspective offers perhaps the most appropriate avenue for understanding why 'negative' conditions, such as the poverty of 'the slum' or 'the local community' in the 'South', have become so powerfully aestheticized and turned into tourist attractions.

Therefore, we should not lose sight of the fact that at the heart of the rising popularity of 'slum tourism' and 'community-based tourism' is a common, omnipresent reference: poverty. As Julia Meschkank clearly demonstrates in her empirical study on the Indian urban area of Dharavi, 'Tourists perceive the slum first of all as a *place of poverty*', which is, at the same time, 'positively linked with the value of community' (2011: 55; emphasis added). Meschkank's conclusion represents a broader tendency in tourism: the 'slumming' of urban neighbourhoods, together with the imaginary of the 'pure' 'local community' in the 'South', legitimizes the tourism-related organizations' efforts to capitalize on poverty. This capitalization, she continues, is supported and reinforced by a pre-existent and natural state of homogenization in tourism. In practical terms, preconceived expectations of poverty influence the 'reality' that tourists ultimately experience and recognize in the tourist space. In the same way that celebrity tours in Beverly Hills are driven by tourists' imaginary of wealth, 'slum tours' and 'community-based tourism' are embedded in a homogeneous, 'westernized' version of poverty that can be toured. This version of poverty negates particularity and accrues totalitarian meaning. In fact, the narratives of poverty dealing with 'slums' and 'communities' in tourism seem to rely more on the assumption of inter-societal homogeneity, without much regard for their specificities. As Baumann (1996: 8) attests in the context of the Southall area in Greater London: 'by conventionalizing individuals and, I also suggest, poverty 'as "belonging to" . . . a pre-defined "community" [or "slum"], one runs the risk of tribalising'. This is a process that relies on a high degree of stereotyping based on the conceptualization of the homogeneous Other. Finally, poverty is semantically charged with 'slum' and 'community' culture in the 'South'. The overall point to emphasize here is that the discourses and performance of poverty in 'slum' and 'community-based' tourism fail to integrate other versions and signifiers of poverty than those resulting from an authorized, universal truth. It is this latter suggestion that I want to pursue further. How are the meanings of poverty defined in the global and non-governmental era? And how are these reproduced in tourism?

The constitution of a problem and the homogenization of differences

The supra-national agencies of development have been at the front line of a new globalizing representation of poverty and the poor, targeting what came to be popularly labelled as the 'developing world'. There is a growing body of literature addressing 'the role of development institutions in constituting poverty as the key development problematic' (Green 2006: 2). Most scholars critically addressing this justify their view by resorting to the importance of social processes of categorization in the ordering of social worlds (Law 1993). According to Escobar (1995), the advent of development after the Second World War brought a new regime of representation that shaped the 'reality' to which it refers. It is in this sense that the traffic of meanings, inherent in development discourses, has progressively appropriated poverty as an organizing concept and the object of problematization: the 'slum problem'; the 'Third World problem'; the 'population problem'. However, the incorporation of poverty as the main development problem came to be a mechanism of power and control; it discursively generated a developing geography as a space of thought, problems and intervention in which development industry is self-evident, necessary, and placed with the expertise of the solutions. It is in this sense that Africa as a category, for example, 'enters Western knowledge and imagination . . . through a series of lacks and absences, failings and problems' (Ferguson 2006: 2), 'where a "traditional African way of life" is simply a polite name for poverty' (ibid.: 21); and so, Africa in general, Canhane in particular, or 'slums' especially, become problem cases in need of a solution that justifies the ascent of an opportune industry of solutions.

International NGOs, donors and national ministries with a vested interest in development all share a conceptual framework that allows them to identify poverty reduction as their goal. However, such a developmental framework holds its common adherence through the promotion of an authorized 'western' representation of poverty, which has become firmly entrenched in global and national discourses of modernity. This knowledge production sets the parameters and determines the representations of poverty in and for development, and it is mostly drawn upon to make policies. Consequently, it reduces areas, populations and their needs to instrumental categories to be applied mostly in cross-developing countries' settings. More importantly, such normative efforts contribute to the constitution of a vast 'South'-wide market of poverty begging for a solution to be explored.

The technically required homogenizing character of poverty is evident in the way the experiences of the poor are promoted as similar across differing social backgrounds and geographical areas. This framework is well illustrated by Deepa Narayan (2001), the co-author of an instrumental World Bank study from 1999 that was used to inform the 2000/01 World Development Report on poverty. In the author's own words: 'there is a commonality of the human experience of poverty that cuts across countries, from Nigeria to Egypt, from Malawi to Senegal' (2001: 40). What is important to highlight in this framework is that poverty is not only widely shared as a developmental problem in the 'South', but operates as a sharing representation of an universalized thing in itself; a homogeneous and tangible entity; an object; a 'numericized inscription' (Rose 1999: 212); a 'total social fact' (Mauss 1990) that can be globally located, assessed, measured and compared. The obvious problem here is that such an objectification negates the incorporation of different versions of poverty, particularly informed by those same people categorized as poor. And since developmental conceptions of poverty must necessarily be matched up with a set of quantifiable measurements (e.g., dollar-a-day poverty line), non-quantifiable aspects of poverty tend to be excluded (Tache and Sjaastad 2010: 1169).

Inescapably, though, experiences of poverty differ from culture to culture, from one region to another, and across time. Referring to the Borana Zone in southern Ethiopia, Tache and Sjaastad argue that: 'Livestock holding, particularly of cattle, is the node that ties different aspects of wealth and poverty together' (ibid.: 1171). In studying 35 villages in Rajasthan in India, Krishna states that poverty is locally defined in terms of the following four stages: having food, sending children to school, possessing clothes to wear outside the house, and retiring debt in regular instalments (Krishna 2004). To give a short example from my research in Mozambique, the relative migratory lifestyle of the fishermen in southeastern Mozambique, dependent upon the location of fish, affects their perspectives on wealth and poverty. As I was told by a 25-year-old fisherman, 'The house is only for sleeping at night' (18 February 2008) and is not part of the fundamental aspects that define poverty and the poor. Contrastingly to my findings, however, Mtapuri's research in

Mashonaland West Province of Zimbabwe indicates that most of the conceptions of poverty by those considered as poor in the region included 'poor dwellings' (2008: 41). This shows how the place of residence, for instance, can obtain different meanings in defining what it is or is not to be poor. Moreover, these two examples of radical disparity come from two neighbouring countries. What this means is that proximity per se does not validate the homogenization of the meanings of poverty. In this regard, in a comparative study between two villages no more than 15 kilometres from each other in western Kenya, Nyasimi *et al.* observed that 'each village had its own indicators of wealth and poverty . . . characteristics of poor homesteads in Ainamoi village could feasibly be considered wealthy by the residents of Kanyibana' (2007: 48). More relevantly for our purposes, Shiva writes:

> subsistence economies which satisfy basic needs by means of self-supply are not poor in the sense that they are wanting. The ideology of development, however, declares them to be poor for not participating significantly in the market economy and for not consuming goods produced in the global economy.
>
> (2005, in Mowforth and Munt 2009: 336)

In such a view, while turning the poor into objects of knowledge and management, such politics of poverty are aimed, fundamentally, at creating consumers.

All of this empirical evidence and debate poses an intense challenge for convergence discourses on poverty, but does not necessarily determine global convergence accounts as entirely 'wrong'. The developmental discourses that explicitly grade populations and countries on a scale from wealthy to poor, from more to less developed, do at least acknowledge and expose circumstances of economic dissimilarity, many rooted in conditions of deprivation. However, such a comparative perspective, leading poverty to a technodiscursive instrument, immediately raises a number of problems. Clearly it invalidates pluralized understandings and meanings; it ignores contextual economic strategies and tactical resource management; and it does not integrate other relationships between materiality, consumption and individual aspirations than those acknowledged by the dominant rationale.

In this sense, poverty becomes a convenient signifier that justifies external intervention and a means of classifying and disposing continents, countries, regions and peoples. These, in turn, become organized as an underdevelopment that is politically and technically manageable, mostly through non-governmental governance. The homogenization of poverty and its workable character are a consequence of an authoritative knowledge that privileges and only recognizes meaning in terms of its instrumentality (Green 2006); that is, its utility for channelling intervention. The constitution of the Human Poverty Index developed by the UN in 1997, for example, reflects the ahistorical, technical and instrumental dimensions aimed at producing workable models. Phrasing it better than I could, Green articulates the situation in these terms: 'What constitutes knowledge about poverty and the demarcation of the poor is a consequence of the power of international development organizations and of the national governments with whom they work' (2006: 14). Along these lines, people and cultures are transformed 'as abstract concepts, statistical figures to be moved up and down in the charts of "progress"' (Escobar 1995: 44).

The development idealization of poverty does not only place a representation of poverty as the problem in developing countries, but institutionalizes such a representation as a way of seeing, perceiving and imagining the 'developing world': it generates a 'reality'. This powerful process drags the 'South' and its problems into the field of 'western' expert knowledge, in ways that can be thus 'western' and technically manageable. This state of affairs contributes to the creation of cultural expectations mainly, but not exclusively, in the 'North' about the 'South', its 'communities' and its 'slums'. Furthermore, not only is a stereotypical image of poverty produced, but also its solution. It is here that tourism plays its role in generating new hopes for modernity. 'Community-based tourism' and 'slum tourism' are two of the most prominent tourism specialities in this agenda.

Tourism and poverty in the non-governmental order

Having said all that, I believe the answer to the leading empirical question – why the tourists in the village of Canhane in Mozambique are persistently led to the shallow well and not to the hut where the residents watch television – is now easy to see. The shallow well is inelegantly offered as a mark that incorporates convincing aesthetic characteristics to connect Canhane to poverty in the visitors' minds. There, the tourists are introduced to the water scarcity problem in the 'community'. Usually frequented by women, the shallow well is probably the most immediate expression of shortage that matches tourists' imagery of poverty, because it congregates and links everyday life and scarcity in the same place. This is not an outcome of Canhaners' tourism enactment. The shallow well is indeed one of the places where women like most to stay because it is a privileged zone for them to socialize with each other, without being called lazy by men. It is where they share the latest rumours in the village, speak about their dilemmas and reinforce links with other women. In fact, the area is symbolically understood as social and feminine among the majority of Canhane residents. As the spot where Canhaners have access to water in the village, the gender representation of space is a consequence of the social attribution of women as water-givers. Hence, the first impressions that tourists have after reaching the shallow well, as illustrated by what a Belgian tourist expressively told me, is: 'poor women!' (6 February 2008). The experience of 'being there' lifts the tourist to an emotional level and legitimates (a specific character of) knowledge of the village and its inhabitants as poor. That is, the residents of Canhane are understood through, and inseparable from, a 'western' imaginary such as poverty.

Significantly, the residents are conscious that such an imaginary of poverty is essentially different from theirs, but they nonetheless embody that 'western' representation of poverty in the ambit of tourism. For example, at an informal gathering, an elder commented loudly and cheerfully: 'the wife [his wife] tells me that tourists are impressed when they see her getting water in the hole . . .'. He interrupted himself to drink more canhu, a fermented local drink. Before he had time to return to his comment, another man cut into the conversation and, at the same time that he looked at me to estimate my attention, he added in a mournful way: 'ahhh, it's Canhane's poverty!' (20 February 2008). His comment was confirmed through body expressions coming from the rest of the group, most of them shaking their heads affirmatively. The elder who started the topic switched his animated mode and participated in the new sad moment. Like many other residents of Canhane, more than just being aware of the representation that the shallow well has in the visitors' minds (as I perceived in that gathering), they strategically validate (and participate in) it by reproducing such a representation as their own.

Although at first sight this seems to contradict everyday life in Canhane, and their idea of the shallow well as social, enjoyable and positive, there is no ambiguity here: it is the outcome of the new politics of the local that leads to the constitution of 'community fronts' in tourism. Particularly when there is water in the hole, the area acquires a social vitality difficult to feel in other places in the village. In this sense, the shallow well means a source of satisfaction for the residents. However, the integration of Canhane in the global market of tourism and development challenges such local collective meanings and positions the residents with regard to the same area in a different way: a space of poverty. As addressed at the beginning of this chapter, neoliberal and non-governmental regimes might elicit new capacities and statuses to historically subjugated peoples. However, to be successful within these regimes, these same peoples have to experience themselves or, especially in tourism, perform self-identification through such capacities and statuses. To put it plainly, the developmental tourism project in the village requires Canhaners' recognition of themselves as poor.

This means that, for tourism, and thus for development purposes, 'Canhane's poverty' is normalized in accordance to contemporary interests. The new norms and representations that emerge from the implementation of the 'community-based tourism' business are moulded to the local and then incorporated as part of a new system of practice for the residents. Consequently, local poverty signifiers – such as lack of cattle, lack of agricultural fields, and/or adults without sons or daughters, husbands or wife/wives – are removed from the representations of 'Canhane's poverty' in and for tourism, in the same way as emblems of poverty coming from the global technocratic order are integrated. And as these new signifiers are integrated, Canhaners subject themselves to, but also valorize themselves in accordance with, the global politics of calculation that homogenize poverty.

In practice, Canhaners' general opinion about tourism can be illustrated in the next phrase: 'It's good for us to receive tourists because they support and help the community' (8 March 2008). This comment, expressed by a female elder, but which represents the overall opinion in the village, gives clues about the principle behind the structure of feeling of the tourism venture: helping the 'community' against poverty and towards progress. For this reason the shallow well became one of the most charismatic tourism sights/sites visited in the village, because of its potential to induce in tourists a sense of moral duty – as the elder said, to 'support and help the community'. Curiously, this phenomenon gives expressive hints for answering Urry's 'interesting question whether it is in fact possible to construct a postmodern tourist site around absolutely any object' (2002: 92). Indeed, the touristic success of the shallow well relies on its ability to be a symbol of (a) poverty informed by subjectivities largely driven by the development rationale.

No wonder then that the members of Canhane, as in many other 'communities' categorized as poor in the developing world, adopt and appropriate for themselves the 'in need' attributes recognized in the non-governmental order that hovers upon them as a way to be eligible for funds and, more specifically, tourism income. In doing so, Canhane represents a global, homogeneous version of poverty but also the potential to solve it, which ultimately became a value for these historically subjugated people. As such, Canhaners participate in, and try to capitalize on, a dominant system of representation derived from a transnational discourse. It is in this sense that various Canhaners strategically incorporate, assume and exercise their position as the 'ones who need to be helped' (16 February 2008) in contrast to what they call 'the mulungus' ('mulungu' is used to describe both the white-skinned person and the dark-skinned Mozambican recognized as having social power through business). Paradoxically, this self-distinction can be understood as an aspiration of membership and inclusion in a globalized world where they could be, at least, placed as (re)producers of otherness or of a difference already intrinsic to 'western' imagery. The imaginary of poverty in this context is used as a rhetorical value for their ambitions. Consequently, (a) poverty serves as an attribute, not a limitation, for the 'community-based tourism' business. The obvious problem here is that this implies Canhaners' adoption of representations of themselves supported by extrinsic forms of knowledge drawn by politics of domination. On the other hand, however, by using stereotypes and icons brought by non-governmental ideals and market ideology, 'Canhane's poverty' becomes simultaneously a problem about which the tourist must act and in which the tourist is the solution. In this view, whereas some social and infrastructural traits of the 'community' are promoted, authenticated and performed, others are not. My point is that such selections are not innocent: they confirm an imaginary around poverty that involves the advancement of moral worthy causes in accordance with development and tourism requisites.

In contrast to the shallow well, the television hut in Canhane is an initiative of a 'local community' member. It characterizes 'community development' through a self-entrepreneurship initiative without any support from development organizations and tourism; which means that it does not have the potential to link tourists and development intervention with social betterment in the village; therefore, it is kept out of the tourism experience.

Through the agency of using tourism to project, in the resident's words, 'Canhane's poverty', the subject-position of the Canhaners resides in emphasizing their poverty condition and, in turn, the potentialities to solve it. Their discourse of poverty is informed by a reflexive, self-validating quality in accordance with a 'higher order' that induces such a condition as a market opportunity: a form of social self-positioning in neoliberalism and non-governmentalism. However, this leads to a further set of problems. First, it reproduces orientalism (Said 1978) that serves to essentialize their status and to subordinate them to a transcendent politics of domination. Second, while it gives hope for inclusion in wider socio-economic systems, by adopting processes of representation that others them, they become reduced to products and specialized (re)producers of imaginaries. Although refusing to embark on theoretical visions that conceptualize cultures as isolated entities rather than as phenomena of interconnection, we might contextualize Canhaners' subjugated status as of those, as Mia Couto put it, 'who look to a mirror that was invented by others' (Zanini 2008: 30). Third, as in every specialized system of production or niche market, the Canhaners emerge to the world as dependants of consumers' wishes and development visions. More problematic, however, the rationale behind their (new) dependency is extrinsic to local systems of reasoning, which increments their vulnerable condition. In the end, Canhaners are being organized, and constituting themselves not only as a market, but also as specialized producers in the development and tourism industries. Moreover, it might be possible to integrate this into a framework that induces colonial and dependency outcomes around an idealized solution to poverty. As addressed by Escobar, the modernization of poverty and the consequent transformation of the poor into the assisted signifies the setting in place of new mechanisms of control over those categorized as poor (1995: 22).

Conclusion

The projection of distinctive landscapes of problems in the 'South' by development organizations and travel agencies produces mapped market opportunities. In this context, the term 'poverty' is reduced to a mere rhetorical underdevelopmental expression that projects a positive moral intention. From the perspective of the travel agencies, the mention of (a) poverty and the promotion of solutions in tourist experience is most often a marketing maneuvre; a communication approach using moral appeals and 'good' reasons in the market segmentation of tourism industry. Furthermore, such packaging of (a) poverty meets an emergent social and market tendency in modern society: the ethical consumer. It is in this sense that the tourists-consumers who consciously choose to go to 'community-based' lodges or on 'slum tours', and to consume products in which their money reverts to the betterment of the 'local community' or the 'slum', have come to be referred to as inherent components of development programmes. This is inherently related to their ability to alleviate the poverty of the populations they visit. In particular, within the model of 'community-based tourism', poverty is an ideological concept that empowers the development sector via tourism. Moreover, such a discourse of poverty is appropriated and reproduced, among other things, at the national, regional and local levels as an opportunity.

The way the Canhaners speak about their poverty must be understood within the broader situational context that gives it relevance and meaning. As shown in this chapter, by consciously reproducing the development and tourists' ideas about poverty, many Canhaners reinforce conceptions of themselves as 'the antithesis of modern men or women located in the Northern industrialized world' (Smith and Duffy 2003: 120). By doing so, Canhaners validate and participate in development ideologies and make tourists' visits (and spending) a positive experience for them, while in turn Canhaners strategically hope to favour their own aspirations.

Poverty as a category induced by the development industry has become a 'reality' performed, as an opportunity, within which, and according to which, some people in the developing world live. The appropriation and performance of (a) poverty by some of those categorized as poor, in the context of 'community-based tourism' and 'slum tourism', constitutes an aspiration of inclusion in the neoliberal world, a world dominated by 'the commodification of everything' (Edensor 2001: 79), and, therefore, a world in which the embodiment and consequent commercialization of every matter, as a certain imaginary of poverty and its solution, can mean a chance for membership and interconnection, even under conditions of inequality and dependence. For this reason, the mythical 'local community' and 'slum' are (re)produced, sold, consumed, valued and, by extension, as Freire-Medeiros (2007) suggests in regard to the 'favela', trademarked for their potential poverty eradication through tourism. Finally, performing poverty in tourism emerges as a modern opportunity for the peoples in 'slums' and 'local communities' in the 'South', involving as it does varying degrees of dependencies with supra-local agencies and their dominant systems of knowledge.

Note

1   This chapter draws upon ethnography research undertaken by the author in the village of Canhane between January and June 2008, and between September and December 2008. The empirical data produced here also draw on several exploratory trips made to the village of Canhane and other parts of Mozambique in 2006 and 2007. During this earlier period, I was in Mozambique for a total of more

than three months. Briefly put, the methodology included: extended periods of participant observation; semi-structured interviews, most of the time taking the form of informal conversations; and bibliographical analysis and archive research, primarily in Mozambique, South Africa, Portugal and Germany.

Bibliography

Asia Adventures (2012) 'Community based tourism in South East Asia'. Available online at http://www.asia-adventures.com/activities/community-tourism-south-east-asia.php (accessed 14 January 2012).

Baptista, J. (2010) 'Disturbing "development": the water supply conflict in Canhane, Mozambique', *Journal of Southern African Studies*, 36(1): 169–88.

Baumann, G. (1996) *Contesting Culture: Discourses of Identity in Multi-ethnic London*, Cambridge: Cambridge University Press.

Butcher, J. (2003) *The Moralization of Tourism: Sun, Sand . . . and Saving the World?* Abingdon: Routledge.

Crick, M. (1989) 'Representations of international tourism in the social sciences: sun, sex, sights, savings, and servility', *Annual Review of Anthropology*, 18: 307–44.

de Kadt, E. (ed.) (1979) *Tourism: Passport to Development?*, New York: Oxford University Press.

Deloitte & Touche, IIED and ODI (1999) *Sustainable Tourism and Poverty Elimination Study*. Available online at www.propoortourism.org.uk/dfid_report.pdf (accessed 4 November 2010).

Edensor, T. (2001) 'Performing tourism, staging tourism: (re)producing tourist space and practice', *Tourist Studies*, 1(1): 59–81.

Escobar, A. (1995) *Encountering Development: The Making and Unmaking of the Third World*, Princeton, NJ: Princeton University Press.

Ferguson, J. (2006) *Global Shadows: Africa in the Neoliberal Order*, London: Duke University Press.

Foucault, M. (2003) *'Society Must Be Defended': Lectures at the Collège de France, 1975–76*, New York: Picador.

Foucault, M. (2008) *The Birth of Biopolitics*, New York: Picador.

Freire-Medeiros, B. (2007) 'A favela que se vê e que se vende: reflexões e polêmicas em torno de um destino turistico', *Revista Brasileira de Ciências Sociais*, 22(65): 61–72.

Goffman, E. (1959) *The Presentation of Self in Everyday Life*, New York: Anchor Books Edition.

Graburn, N. (1983) 'The anthropology of tourism', *Annals of Tourism Research*, 10(1): 9–33.

Green, M. (2006) 'Representing poverty and attacking representations: some anthropological perspectives on poverty in development', paper presented at the International Conference on Chronic Poverty, Manchester, 7–9 April 2003. Available online at www.sarpn.org.za/documents/d0002384/Poverty_development_GPRG.pdf (accessed 10 October 2010).

Hagenaars, A. (1991) 'The definition and measurement of poverty', in L. Osberg (ed.) *Economic Inequality and Poverty: International Perspectives*, Armon, NY: M.E. Sharpe.

Krishna, A. (2004) 'Escaping poverty and becoming poor: who gains, who loses, and why?', *World Development*, 32(1): 121–36.

Law, J. (1993) *Organizing Modernity: Social Ordering and Social Theory*, Oxford: Wiley-Blackwell.

Li, T. (2007) *The Will to Improve: Governmentality, Development, and the Practice of Politics*, Durham, NC: Duke University Press.

Manfred, R. (2010) 'Poverty tourism: theoretical reflections and empirical findings regarding an extraordinary form of tourism', *Geojournal*, 75: 421–42.

Mauss, M. (1990) *The Gift: The Form and Reason for Exchange in Archaic Societies*, New York: W.W. Norton.

Meschkank, J. (2011) 'Investigations into slum tourism in Mumbai: poverty tourism and the tensions between different constructions of reality', *GeoJournal*, 76: 47–62.

Mowforth, M. and Munt, I. (2009) *Tourism and Sustainability: Development, Globalisation and New Tourism in the Third World*, Abingdon: Routledge.

Mtapuri, O. (2008) 'Exploring local conceptions of poverty, wealth and well-being: field evidence from Mashonaland West Province of Zimbabwe', *Africa Development*, 23(3): 35–54.

Narayan, D. (2001) 'Voices of the poor', in B. Deryke, R. Calderisi and C. Sigden (eds) *Faith in Development*, Oxford: World Bank and Regnum Books International.

Nyasimi, M., Butler, L., Burras, L., Ilahiane, H., Schultz, R. and Flora, J. (2007) 'Differentiating livelihood strategies among the Luo and Kipsigis people in western Kenya', *Journal of Ecological Anthropology*, 11: 43–57.

Patullo, P., Minelli, O., Hourmant, P., Smith, P., Viesnik, L. and Dall, A. (2009) *The Ethical Travel Guide: Your Passport to Exciting Alternative Holidays*, London: Earthscan.

Planeterra.org (2012) 'Community based tourism'. Available online at www. planeterra.org/pages/community_based_tourism/37.php (accessed 9 January 2012).

Rolfes, M. (2010) 'Poverty tourism: theoretical reflections and empirical findings regarding an extraordinary form of tourism', *GeoJournal*, 75: 421–42.

Rose, N. (1999) *Powers of Freedom: Reframing Political Thought*, Cambridge: Cambridge University Press.

Said, E. (1978) *Orientalism: Western Conceptions of the Orient*, London: Routledge and Kegan Paul.

Salazar, N. (2009) 'Developmental tourists vs. development tourism: a case study', in A. Raj (ed.) *Tourist Behaviour: A Psychological Perspective*, New Delhi: Kanishka.

Shiva, V. (2005) 'Hacer que la pobreza sea historia, y la historia de la pobreza', *Znet*. Available online at www.zmag.org (accessed 23 October 2010).

Smith, M. and Duffy, R. (2003) *The Ethics of Tourism Development*, Abingdon: Routledge.

Smith, V. (ed.) (1989) *Hosts and Guests: The Anthropology of Tourism*, Philadelphia, PA: University of Pennsylvania Press.

SNV (2007) *A Toolkit for Monitoring and Managing Community-Based Tourism*. Brooklyn, NY: SNV and University of Hawaii. Available online at www. snvworld.org/en/Documents/Knowledge%20Publications/A%20toolkit%20for%20 monitoring%20and%20managing%20community-based%20tourism.pdf (accessed 12 November 2010).

Stronza, A. (2001) 'Anthropology of tourism: forging new ground for ecotourism and other alternatives', *Annual Review of Anthropology*, 30: 261–83.

Suriya, K. (2010) 'Impact of community-based tourism on household income, poverty reduction and income distribution at the village level in Thailand', paper presented at the Rimini Conference in Economics and Finance, Rimini, Italy, 11 July.

Tache, B. and Sjaastad, E. (2010) 'Pastoralists' conceptions of poverty: an analysis of traditional and conventional indicators from Borana, Ethiopia', *World Development*, 38(8): 1168–78.

Taylor, C. (2002) 'Modern social imaginaries', *Public Culture*, 14(1): 91–124.

Tourism Concern (2009) 'Tourism in focus', *In Focus*, spring edition. Available online at www.tourismconcern.org.uk/uploads/file/In%20Focus/Tourism%20in%20Focus %20Spring%202009.pdf (accessed 7 March 2010).

Urry, J. (2002) *The Tourist Gaze*, 2nd edn, Thousand Oaks, CA: Sage.

Weaver, D. (2010) 'Community-based tourism as strategic dead-end', *Tourism Recreation Research*, 35(2): 206–8.

Zanini, F. (2008) 'Conversa com Mia Couto', *Jornal Savana*, 7 November: 30.

8 Negotiating poverty

The interplay between Dharavi's production and consumption as a tourist destination

Julia Meschkank

Introduction

Slum tourism is generally seen as poverty tourism, and so is discussed from a moral-ethical standpoint. This seems logical if one considers the endorsing of sightseeing in a city's poorest neighbourhoods to be an example of exploitation for commercial ends. Slum tourism is also seen as addressing a common impulse people have for seeing what is most 'real' about a city they choose to visit. The Brazilian favelas, South African townships and Indian slums have very different semantic positions regarding their representation of local reality. Studies have considered the 'real' black Africa (Rolfes *et al.* 2009; Rolfes 2010), the 'real' exotic Brazil (Freire-Medeiros 2007) and the 'real' poor India (Meschkank 2011), and each has focused on places that met the UN-Habitat criteria (2003) for slums. These criteria include: restricted access to safe water sanitation, provisionally built and temporary housing, high population density and insecure rights to residence. In addition to such a formalized perspective, mass media, scientists and laypersons have all found ways to interpret representative characteristics of slums, including such things as squalor, desperation, stagnation, crime and disease. This is a background of negative observational schemes defining slums, townships and favelas not only as places of poverty, but also as places of despair. It is hardly astonishing that slum tourism in scientific discourses is referred to as negative sightseeing (Welz 1993).

This is a form of tourism, nonetheless, which has emerged and become successfully established in many cities the world over. The phenomenon has historical forerunners in the Global North; however, since the 1990s the Global South has seen professionally run slum tours operating in Mexico City, Manila, Nairobi, Rio de Janeiro, Cape Town and Johannesburg (Steinbrink and Pott 2010; Steinbrink 2012). It has become highly organized and attracts people in their thousands. In 2006, a tour of a township in South Africa's Cape Town was attended by approximately 300,000 people (Associated Press 2007). In contrast, slum tourism in Mumbai, a relatively recent phenomenon, has only one professional and regular tour operator – Reality Tours and

Travel. The agency was founded by Chris Way (UK) and Krishna Poojari (India) in January 2006, and brings about 7,000 tourists a year to the well-known inner-city slum called Dharavi.

Why would a branch of tourism be successful if it is based on organized sightseeing in areas of suffering and hardship? The majority of existing empirical studies on this topic focus on this very question: why do tourists participate in slum tours? And the main motivational factors appear to be an interest in a country's culture, an interest in a country's living conditions and the desire to experience the complexity and diversity of a given location (Rolfes 2010).

Urry (2002) suggests that tourists want to see what they expect to see; therefore, another motive must be an interest in seeing slums as they are expected to be, which is as places of poverty, despair and suffering (Rolfes *et al.* 2009; Rolfes 2010). Accordingly, in anticipation of seeing a slum and sensing the implicit accusations of voyeurism and exploitation, tourists express moral doubt and a sense of guilt. Typically, tourists justify their decision to participate in a slum tour by claiming the desire to experience the 'real life' of a city (Rolfes 2010: 17; see also Meschkank 2011). The providers of slum tours attend to this and market their products as 'reality tours'; that is, tours that will show the 'truth' of slums, favelas or townships. Previous empirical studies have revealed how tour companies seek to show the 'real' slum through a transformation of the negative semantic field that surrounds touristic notions of poverty (see Freire-Medeiros 2007, 2009; Rolfes *et al.* 2009; Rolfes 2010; Meschkank 2011; Dyson 2012). These tours therefore do not generally emphasize depictions of pain, suffering and hardship, but rather seek to present slums positively, focusing on aspects such as development initiatives, commercial and technical infrastructure, the multifarious and often informal economic activities of residents, and social and charitable projects occurring within slums.

This chapter seeks to illustrate and analyse the transformation of negative poverty and place-specific semantics that has occurred in Dharavi. It refers to an empirical case study carried out there in February and March 2009. This analysis was undertaken utilizing perspectives from Luhmann's communication theory (1995) as adapted to tourism studies by Andreas Pott (2007). This theoretical model considers tourism as an example of societal communication, and tourist places as forms of meanings, not only socially constituted and negotiated, but also, more widely, constitutive for the (re)production of tourism communication. Tourist places are seen not as fixed entities but rather as frameworks that provide a contingent, but nonetheless relatively resistant, continual supply of themes and images. Within these frameworks, and by utilizing them, tourists and tourist organizations orientate themselves to one another. The selection of themes and images that forms the place-related semantic is contingent, although not arbitrary, and occurs as the result of social negotiation processes that are taking place between the consumers and producers of tourist spaces.

The research engaged a qualitative and multi-perspective design, which included participant observation and qualitative interviews (with nineteen tour participants and with the founders of the tour company). The focus was twofold: (1) to investigate how – that is, with which main distinctions and observational frameworks – tourists and tour providers observed Dharavi; and (2) to investigate how the observational frameworks (and identified place-related semantics) of the producers and consumers referred to one another. The first section of the chapter presents the theoretical premises, arguing that tourist places are not only socially constructed, but are also constitutive features of tourism communication. The following section sets out the results of the empirical study, focusing on the construction of the different place-related semantics operating in the context of tourism communication regarding Dharavi. The third and final section contains an interpretation of the results once again, by utilizing Andreas Pott's concept of place-related semantics.

Place-related semantics as frameworks that orientate the complex interplay between the production and consumption of tourist spaces

How tourism and communication are closely bound becomes clear when one realizes that the tourist industry deals in an intangible service that is sold essentially via mediated information and imagery. Tourist companies, tourism organizations and the mass media produce images that drive expectations with promises of relaxation and an awakened wanderlust. In relation to marketing, the term 'communication' refers to the transmission of information. This chapter draws specifically on Niklas Luhmann's (1984, 1995) theory of social systems, which uses the term to refer to ultimate and indivisible elements of society. Luhmann's theory has underpinned other recent approaches to tourism research (Pott 2007; Farías 2008), which have conceptualized tourism as a context of self-referential communications in which communicative events refer back to one another, build up one another, and connect with one another. This approach has provided insights into tourism's evolution and its organization by drawing focus on to, and providing clarification of, the internal structures that enable and organize the reproduction of tourism communication (ibid.). One result is that attention in tourism studies has been drawn to consider the argument that tourist places, while being socially constructed, are in fact equally contributing to organizing the process of tourism communication generally.

It is evident and widely accepted that tourist places are socially constructed. Squire (1994: 5) points out that 'landscapes become tourist places through meanings ascribed to them by visitors and promotional agencies'. Readings of places often, in turn, refer to specific meanings created by politics, mass media, films and books. Many studies in tourism research have focused on the social construction of tourist destinations and have addressed a range of issues, including the development and improvement of marketing strategies

(Nigel *et al.* 2004; Govers and Kumar 2007), the representation and narration of tourist places (Hughes 1992; Selwyn 1996; Crang 1997; Selby 2004; McCabe and Duncan 2006; Meethan 2006), the embodied performative production of tourist places (Edensor 2001; Baerenholdt *et al.* 2004) and the discursive embedding of tourist places in hegemonic power relations (Hall and Tucker 2004).

The analysis presented here also discusses the social construction of slums as tourist destinations; in addition, it seeks to demonstrate how place-related semantics contribute to the organization of the (re)production of tourism communication more widely. Drawing on the work of German geographer Andreas Pott (2007), tourist places are considered to be/as place-related semantics, which organize and structure tourism communication by providing a framework within which tourists and tourist organizations orientate themselves. Pott (ibid.: 130–1) points out that the observational frameworks of tourism are generally codified with reference to spatial distinctions and formations (e.g. here/there, in/out). In a following step these are given meaning and thus become touristically formed, reformed and (re)interpreted. This results in generalized and, via repetition, condensed forms of meanings – place-related semantics. These support the orientation and structuring of tourism communication by providing a relatively resistant and continual supply of themes, images and distinctions for the destination at issue. They limit the arbitrariness of how to interpret and represent a destination by allowing a space for selection within which a certain degree of freedom is given (ibid.: 188). Orientations within such a framework arise as tourists and tourist organizations either accept the dominant place-related semantic, or consciously distance themselves from it and demand and provide alternative programmes (ibid.: 144).

Place-related semantics are not fixed entities existing in and of themselves, but are socially constructed and therefore the contingent results of processes of meaning-making. Relying as they do on processes of social negotiation, they are anything but arbitrary. Tourist organizations cannot simply interpret and represent a destination as they please. Rather, as I have argued, they must refer to the prevailing images and expectations held by visiting tourists – either accepting them or consciously distancing themselves from them.

This theme has recently been discussed in tourist studies in response to demands that more attention be paid to considering both sides of the touristic process – the dynamics of place production and place consumption. Studies in tourism have overemphasized processes of place production at the expense of paying attention to matters regarding place consumption (Young 1999; Edensor 2001; Meethan 2006). And this is the case even though prominent concepts, such as Urry's *tourist gaze* (2002), have successfully clarified the central importance of tourist perception. In accordance with Crang (1997), Meethan (2006: 5) has pointed out that, 'if we see gazing as an active rather than passive process . . . it is incorrect to assume that the intentions of producers are simply absorbed whole and unmediated by passive consumers'. Similarly,

Young (1999: 375) has engaged with the question: 'how (do) tourists reconcile potentially conflicting representations of place', when it is given that they are actively bringing their own understandings and interpretations to the places they visit? The prominent role of tourists, and the call for this to be acknowledged, are clearly relevant. This is made clear when one considers that the success tourist organizations might have with their interpretations of place relies on tourists' perceptions. For as Pott (2007: 157) points out, the semantic contents being communicated in brochures and with imagery will only prove useful or be considered somehow true when perceived as such by consumers. He further argues that the tourist perception may be preformed, but it can hardly be considered to be predetermined. Tourists always have choices about how they perceive a place and how they might charge with meaning those perceptions of that place (ibid.).

Accordingly, new approaches in tourism research are putting emphasis on the concept of the tourist, not as an individual who is lazy and 'dumb', but rather as an active and intelligent consumer, interpreting, negotiating and creating their own particular meanings (Meethan 2001; Wickens 2002; McCabe 2005). Accepting this naturally leads to assigning more focus to the relationships between production and consumption. Examining the complex and dynamic interplay between the producers and consumers of tourist spaces when investigating slum tourism is particularly rewarding because, here, tour companies generally advertise agendas that actively seek to challenge and transform the expectations and images held by tourists. These images and expectations are in the most part derived from second-hand sources such as the print press, television, popular cinema and books.

The following analysis of tourists' and a tour agency's statements uses as a starting point the theoretical basis that socially negotiated, place-related semantics structure and organize tourism communication. Thereby, it seeks to answer the following questions:

- With which main distinctions and observational frameworks do tourists and Reality Tours and Travel observe Dharavi?
- Which place-related semantics are thereby constructed?
- Is poverty the observational scheme that structures the whole context of slum tourism communication?
- How do the identified observational frameworks and place-related semantics refer to each other?

Additionally, the analysis also addresses the following points:

- How were prevailing images about slums addressed and modified by the tour operator's programme?
- In what ways did tourists handle the challenge of their expectations being contradicted?

Slum tourism in Dharavi: results of an empirical case study

'A shadow world' – the place-related semantic created before the tour

> What images do you have from Dharavi or from slums in general?
>
> (Interviewer)

> Well, people living under plastic sheets, washing in sewers, no fresh water, very little food, disease, death.
>
> (Tourist)

The interviews revealed that, predominantly, tourists participating in a Dharavi tour expected to see poverty. They perceived the slum first of all as a place of poverty. Further questioning revealed that they possessed a set of negatively connoted characteristics integral to their concepts of poverty, which mostly related to poor living conditions. Dharavi was preconceived in the minds of tourists before undertaking a tour as a place that would be a provisional settlement, dirty and overcrowded, lacking appropriate hygienic and sanitary conditions, and without adequate public infrastructures such as running water and electricity. Tourists also expected open sewers, and that private toilets would be rare. Many tourists also assumed Dharavi would be diseased, containing cases of malaria, cholera and typhus. Some expected Dharavi to be an environment highly unconducive to economic activity; additionally, some thought that Dharavi's residents would not have access to a labour market, and therefore would be begging.

Some also expected the standard of education in Dharavi to be poor and that there would be a lack of educational infrastructure such as schools. Indeed, interviews revealed that negatively connoted views had led some tourists to deduce that residents would not only be poorly educated, but also generally of low intelligence. Owing to negative expectations, some tourists thought life in the slum would be a struggle for survival. Some qualified this by saying that they imagined slum residents to be dependent on manual labour for survival, and therefore unable to gain an education or participate in intellectual activities: 'First of all you care about your body and after that you care about your mind. And I think the people are basically busy with their body, how to keep it alive' (tourist).

The statements from tourists before tours invariably highlighted that poverty was semantically charged with negatively connoted characteristics. As such, one can talk of a specifically negative semantic of poverty. This leads to the construction of a place-specific semantic, which is initially structured through the lens of a negative poverty observational scheme.

'A place of enterprise, humour and non-stop activity'

Communicative links: findings regarding the place-related semantic created by the tour agency Reality Tours and Travel

> We are a unique tour and travel agency based in Mumbai, India that specializes in guided tours of Dharavi – Asia's biggest 'slum' – a place of poverty and hardship but also a place of enterprise, humour and non-stop activity.
>
> (Reality Tours and Travel website)

With findings similar to those from other empirical studies – Cape Town (Rolfes *et al.* 2009; Rolfes, 2010) and Rio de Janeiro (Freire-Medeiros 2007) – it was seen that the company taking tours through Dharavi aimed to correct the tourist public's perceptions, and challenge the negative semantic of poverty generally. Indeed, the company's central objective was to achieve a trans- formation and improvement of the negative place-related semantic of Dharavi. This position was also presented personally by the tour company owners and tour company employees/tour guides during discussions undertaken for the purposes of this research. The name Reality Tours and Travel further alludes to the company's aim to navigate to a 'real' or 'more real' image of the Dharavi slum. Thereby, Reality Tours and Travel refers back to a negative image of slums being places of poverty (in the sense of suffering, hardship and despair). The tour agency considers such an image to have been drawn in the minds of tourists through exposure to national and international media. They assume all international tourists will have had such exposure and will hold negative images of slums.

In order to achieve an image transformation, Reality Tours and Travel has had to respond to the predominant place-related semantic. What assumptions does Reality Tours and Travel make regarding associations tourists will have in relation to slums when they arrive in Dharavi? Furthermore, how does Reality Tours and Travel use prevailing imagery held by tourists to form points of reference? Considering that its stated objective is a correction of these images, how does Reality Tours and Travel respond to the expectations held by tourists, and which observational frameworks does the company exploit in order to structure tourists' perceptions during a tour?

Participatory observation during tours, as well as interviews with Chris Way and Krishna Poojari, the tour company's owners, showed that, according to Reality Tours and Travel, tourists perceive Dharavi as a place of poverty, in the sense of hardship and despair. The owners state that they believe that the tourists have a mental picture of poverty that is connected with negative attributes: in particular, general passivity and crime. Accordingly, the tour company assumes that tourists believe Dharavi's residents to be lazy, inert people incapable of changing their situation:

Basically, what happens when you say the word 'slum'? That name gives all the negative images: that people are just poor or doing nothing, that they are sitting around, that there is a high crime rate, that children don't go to school, and this kind of stuff.

(Krishna Poojari)

Slum tours are therefore arranged with these assumed associations in mind, and particular sights and locations are chosen. The tour company aims to correct the negative associations present in the minds of tourists by employing observational frameworks capable of responding to the (assumed) preconceived expectations. The observational frameworks exploited during tours embody oppositional stances to the expectations held by tourists. For example, in order to counteract the notion that slum residents are passive and lazy, a central focus of tours is the economic activity going on in Dharavi:

I am talking about the people, how the people are working. Because most of the people think that slum people are sitting quiet, that they are doing nothing, that they might be thieves or robbers. But it is not like that. They are working. They are working in very poor conditions, but they are working very hard.

(Tour guide)

Dharavi is presented to tourists as a place of high economic productivity, which contains more than 10,000 small-scale industries generating an annual turnover of US$665 million. The importance of entangled local, national and global relationships to these economic activities is exposed and their importance discussed. At the beginning of a tour, the slum's recycling area – the '13th Compound' – is featured. This is where urban waste products are separated and items recycled. Visits to areas where the slum's textile and leather industries can be seen in action are also featured parts of the slum tours. In addition to the detailed descriptions of the production processes and their integration into regional and global value-adding chains, the tours focus on poor working conditions. The overriding impression given to tourists is that Dharavi's residents are honest, hardworking people, pursuing jobs despite poor working and living conditions, hoping just to cover the cost of living.

Another image that the tour company refers to is that of slums as places of organized crime and religious violence. Tour guides state that Dharavi was controlled by Mafia-like organizations until the 1990s; however, this influence was weakened by government initiatives and interventions. The tour then constructs the observational scheme of community; this is placed in contrast to tourist expectations of crime and antisocial behaviour. They do this by emphasizing a presentation of the harmonious cohabitation of members of different religious and ethnic groups, as well as drawing attention to the friendly manner residents have towards strangers:

But here there are negative sides . . . there are open drains, there is a lack of sanitation, people live in tiny houses and the working conditions are quite poor. You can see children playing at the garbage, they jump inside. And electricity wires hang everywhere, that is quite dangerous. But still there is a huge sense of community here. People are very friendly here. They always welcome outsiders.

(Krishna Poojari)

Another feature activated as a mode of observation during the tours is the state of education in Dharavi. Once again, this is an aspect of the tour that ties in with the tour company's assumption that tourists in general expect Dharavi residents to have a low standard of education. Tour guides never seem to tire of stressing the point that Dharavi's residents have a strong belief in education. Guides highlight that there is a relatively good provision of educational infrastructure that is used by 85 per cent of Dharavi's children. They note also that 15 per cent of school graduates from Dharavi go on to gain higher qualifications and work in banks or for multinational companies. Additionally, they emphasize that many of the high achievers from the Dharavi education system remain living in Dharavi, even if they have found well-paid work (as teachers, doctors, officials etc.) in other city areas.

The attention of tourists is also drawn to redevelopment efforts undertaken by government and private agencies, particularly the implementation of initiatives such as the provision of basic structures that bring running water and electricity to Dharavi. Tours also discuss planned redevelopment projects, which introduces another observational scheme: development in contrast to stagnation. This scheme is established and referred to repeatedly during tours as guides stress the positive effects of developments in areas such as employment, education and social networking/community development, thereby painting a positive picture of a slum full of hope.

'A highly innovative area'

Findings regarding the place-related semantic created after tours

What surprised me is the bustle of the slum. The bustle in terms of that there is trade, that there are markets and that there is a proper life. It is not like as it is often imagined that people are lying around in the dirt, vegetating and go begging. It is an area, slum – I don't want to use that word. It is a less developed area, in which just the same intelligent, talented and highly creative people live.

(Tourist)

Although there were exceptions, the majority of tourists remained dismayed at the living conditions they observed during tours. In particular, they were disturbed by the high population density, and the dangerously poor sanitation and general lack of hygiene. For many tourists these were reasons enough to continue to consider Dharavi as a place of poverty. The poverty observational scheme thus remained relevant after tours. However, analysis of the interviews also revealed that all of the tourists accepted the (economic) activity observational scheme. Each of the interviewees was impressed by how hardworking and highly productive the inhabitants seemed to be. Interestingly, many anticipated that Dharavi's residents would be passive, unemployed and begging. However, they did not mention this in their pre-tour interview, which highlights the fact that expectations often work implicitly, and special observational operation is required to ensure that these presumptions become a subject of communication. Tourists themselves often first became aware of their own negative assumptions regarding poverty when confronted by the tour's specific observational frameworks designed to do exactly that. Their expectations were revealed by their participation in the tour. For example, tourists became conscious of the expectations they implicitly carried regarding (economic) passivity, due to a specific observational focus applied to the opposing sense, (economic) activity.

Additionally, interviewees mentioned as relevant what can be classified as comprising the community observational framework. However, it became clear during interviews that all tourists held different conceptions regarding what the word 'community' meant. For some it was related to the fact that they saw different religious groups living together in harmony, which challenged their expectation that they would see religious violence in the slum. For others, seeing the slum residents giving one another mutual support and assistance confounded their expectations that antisocial behaviour would predominate and that there would be a visibly high incidence of crime. By observing community, regardless of how they identified its signifiers, most tourists realized that they had expected to see more antisocial behaviour, violence and crime: 'Just because they are poor, it doesn't mean that they can't have friends and relationships and things like that' (tourist).

Corresponding to the reflections noted regarding economic industriousness and a sense of community, the tourists interviewed also demonstrated critical reflection regarding Dharavi's levels of education, and once more it became apparent that tourists realized the presence of their negative expectations. Tourists were amazed once it was pointed out to them during tours that residents of Dharavi, in general, possessed a relatively good standard of education. This amazement was not only observed when tourists saw the provision of an educational infrastructure, but was also present when tourists experienced the general standard of education among the slum's residents:

They were educated. And I saw it also in our tour guide: when we entered his house someone was asking if this was his kitchen. And he replied, 'Yes, and it is also our living room and at night it is where we sleep.' And it is strange. If I would have seen this guy, talking with him, and then had to make a single sketch of what his house would look like, I would have imagined it to be much bigger and with his own room. Then I found out that it is a cliché. It is the worst cliché that you can have: but that poor people can be very intelligent.

(Tourist)

Another topic raised by tourists after tours is given the heading 'Redevelopment efforts'. One third of the interviewees were positively surprised by living conditions observed in the slum. On the one hand, many tourists realized when looking at government-built, high-rise buildings that they had actually only expected provisional and temporary dwellings in the slum, such as tents and huts. As a result of seeing such high-rise government housing, some came to the conclusion that Dharavi should not be called a slum:

> More by chance, I might not automatically call it a slum, especially some of the areas. The area where we saw the pottery and which he called the more Hindi area seemed to be very clean, paved and with high-rise buildings.
>
> (Tourist)

By contrast, a few tourists identified the high-rise area of the slum as demonstrating a negative influence of development. Regarding a planned development project for more high-rise apartments in Dharavi, one tourist expressed concerns, saying that residents would be offered a more modern but potentially more isolated life in a high-rise building:

> Because going back to this thing about re-housing people in high-rise blocks, which is the easy way out. I don't think it is the answer. They lose their communities, they lose their trades, and they lose their history. You know, in western Europe we have done it and now it has been a disaster.
>
> (Tourist)

Given that statement, it could be said that this tourist saw a negative future for Dharavi's residents in the planned 'modernization' of Dharavi. However, when we look at the negative to positive observational frameworks, the majority of the interviewees accepted the development observational framework presented by the tours and went on to perceive a positive future for the people of Dharavi: 'Because it is so much industry, I would say that it is not hopeless like the images I see from Africa with you know, really poor people. I think many of these kids have a future' (tourist).

The above quotation illustrates another aspect of the post-tour observational frameworks, and that is that tourists must somehow come to grips with the irritation of having their expectations contradicted. Many of those interviewed resolved their irritation by deciding to relocate true poverty in the sense of suffering, hardship and despair to Africa or South America. Another response tourists had to this challenge to their expectations was to contest Dharavi's claim to be representative as a slum: 'I think it is kind of a special slum, because there is such a high level of commercial activities. So I don't know if it is representative for all the slums in Mumbai' (tourist). Other tourists doubted Dharavi's status as a slum generally: 'I have seen lots of people working and kids playing. I have just seen the normal life, I think. Normal Indian village or neighbourhood' (tourist).

Conclusion

Tourism has been considered to be a societal form of communication. Place-related semantics have been defined as structures organizing and structuring the (re)production of this communication, by providing a supply of terms, images and themes used by tourists and tourist organizations to orientate themselves. It has been stressed that these place-related semantics are socially negotiated forms: contingent and not arbitrarily determined. The aim of the analysis was to outline the main distinctions and observational frameworks utilized by tourists and tour operators within the context of tourism communication designed to observe the Dharavi slum. So that the relationship between the production and the consumption of Dharavi as a tourist destination might be further clarified, special emphasis in the analysis was put on observing the ways in which observational frameworks and place-related semantics referred to one another. The empirical results demonstrated how prevailing images about slums were addressed and modified by the tours and, additionally, how tourists handled the challenge of being confronted by their own expectations and having those expectations contradicted.

From the results of the empirical analysis, it is clear that tourism communication related to Dharavi is enabled and organized by the utilization and referencing of a place-related semantic that is, above all, a semantic of poverty. Poverty was shown to be the predominant observational scheme, structuring and organizing the context of slum tourism in Mumbai, limiting the arbitrariness of social connections and simultaneously offering a range within which selections were made with a degree of freedom regarding choices of how one might perceive and how one might represent Dharavi.

As the analysis demonstrated, images held by tourists before a tour were ones that portrayed Dharavi to them as a place of poverty, and poverty was understood to mean suffering due to want. It was expected that the slum would conform to these preconceptions and show images of people in a state of apathy, lawlessness, stagnation, despair and desperation. The stated objective of Reality Tours and Travel was to confront and correct these negative semantics of poverty and place. In order to market their product and achieve their objective, chosen sites and themes representing Dharavi during the tours needed to refer to the expectations held by tourists. The fieldwork presented here has shown that the company has done this by establishing observational frameworks standing specifically in opposition to these expectations. Responding to an image determined by characteristics such as passivity, crime, poor living conditions and a poor standard of education, Reality Tours and Travel engages – as predominant observational frameworks during its tours – images in Dharavi of economic activity, community, redevelopment efforts and a good standard of education. The fact that many tourists only realized the nature of their expectations/held stereotypes while observing Dharavi through the observational frameworks as established by the tour operator indicates clearly that the frameworks chosen by Reality Tours and Travel are responses that accurately identify and connect up with the expectations held by tourists. Furthermore, the observational schemes integral to the tour are accepted by many tourists because, during the tour, these schemes become actual, authentic experiences (see Meschkank 2011).

Poverty remains the dominant observational framework during tours, even though it is not explicitly referred to in the sense of a pointing at the misery of slum residents. As they walked through Dharavi, tourists observed dangerously poor living conditions, which after the tour led the majority to continue to perceive Dharavi as a place of poverty. However, what did change was the perception of poverty itself, and the term became charged with different, more textured meanings. Life in Dharavi was still conceptualized in the minds of tourists as impoverished, but it was characterized less by apathy, crime, stagnation and desperation and more by economic industriousness, a sense of community, notions of development and notions of hope. For the majority of tourists, a more positive semantic of poverty had developed. This transformation illustrates that semantics of poverty and place are not fixed entities existing in and of themselves, but rather that they are contingent meanings, socially negotiated.

The empirical data indicate that tourists did not simply absorb the readings presented by the tour operator; rather, they actively interpreted and contested the way Dharavi was represented. Empirical results showed that the positive semantic field of Dharavi did not lead to a transformation of generally held touristic notions of slums or poverty. Despite notions of Dharavi having changed, prevailing images about slums were reproduced. Dharavi was no longer considered a real slum, as real slums were relocated elsewhere. A paradox emerged: the slum Dharavi, touristically formed, reformed and (re)interpreted by its image transformation, had simultaneously had its slum status called into question. Thus, the concept of true slums and true poverty remained a relevant tool for imaging and ordering the world socially and spatially into poor and rich, stagnation and development, despair and hope.

Bibliography

Associated Press (2007) 'Township tourism booming as visitors want to see "real" South Africa', *USA Today*. Available online at www.usatoday.com/travel/destinations/2007–01–04-south-africa-township-tourism_x.htm (accessed 15 November 2010).

Baerenholdt, J., Haldrup, M., Larsen, J. and Urry, J. (2004) *Performing Tourist Places*, Aldershot: Ashgate.

Dyson, P. (2012) 'Slum tourism: representing and interpreting "reality" in Dharavi, Mumbai', *Tourism Geographies*, 14(2): forthcoming.

Crang, M. (1997) 'Picturing practices: research through the tourist gaze', *Progress in Human Geography*, 21(3): 359–73.

Edensor, T. (2001) 'Performing tourism, staging tourism: (re)producing tourist space and practice', *Tourist Studies*, 1: 59–81.

Farías, I. (2008) 'Touring Berlin: virtual destination, tourist communication and the multiple city', unpublished dissertation, Humboldt University, Berlin.

Freire-Medeiros, B. (2007) 'A favela que se vê e que se vende: reflexões e polêmicas em torno de um destino turístico', *Revista Brasileira de Ciências Sociais*, 22(65): 62–72.

—— (2009) 'The favela and its touristic transits', *Geoforum*, 40(4): 580–8.

Govers, R. and Kumar, K. (2007) 'Promoting tourism destination image', *Journal of Travel Research*, 46(1): 15–23.

Hall, M. and Tucker, H. (2004) 'Tourism and postcolonialism: an introduction', in M. Hall and H. Tucker (eds) *Tourism and Postcolonialism: Contested Discourses, Identities and Representations*, Abingdon: Routledge.

Hughes, G. (1992) 'Tourism and the geographical imagination', *Leisure Studies*, 11: 31–42.

Luhmann, N. (1984, 1995) *Social Systems*, Stanford, CA: Stanford University Press.

McCabe, S. (2005) 'Who is a tourist: a critical review', *Tourist Studies*, 5(1): 85–106.

—— and Duncan, M. (2006) 'Tourist constructions and consumptions of space: place, modernity and meaning', in P. Burns and M. Novelli (eds) *Tourism and Social Identities: Global Frameworks and Local Realities*, Oxford: Elsevier.

Meethan, K. (2001) *Tourism in Global Society: Place, Culture, Consumption*, Basingstoke: Palgrave.

—— (2006) 'Introduction: narratives of place and self', in K. Meethan, A. Anderson and S. Miles (eds) *Tourism Consumption and Representation: Narratives of Place and Self*, Wallingford: CAB International.

Meschkank, J. (2011) 'Investigations into slum tourism in Mumbai: poverty tourism and the tensions between different constructions of reality', *GeoJournal*, 76(1): 47–62.

Nigel, M., Pritchard, A. and Pride, R. (2004) *Destination Branding: Creating the Unique Destination Proposition*, London: Butterworth-Heinemann.

Pott, A. (2007) *Orte des Tourismus: Eine raum- und gesellschaftstheoretische Untersuchung*, Bielefeld: Transcript.

Rolfes, M. (2010) 'Poverty tourism: theoretical reflections and empirical findings on an extraordinary form of tourism', *GeoJournal*, 75(5): 421–42.

——, Steinbrink, M. and Uhl, C. (2009) *Townships as Attraction: An Empirical Study on Township Tourism in Cape Town*, Potsdam: Universitätsverlag.

Selby, M. (2004) 'Consuming cities: conceptualising and researching urban tourist knowledge', *Tourism Geographies*, 6(2): 186–207.

Selwyn, T. (1996) *The Tourist Image: Myths and Myth Making in Tourism*, Chichester: John Wiley.

Squire, S. (1994) 'Accounting for cultural meanings: the interface between geography and tourism studies re-examined', *Progress in Human Geography*, 18(1): 1–16.

Steinbrink, M. (2012) 'We did the slum! Urban poverty tourism in historical perspective', *Tourism Geographies*, 14 (2): forthcoming.

—— and Pott, A. (2010) 'Global slumming: zur Genese und Globalisierung des Armutstourismus', in H. Wöhler, A. Pott and V. Denzer (eds) *Tourismusräume: Zur soziokulturellen Konstruktion eines globalen Phänomens*, Bielefeld: Transcript.

UN-Habitat (2003) *The Challenge of Slums: Global Report on Human Settlement 2003*, Nairobi: UN-Habitat.

Urry, J. (2002) *The Tourist Gaze*, 2nd edn, Thousand Oaks, CA: Sage.

Welz, G. (1993) 'Slum als Sehenswürdigkeit: "negative sightseeing" im Städtetourismus', in D. Kramer and R. Lutz (eds) *Tourismus-Kultur, Kultur-Tourismus*, Münster: Lit-Verlag.

Wickens, E. (2002) 'The sacred and profane: a tourist typology', *Annals of Tourism Research*, 29(3): 834–51.

Young, M. (1999) 'The social construction of tourist places', *Australian Geographer*, 30(3): 373–89.

9 Reading the Bangkok slum

Ross King and Kim Dovey

Introduction: Bangkok in the tourist gaze

> Method of this work: literary montage. I have nothing to say, only to show.
> (Benjamin 1982: 574)

Walter Benjamin's method was to set images, both visual and textual, against each other in a technique that Susan Buck-Morss (1989) labelled the display of 'dialectical images' – one image would stand against another, calling into question the message or meaning that each would convey. Meanings are destabilized and so, likewise, are our assumptions about the world we perceive.

What follows are images of the Bangkok slums. We know from our own observations on many fieldwork visits to the city that these are typical scenes that Bangkok's tourists will often pause to observe, perhaps to contemplate and very often to photograph. Our suggestion is that, as the observer attempts to 'read' the messages that these scenes might convey, other images – both immediately presented and remotely recalled (imagined) – will cross-cut, in the sense implied by Benjamin/Buck-Morss, what is before the eye or in the photographed image. As a virtual tour of the city's slum, this chapter attempts to enable reflection on the aesthetic dimensions of slums and on how slums become subject to the tourist gaze.

This somewhat attenuated photo essay is concluded with some comments on possible responses to the Bangkok slum, whether directly confronted or vicariously experienced through the photographic image.

Glimpses of the slums

The disruptive slum

Figure 9.1

Bangkok tourists will most typically seek out the palaces, the golden 'wat' (temples), towering 'prangs' and 'chedis' (sacred monuments). They will also take boat tours along the grand Chao Phraya River lined with the best of photo opportunities: Wat Arun, Wichiprasit Fort, the Grand Palace. Wat Pho (home of the huge reclining golden Buddha) is adjacent to the Grand Palace but hidden from the river behind a wall of once formal, now informalized, riverside settlements – the slums. The slums are an interruption that spoils an otherwise nice picture. The tourist notices the slum with camera poised while waiting for it to disappear. In time, these riverside slums will be commented on and photographed. The image here is 'dialectic' – it displays different, counterposed images that stand against each other, each seemingly undermining the world represented in the other (Figure 9.1).

Khlong Bangkok Noi

Figure 9.2

Visitors to Thailand are also likely to take a boat trip through the labyrinthine canals or 'khlong' that intersect the main river, lined with informal housing extending over the water with a visible social life on the water's edge. Such waterfront communities are seen as remnants of a traditional Thai authenticity that is no longer found in the streets; one can hear the tourists say: 'this is the real Bangkok'. The 'authentic' Thai lifestyle is consumed from the safe distance of the boat as locals bathe and hang out in the traditional open pavilions ('sala') over the water, and floating shops ply their trade. While dilapidation is often evident and even severe, the crowding and the 'real' slum remain hidden behind the more commercial and partly tourist-focused informal activity at the water's edge (Figure 9.2).

Khlong San Saeb (1)

Figure 9.3

A walk along the mostly traffic-clogged 'soi' (side streets) can suddenly present the observer with a glimpse of a 'khlong' such as Khlong San Saeb, the original artery on which the city grew eastwards into its hinterland. The response can be one of shock: first, a green, almost bucolic Bangkok is immediately juxtaposed with frenetic, inhospitable, commercial-corporate Bangkok. The tourist photographer may try to exclude the high-rises or else to capture the dialectic of inconsistent realms. Second, there is the shock of a low-income, informal settlement within metres of the city's most expensive real estate. Since tourists typically seek information in guide books, here they might find a subsequent shock when they realize that, in the heart of Buddhist Bangkok, these are Muslim settlements. These are the settlements of the Muslim prisoners of war brought to Bangkok in its early days and who dug this canal – a dialectic of opposed yet mutually defining cultures (Figure 9.3).

Khlong San Saeb (2)

Figure 9.4

Khlong San Saeb is also a water taxi route and a fast connection from the commerce of Siam Square to Fort Mahakan in the ancient city centre of Rattanakosin. The taxis speed past a variegated series of informal row houses in a range of materials and forms, each with a display of domestic paraphernalia. Locals wear face masks to filter smells of putrid water, and waterproof curtains prevent splashing as tourists crane to catch fleeting glimpses of everyday lives. These momentary flashes of other lives can be mere spectacle or disturbing, as can the act of photographing and publishing (Figure 9.4).

Khlong Toei (1)

Figure 9.5

There are no tourist trips through the Khlong Toei slums, one of Asia's largest. They are, however, often visited by student groups, which can be seen as a growing segment of the tourism industry, patronized by schools and universities of the West, and hosted by NGOs of the 'developing' world. The comment from a Princeton undergraduate visiting the Khlong Toei slums illustrates the response:

> It is home to over 120,000 people – a claustrophobic maze of one-room dwellings stacked on top of each other and crammed side by side, insulated only by shifting layers of tin sheeting and particle board. Refuse of every sort is disposed of in uncovered trenches that line the alleys between homes; the trenches are less than one foot deep, so trash and other waste tends to seep beneath the floor boards and onto the front steps of residents' homes. Lethargic dogs with disfiguring skin and eye diseases drink and eat from the trenches, and then, in search of food, linger in doorways and sidle up to passers-by.

(Cited in King 2011: 154–5)

Outrage and revulsion at the obscenity of poverty – the 'shock of the real' – is evident in the young woman's reaction and in the image (Figure 9.5), where the immensity of the Port-Bangna Expressway stands astride an assemblage of apparently scavenged remnants, juxtaposed in turn with formal buildings immediately behind. A bewildering, incomprehensible order is manifested, for how could such an accretion of elements come about? Is this of some different order of reality?

Khlong Toei (2)

Figure 9.6

Despite the vastness of Khlong Toei and the plethora of passageways through which its denizens could escape in times of danger, there are very few obvious entry points. This is one of them. Yet, look again; the two men at the street sign can themselves be seen as a sign: no 'farang' (foreigners). One enters with sentiments of both voyeuristic intrusion and dread. We are standing at the edge of something alien to our experience – another world, another humanity, an abyss. The seeming porosity of the slums is misleading – few tourists will pass this point (Figure 9.6).

Sukhumvit soi 71

Figure 9.7

The slums spread as demand exceeds supply. The vast domain of the Khlong Toei slums extends northwards, across the tourist realm of Sukhumvit road and into the shophouse land of its 'soi' or side streets. This is not a construction site but a deconstruction site – assumptions and understandings (what is formal? what is informal? what is a slum?) are confronted, challenged, deconstructed. While there is no written history of this building (or is it buildings?), it was a three-storey (or was it four-storey?) shophouse row from the 1970s, 1980s or 1990s. One will assume that it is 'formal' in that it is owned, pays taxes and has municipal service connections. It is also informalized, as poor occupants have adapted its spaces and extended outwards from its façade; there is a mélange of signboards of present or departed businesses and other screens across other balconies to seize some privacy. Formality is informalized (Dovey and King 2011) (Figure 9.7).

Khlong Phrakhanong

Figure 9.8

The slums can also be interstitial, inserted into bits of left-over space, enjoying varying degrees of legality, semi-legality and illegality, though almost always displaying some form of informality. Khlong Phrakhanong, on the edge of the Khlong Toei slums, is photographed from the elite boulevard of Sukhumvit road. Here one sees, as in the first image of Khlong Toei (Figure 9.5), how the massive (and largely futile) effort to solve the traffic problem for middle-class commuters creates a vacuum where the now rare floating houses fill an interstice. The formal city creates the interstices, but also the condominiums, corporate towers and elevated viewing points on to the informal settlements that fill them (Figure 9.8).

Ban Panthom

Figure 9.9

The tourist on the tourist streets of Sukhumvit, Silom or Charoen Krung will almost inevitably wander from the 'soi' into one of the deeper and smaller 'trok' (laneways), where the attraction is at once the sense of entering into a more 'authentic', 'backstage' part of Bangkok urban life yet also the ambiguity of the place – is it private and can I walk here? A young child is playing in a portable pool set up on the street along with potted plants, tricycles, birds, a Coca Cola machine and women engaged in production (subsistence, informal, formal?) This scene mixes nostalgia with a revelation of how liveable and quiet urban life can be in the absence of cars, while the city roars just 30 metres away. While there are slum conditions here, there is also much highly liveable housing (Figure 9.9).

The anti-slum

Figure 9.10

One cannot understand Bangkok slums without reading their counter-imagery. In a 'soi' off Sukhumvit is an image of the anti-slum; the desire that it seeks to fulfil is to escape the other reality of Bangkok streets into a purified upper world from where the view is likely to be down on to the slums. This imaginary city of middle-class dreams is a backdrop to some orange-shirted motorcycle taxi riders resting under an informal shade. Their orange shirts are particularly poignant since they are likely to come from the rural north-east (the base of the insurgent Red Shirts of recent political turmoil) and to live in the slums, yet their job is to ferry the Bangkok middle-classes (the Yellow Shirts) through the choked traffic (King 2011: xix–xxvii) (Figure 9.10).

Conclusion

> Don't ask what it means. Ask how it works.
>
> (Gilles Deleuze, quoted in Buchanan and Marks 2000)

Images are captured and framed for certain purposes. We have asked ourselves how images of slums work on us, but also how do we work on them? Tourists visit Bangkok for its golden temples, grand palaces and shopping malls, perhaps for its street markets and nightlife. They do not visit for its poverty, slums and inequality, or for the signs of political violence that might variously be seen as both cause and effect of that inequality. Yet, the slums and the lives of their inhabitants will be inescapable and the tourist becomes, albeit accidentally, the slum tourist. Some of the images presented above may be typical of those they have on their cameras at the end of the day. Others will reflect the fact that most of the slums are invisible to the tourist gaze, protected by a potent mix of the slum dwellers' desire to escape eviction and the desire of authorities to maintain an image of law and order (Dovey and King 2011).

As tourists read these images of slums, trying to make some sense of what they have seen, their readings may or may not approximate to those that we have sketched above. How they (and we) read this imagery will always tell more about the reader than about the scene photographed. That reading, we suggest, will inevitably lead to uncertainty. First, there is the question of the aesthetic – is it observed for its visual complexity, its surprise, because we are looking for 'the authentic' – are we moved by some idea of 'beauty', or more by the horror of Bangkok, the 'sublime'? Second is the question of explanation – how can we explain this unequal, complex, chaotic world to ourselves? How do we account for the sort of incomprehensible world represented in Khlong Toei or Sukhumvit soi 71 (Figures 9.5, 9.6 and 9.7)? Our understanding of the production and reproduction of both society and built environment is challenged. We leave with little to hold on to. Third, and most unsettling, is the moral dilemma. We are the intruders, the voyeurs – why have we photographed these people and places? If we 'take' pictures, do we make a promise to 'give' something back? Is it okay as long as we get no pleasure? What about the inevitable pleasure of the sublime – of being close to danger when we are guaranteed to be safe; the adrenaline shock of the real? Do we depart erasing this world from consciousness or outraged at our impotence to change it? Slums offer a challenge to our sense of reason and morality as well as our sense of beauty or place (Dovey and King 2012). Whether it produces shock, horror, pity, delight or political activism, slum tourism is unlikely to abate and seems destined to open slum settlements to western eyes. The question of how much it may open western eyes (and pockets) to the enduring problems of poverty is more complex, but the prospect is enticing.

Bibliography

Benjamin, W. (1982) *Gesammelte Schriften: das Passagen-Werk*, vol. 5, ed. R. Tiedemann and H. Schweppenhuser, with T.W. Adorno and G. Scholem, Frankfurt: Suhrkamp Verlag.

Buchanan, I. and Marks, J. (2000) 'Introduction', in I. Buchanan and J. Marks (eds) *Deleuze and Literature*, Edinburgh: Edinburgh University Press.

Buck-Morss, S. (1989) *The Dialectics of Seeing: Walter Benjamin and the Arcades Project*, Cambridge, MA: MIT Press.

Dovey, K. and King, R. (2011) 'Forms of informality: morphology and visibility of informal settlements', *Built Environment*, 37(1): 11–29.

—— (2012) 'Informal urbanism and the taste for slums', *Tourism Geographies*, 14(2): forthcoming.

King, R. (2011) *Reading Bangkok*, Singapore: NUS Press.

Part III

Slum tourism and empowerment

10 Favela tourism

Listening to local voices

Bianca Freire-Medeiros

Introduction

A growing body of research that investigates a range of unfolding dimensions of slum tourism in Rio de Janeiro, Cape Town, Mumbai and elsewhere is being produced by senior scholars and a large number of graduate students from different disciplines and places of origin. A significant percentage of this milieu is, in fact, represented in this book.

Despite our cultural, theoretical and methodological differences, I believe that we researchers are all more or less explicitly debating whether slum tours ought to play the roles they currently play. Some opponents identify these tourism practices as 'poverty tours', and accuse them of being inappropriate altogether because they objectify poverty and deny local residents autonomy and dignity.[1] The central metaphor here is that of a safari or a zoo showcasing poor people. Others hold, instead, that the problem with such tours is not ontological but pragmatic: slum tours are neither good nor bad in principle; it all depends on the actual practices and uses, which differ from place to place (see Selinger and Outterson 2009). According to this view, slum tours have the potential to benefit local residents socially and economically. It is acknowledged, however, that (1) in most cases the level of democratic involvement of the local population in tourism initiatives is very low or completely non-existent; and (2) more often than not professional tourism companies are basically the only ones collecting the profits (Ramchander 2004, 2007; Freire-Medeiros 2006, 2009a, b, 2012; Rolfes 2009, 2010a, b).

It is important to note that both opponents and supporters of slum tours seem to be moved by a broad concern for the local population's dignity and self-esteem as well as for the extent to which their economic disadvantage is being exploited by the tourism market. In other words, both groups seem roughly to share a conception that poverty is unjust to some extent, that decent material conditions of life are a human right, that exploiting other people's misery as a tourist attraction is outrageous and that socially and economically vulnerable human beings should be met with solidarity and not simply be gazed upon.

This commendable concern, however, does not necessarily translate into academic investigations. Local populations whose places of residence are being turned into tourist destinations inspire frequent anxiety at these developments, but their active role in this process is not so often examined. When constructing their analyses and critiques, only a few researchers take into account the expectations, opinions and reactions expressed by the very population that they accuse others – in this case, tourism promoters and tourists – of objectifying. I believe that there are at least two sets of reasons for the scarcity of investigations that focus on slum/favela/township residents as social agents and as integral parts of the slum tourism phenomenon.

The first set of reasons has to do with what one could call operational factors. When choosing to focus on residents – and not only on the so-called hosts, but also on those indirectly involved in the process – the researcher would have to deal with a large area of investigation, much larger than when the focus is placed upon tourism operators, guides or tourists. Either from a micro-sociological or structural perspective, dealing with a greater number of subjects means mobilizing more human resources and/or spending a longer period in the field. In times of financial cuts, this is simply not feasible.

The other set of reasons can be identified as socio-epistemological factors and includes, among others, the obvious distances existing between researcher and local residents related to social class, lifestyle and language. Different authors, myself included, have pointed out that the interaction between slum tourists and locals is mainly visual and rarely verbal due to the existing language barrier (Jaguaribe and Hetherington 2006; Freire-Medeiros 2006, 2009a, 2012; Menezes 2007, 2010). However, there seems to be no reflection on the implications of this barrier when it is placed between researcher and residents.

A considerable number of researchers come from the North Atlantic, English-speaking world and may not have the appropriate language skills to approach local residents and conduct a qualitative investigation. This might be critical in the case of favela tourism, which demands knowledge of the (obscure) Portuguese idiom, but it also holds true of other field situations where residents may speak English. After all, sharing the same idiom does not necessarily mean being able to communicate properly and fully. 'Fluency in English is virtually synonymous with literacy in a context where orality still determines the consciousness of millions', observes Graham Pechey (1994: 158). 'Speaking English', he accurately argues, 'is for many rather like modulating from the spontaneity of everyday speech to that quasi dramatic expository mode in which one explains oneself to an outsider' (ibid.). One could point to equivalent limitations for scholars who are native speakers of Portuguese and who find themselves still unable to understand fully the vocabulary – and the eloquent silences – used in the context of the favela. I confess that communication in the broadest sense was a challenge that I faced from day one during the five years I spent researching favela tourism.

Needless to say, high-quality research within the field of slum tourism studies is being conducted despite time and economic constraints on researchers who are not 'from within'. But the fact is that a gap remains to be filled when the topic is the opinions, demands and expectations of those whose poverty is being commodified in the tourism market. With this in mind, the ostensible subject of this chapter is tourism as seen through the eyes of those who live in Rocinha, advertised in the tourism market as 'the largest favela in Latin America'.

The historical conditions for the appearance of favelas as empirical realities and as objects of discourse by a plethora of social actors are numerous, and have been competently retraced by scholars such as Machado da Silva (1994), Leite (1997, 2000), Zaluar and Alvito (1998), Valladares (2000, 2005), Valladares and Medeiros (2003) and Burgos (2004), to name but a few. Still, I believe that it is important to highlight that, if since the beginning favelas have presented considerable internal differences both in their physical and social space (Lopes 1955; Machado da Silva 1967; Leeds 1969), nowadays such diversity has been taken to even further extremes. As Preteceille and Valladares argue (2000: 15), 'there are "favelas" within favelas and they differ from each other in terms of the profile of their residents as well as urban conditions'. This empirical diversity of the 1,020 existing settlements, nevertheless, is subsumed by encompassing narratives that produce what I call the travelling favela: a global trademark and tourist destination (Freire-Medeiros 2008, 2009a, b, 2012).

Since the early 1990s, Rocinha has been incorporated into a repackaged and recoded tourist image of Rio de Janeiro, which includes, for the local elites, desolation – favelas as an iconic image. What do the inhabitants of Rocinha think about the presence of tourists in their place of residence? Do they perceive this presence as something that humiliates and objectifies them or as a possibility of empowerment? What nuances are constructed and revealed between total endorsement and unconditional disapproval? In addition to the field observations and the frequent informal conversations that were part of our research routine,[2] I and a research team of enthusiastic young students carried out 178 semi-structured questionnaires with residents from different parts of Rocinha, including those visited by tourists and those ignored by them. We started with contextualizing questions: when s/he had begun to see tourists in Rocinha, how (or if) this presence changed her/his daily lives and if s/he had had any contact with a tourist. We then asked their opinions about the tourists' presence and gave them an incentive to speculate on the tourists' motivations to visit the locality. The third block of questions placed the residents as tourism promoters: 'if you could be a tourist guide for Rocinha, what would your tour look like?'; 'How much would you charge?'; 'If the tourists wanted to buy souvenirs, what would you recommend?' Following these, there were specific queries about the photographic gaze. The interviewees were seen as tourists themselves when asked if they travelled and, if so, where to – and if they liked to take pictures and which kinds of souvenirs they usually bought. We finished asking what s/he expected from tourism in Rocinha and what were the most positive and the most negative aspects of her/his neighbourhood – not with regard to tourism activities, but in general terms. My team and I made it clear that we had no connection to the tourism agencies, and introduced ourselves as students interested in understanding tourism in Rocinha. We reassured them that interviewees would not be identified by name.

Welcome to Rocinha

Rocinha is located between São Conrado and Gávea, the latter boasting Rio's highest Human Development Index, while Rocinha has the fourth worst. Gávea's per capita income is ten times that of Rocinha (IPP 2003), and, despite a considerable increase in the quality of living in the favela in the last decades, 21.89 per cent of its population still lives below the poverty line with a monthly income of US$35 and under (FGV 2004). Due to extreme levels of population density, Rocinha has the highest rates of tuberculosis in the state of Rio de Janeiro.

Still, 'Rocinha's case is many times referred to as an element of relativization of the current view that takes favelas as a space dominated by poverty' (Pandolfi and Grynszpan 2003: 55). As a matter of fact, no other place that goes by the name of 'favela' boasts such an incredible number and variety of businesses as are found in Rocinha: three banks, thirty-odd stores selling building materials, beauty salons, health clubs, pharmacies, motorcycle stores, cellular phone and DVD rental stores, a mini shopping-mall, pizza delivery places, several restaurants (including a sushi place) and three travel agencies. More than a few businesses accept debit and credit cards, a feature that Valladares (2005: 154–5) highlights as evidence of the local population's participation in the national consumption market – a market that is deeply influenced by real or imagined foreign objects and trends that assume local incarnations, versions and uses.

Services also abound: residents can count on three public schools and several daycare facilities, a post office, five bus lines that reach the city centre and other main points in town, and 600 motor taxis working mostly within the locality (an essential service if one remembers that most streets are narrow and precariously paved). There are three neighbourhood associations, three women's associations and one local merchants' association. In the early 2000s, an old abandoned hotel next to the Samba School was turned into a public building and nowadays houses the Citizenship Centre, where city government has established service outposts and where several training, education and health centres are held.

According to the 2000 IBGE census, 97 per cent of households had at least one TV set and around two thousand of them had telephone lines. There are at least three 'rádios comunitárias' (community radios), two locally produced newspapers and cable television, including vicinity-based channel TV ROC. From 2009, residents started to enjoy a free wireless Internet service provided by the state.

Since early 2010, significant improvements have been conducted at Rocinha as part of the Growth Acceleration Programme (Programa de Aceleração do

Crescimento: PAC) sponsored by the federal government, with investments of around US$120 million. In an area previously occupied by hundreds of precarious shacks with open sewage, a major sports centre has been erected with a semi-Olympic-sized swimming pool and other facilities. The project also includes the reurbanization of certain areas, the opening of roads and the construction of two funiculars on rails, which are supposed to enable garbage collection on the upper part of the favela. Most of these services and opportunities, however, are not equally distributed within Rocinha itself. The community is informally subdivided into several very socio-spatially diverse sectors – twenty-five of them in total. In general terms, those living in the sections closer to the main vehicle arteries or in the bottom of the favela are in a much better situation than those in less accessible regions located on the peaks of the hills, where water provision is intermittent and mudslides are frequent.

In this sense, it is possible to say that wealth and poverty articulate a growing diversity not only in the surroundings of Rocinha, but equally within its territory. Such internal and complex heterogeneity demands that tourism promoters face the problematical challenge of accommodating Rocinha to the expectations of tourists who more often than not come inspired by and in search of the travelling favela, an imaginary space that is expected to be, among other things, homogeneously poor. This inevitable distance between 'reality' and 'expectations', 'empirical plurality' and 'tourism reductionism', while intrinsic to tourism narratives and practices (Rojek 1994; Urry 1995), in the case of favela tourism assumes even more problematic contours, precisely because most promoters morally justify their business as an opportunity to deconstruct the stereotype of the favela as the main locus of poverty (Freire-Medeiros 2007, 2009a, 2012; Rolfes 2010a, b). Fighting this negative label without replacing it with a romanticized view of the conditions of living in the favela seems to be as much of a challenge as it is to expose the realities of poverty without giving incentive to objectifying approaches.

'There is a danger even in writing of "the poor" for it suggests, at the very least, that poor people have more in common than not, that they share interests, beliefs, wants, complaints, or a common culture', advises Stephen Pimpare in his *A People's History of Poverty in America* (2008: 10). But poverty does need to be essentialized and fetishized (and often 'ethnicized') in order to be marketable. In the tourist market, it is fundamental to speak of Rocinha as being 'the favela' and 'the favela' as being 'the territory of the poor'. Fetishized by tourism narratives, the necessarily relational and relative character that poverty possesses becomes even more obscured. However, if the travelling favela that tourism re-edits on a daily basis could be considered 'unreal' in regard to a number of features, it still mobilizes real bodies and its reverberations are to be experienced in empirical places. So it is time to de-essentialize and de-fetishize poverty by listening to some of those who are affected by, and are part of, the touristic Rocinha.

'Favelado ain't no sucker'

When we first met, Lina was 55 years old and had been working for several years as a house cleaner in different parts of Zona Sul, where the better-off live. A decade-long resident of Rocinha, she was very enthusiastic about our research project and gave us a long and fascinating interview that I partially share here:

> I've been seeing tourists in Rocinha for as long as I can remember, but now it has become a lot more visible ... Their presence is a welcome contribution, I think it's phenomenal! The community is marginalized in every possible way, even people from here look down at Rocinha, and now people come from abroad and make a point of visiting – look how splendid! Meanwhile people from here are afraid, right?

When we asked why tourists were interested in visiting Rocinha, Lina smartly replied:

> I am the one who should be making that question! I am curious to find out; I'd like to know their language just to ask that, to talk about it, because it's very interesting. I'm dying to know! Does this happen in every favela? What is it about Rocinha? This is just like any other favela, right? And the people from here [other Rocinha residents? Residents of Rio? Brazilians in general?] don't give Rocinha the right value.

According to the script suggested by Lina, there ought to be even greater interaction between tourists and Rocinha residents, perhaps through the spread of B & Bs in the community, as has already been occurring in other favelas where drug-trafficking is not so ostensive. The security/risk factor is taken into account by Lina:

> It [favela tourism] should be more organized. They [the tourists] could spend the night here and have a more intense experience. But if there is an invasion [police], a shooting, what is there to be done? It's complicated, right? I'd show them where there is nature, but there isn't much of it left ... I'd do a night tour so that they could see the moon. Now if they want to see the terrible poverty [*miserê*], I'd take them to see the sad, hurtful side, which makes you say 'my God, does this exist?!' Yes it does, right here, so close to the *asfalto* [the paved streets below where the better-off live]. Then we'd go by the Valão [an area crossed by an open sewer channel], the Roupa Suja, see all the human and material misery ... I wouldn't charge any money for this tour.

There seems to be a common understanding that residents of tourist areas are not exactly interested in receiving tourists as guests and engaging in cultural exchanges, but rather in receiving money brought by tourists. In this sense, tourists become a necessary evil – it is an evil because their presence is disruptive and yet a necessary one because their money is needed. In the case of favela tourism, the utterances of Lina and our other interviewees do not fit comfortably into this framework, as I will attempt to demonstrate.

In our studies on Rocinha as a tourist destination, Dwek (2004), Carter (2005), Machado (2006), Serson (2006) and I come to very similar conclusions regarding the economic impact of tourism locally: the commercial relationships between residents and tourists are informal and sporadic, if existent; there is no distribution of profits – the capital generated is only marginally reinvested in the favela, and always by way of charity. However, like Lina, most of the inhabitants of Rocinha who were our interviewees (84 per cent) sympathize with the presence of tourists (see Figure 10.1).

Within the set of answers classified as 'positive and negative' (3 per cent) are those that suggest a positive evaluation of favela tourism as an idea, but indicate a dissatisfaction with how tours actually take place. In other words, tourists are not rejected, yet there is a demand for an alternative form of touring, different from the ones currently being promoted in Rocinha:

> I think it's a waste, because it could be something a lot better and beneficial to the community as a whole. As it is, only one person or another are being benefitted, only some interests are satisfied, and although there have been changes it is still just like a sightseeing visit, like going to the botanical gardens or the museum. It only benefits those who want to visit the favela and those who organize these tours. There are some places I don't see them visiting, like social assistance programmes for example

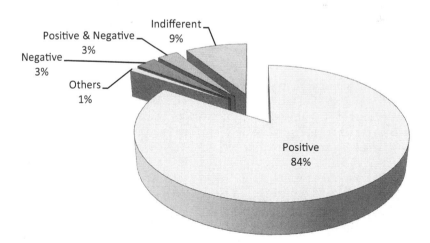

Figure 10.1 Residents' perceptions of tourists' presence in Rocinha
Source: author's own data.

. . . Tourism here doesn't bother me, doesn't speak to me, I have nothing to say about it, but it saddens me a bit. Here is a good chance and it goes by just like that.

(Rosa, 45, grade school teacher)

One should keep in mind that an answer classified as 'positive' can also be the expression of an extremely varied array of justifications. These justifications can undoubtedly be based on economic motivations related to sporadic or potential gains, but not exclusively. Carla, 20, a supermarket cashier, remarked with a smirk:

I think it's [favela tourism's] actually a good thing. Once my daughter was at the doorstep of my mother-in-law's house and a tourist went by and gave her R$50, so they do help in this way, they see children and give them money.

But money does not even need to be earned or seen to confirm tourists' good will: 'if they're coming, they can only mean to help', pronounced a local resident used to the transit of tourists streaming past his front door. On other occasions, 'making cash' off tourists may be experienced as a way to subvert the asymmetry of the relationship. Laughing, Val, a 23-year-old housewife, told us of the following episode:

A friend of mine owns a really tiny bar. The tourist ran inside [the bar] dying to use the toilet, so he gave her R$50 just to use it! I thought that was soooo cool! I think it's funny that they act like that. They're clueless really! Think about it: R$50 just to use the toilet!

Material gains, according to many to whom we spoke, can also come in forms other than cash. The owner of a stand in the area known as Laboriaux told us that:

They [tourists] climb up to the *laje*, do some filming, that sort of thing . . . They [the guides] ask the house's owner, who's my father-in-law, for permission. They [tourists] pay if they want to, sometimes they give a treat. Once, one of them gave away a camera, one of those professional photographers use.

(Carol, 46, vendor)

As Viviana Zelizer (2005) so accurately demonstrates, money is neither culturally neutral nor socially anonymous. The economic arrangements that take place within the touristic Rocinha do not simply call up considerations of cost, profits or gains. They inspire the residents to discuss the various forms and representations assumed by any money that is actually or potentially brought in by those who visit the favela. In this sense, the money given by tourists might be considered a windfall, which, as welcome as it is, should not be regularly counted on, as in the case of Carla and Val, or may assume other material forms, as in the case of Carol.

Whereas 'interest in economic gain', in its broader sense, often appears as a justification in the discourse of favela dwellers, in many other cases supporting tourism means investing in a supposed counter-stigma, a possibility opened up by the presence of foreigners. After seeing the favela through their own eyes, tourists allegedly become capable of demystifying the violent image of the favela tirelessly projected by the elite and the media:

> [Tourism] is good because it shows that Rocinha is more than just violence and shootings. There is more to Rocinha than that. There are many good things, many social, artistic and cultural projects – basically, there are many good social projects there in Rocinha. I have seen [tourists] helping the community – like it or not, they end up helping, directly or indirectly. They bring their eyes into the community.
>
> (Marcelo, 28, baker)

One should keep in mind that, in April 2004, less than two years before these interviews were conducted, the then Deputy Governor of the State, Luiz Paulo Conde, proposed that, for security purposes, public power should erect a 10-foot-high wall that would completely ring not only Rocinha but also Vidigal, another favela nearby. The physical proximity between the visitors and those visited through favela tourism, despite all of its limitations, is perceived as capable of countering the interpretative package that points at all favela residents (especially its youth) as inevitable accomplices of criminals:

> I think it [tourism] is great. It shows that Rocinha is different from what people see on TV, that it is not a seven-headed beast because of drug trafficking and things like that. And tourists are here to reduce that, this whole story of saying that Rocinha is just about drug trafficking. There is culture inside the community, lots of interesting things going on, and tourists just began noticing it. Rocinha is not just trafficking, deaths, that kind of thing. It is more: art, culture, dancing. So tourists are really enjoying that . . . I hope they don't come looking for the trafficking thing. I hope they get to see all the work getting done. This is what we expect from them: that when they go back to where they live they'll show the good things about Rocinha and not the bad things.
>
> (Fred, 22, student)

At the time of the research, Andrea was 26 years old and worked at a dentist's office. A few weeks before, while watching TV at home, her husband had been hit by a stray bullet during a confrontation between policemen and bandits. She also believes in the potential of tourism to develop a counter-stigma:

[The presence of tourists] is good for the community, it helps against the idea that it's a violent place. I have friends who, when I mention I'm from Rocinha, they say they would never go there, because they think there are gunfights every day, all the time. So with tourism people lose that impression that it's all just violence. Violence happens, it happened to us, but Rocinha is not only that.

Countering media and commonsense representations that repeatedly activate the metaphor of war (Leite 2005) in their interpretations of the favela, many dwellers have started employing the representations made by tourists. In this sense, it should not come as a surprise that, when asked to picture themselves as guides, 79 per cent said they would highlight the most positive aspects of Rocinha: the commercial area, the view to the ocean and the woods and the arts-and-crafts market. Even though they assume it is precisely poverty and violence that constitute the key attractions of Rocinha as a tourist destination, many locals insist that the more negative aspects (shacks, garbage, spatial disorder, guns) should not be associated with the touristic favela. Let us see a few examples.

In your opinion, why are tourists interested in visiting Rocinha?

Because Rocinha is known everywhere . . . And when people come from another country, they are interested in seeing our poor communities, in Rio de Janeiro and in Brazil, and seeing it for themselves. For good or bad, they [the tourists] are comparing our community to theirs. So they want to see the difference. That is their curiosity.

(Sheila, 25, store vendor)

Because out there Rocinha is the most talked-about favela, the wars [conflicts between bandits and police as well as between different commandos] and so on . . . I think they come here to compare their daily lives to ours, they have better living standards, they want to see the class difference.

(Rodrigo, 42, carpenter)

I think they want to know, right? It's curiosity. It's the same thing when we go to Búzios [a popular beachside destination for the Rio affluent] . . . Rocinha is much talked about . . . There are interesting things in Rocinha, although people discriminate a lot against the favela. I think that's why they are interested in coming and finding out. I don't know if there are favelas in their countries. So I think they come here for that reason too.

(Everson, 27, security guard)

If you were the tourist guide, what would your tour be like?

I'd show the positive things I know in Rocinha. There is the Samba School, the Casa da Paz which works for the community, the [Neighbours'] Association and also the view.

(América, 33, telemarketing operator)

I'd show the Samba School, the people who make the costumes, the children's orchestra, the musical school. There is a clothing factory where seamstresses make clothes for export, two NGOs, one active in social works and another one which offers drug rehab support.

(Madalena, 68, retired)

There are lots of things to show. There is the Casa de Cultura, the area with the handicraft people, then Rua 1, which leads to a view of Gávea and the Lagoa, the internet cafés where people access the Internet. I would walk through the narrow streets and alleyways, take them to the community radio stations, and here to TVRoc.

(Carlinha, 33, telemarketing attendant)

Obviously, there are those who believe it is important to show that 'the coin has two sides', as explained to us by Maicon, a shop vendor: 'You have to show the reality of Rocinha, the daily life, the good things and the bad things. There are still mud-and-stick houses, wooden shacks . . . You have to show everything, everything. The good and the bad.' Even in these cases, there seems to be no intent to displease tourists or insult them, but to reveal the favela in its complexity. Antonio's utterances and his effort to reconcile the different realities of the favela illustrate how poverty tourism can lead locals to re-evaluate their own identities:

Rocinha is a huge place, there are many beautiful spots . . . I'd also take them to meet some traditional characters from the community and some houses that still represent what Rocinha was 20 years ago. People who make the climb up to Rocinha have to see all this, to have a notion of what life is like. There is this contrast, so it is a reality that must be reconsidered.

(Antonio, 30, barber)

The local leaders who were willing to establish a dialogue with our team were not intent on rejecting tourism but were, rather, opposed to the manner in which agencies active in Rocinha had exploited it as a tourist destination. As he made clear during a long interview with our team, and according to his statements to the press, William de Oliveira, at the time President of the main Neighbours' Association, was not opposed to tourism in Rocinha, but to how the favela is presented and, most of all, how profits have been shared: 'They go up to see the Christ [the Redeemer, the statue], they pay. They go up the Sugar Loaf, they pay. They come here, they take.'

'The community does not ignore the tourist', observes Toninho, a tourist guide and a resident of Rocinha: 'They even attempt to interact – "hello man, how are you?" [in English] [laughter] – they try to tell something of their stories, but there is the language barrier . . . Residents do not ignore the tourist, they ignore how things work.' But who, of all those composing this scenario, actually knows 'how things work'? As I have discussed in previous opportunities, certainly not the tourists, who are unaware, for example, that the money paid for the tour is not directly channelled to the community. Tourism operators? In the opinion of guides with whom we talked, as well as of souvenir vendors, save for the rare exception there was a belief that tourism operators are concerned with little else but their businesses. What about guides? They are equally unconcerned, it seems – despite the strategic position they occupy, they do not constitute a group per se. The majority cannot name more than a half a dozen colleagues who work on a day-to-day basis on the same job and at the same place. How about myself and my research team?

My team and I, despite our welcome in Rocinha and the network we forged, were always perceived as 'something else', neither local nor gringo. Moreover, the speed and intensity of the transformation of the field of favela tourism never ceased to surprise us. One of these surprises was the revelation that most residents (76 per cent of interviewees) were unaware of the fact that Rocinha tours were charged for. Even when they knew the tours were not for free, they rarely knew what the rates were (operators usually charge R$70 per person). We, the researchers, frequently found ourselves interfering in the reality we were studying, telling interviewees the prices the agencies charged, to which many reacted with indignation: 'Oh, is that so?! I wish I had a job like that!' Others, such as Rambo, 25, a store vendor, made completely inflated estimates of value: 'I think I would charge pretty well. Like about R$500 each . . . What they [the agencies] charge is quite little.'

However, 70 per cent of the interviewees responded, like Lina, that they wouldn't charge at all for the tour. 'No, I am not the type who charges anyone', answered Iara, 49, a house cleaner. And she justified this by saying: 'It is something you do for love, and love doesn't come with a price tag. It would be a pleasure to do the tour, take them for a stroll, to see Rocinha, I would do that with pleasure.' Leo, 28, a blacksmith, agreed:

> I would not charge anything. I would do it with pleasure, free of charge. The [Mexican] tourists who came here offered me money and I said 'no, I don't want any'. I really dig that they got to know the community where I grew up, where I live. Do the agencies charge? I don't know, they probably have their own expenses, right? I can't say if it's expensive or cheap. They have their expenses too. But I'd do it free, no money charged.

Every time my team and I participated in tours, children and adults were extremely receptive to tourists, enthusiastically waving and attempting a few words in English. Obviously, I do not intend to deny the existence of deeply unequal relationships, but one must realise that favela residents are not the passive receptacles of the curious looks cast by tourists. Hierarchies of power are perceived quite visibly:

> I can't even answer this question [concerning one's opinion of tourism] if I don't know what they are saying out there, what they see here, I don't know! I've never heard the comments they make out there, but if they are saying good things, that's good, I hope they do it more and more, but if they are saying bad things, we'd better stop right here. We don't go there and say bad things. I've never even been where they live! I don't even have the means!'
>
> (Tiana, 28, receptionist)

As keenly pointed out by Georg Simmel (1997) in his analysis of moments of co-presence, reciprocal action does not imply symmetry of power. Reciprocity is present in the most unequal interactions, even in those that seem exclusively and highly hierarchical. Building upon his theoretical musings on the exchange of glances, Simmel defends the idea that interactions are at once active and passive: one cannot avoid taking through the eye without at the same time giving with it. The eye produces 'the most complete reciprocity' of person-to-person, face-to-face exchange (Simmel 1997: 112). In the tours we followed there was never an occasion when we did not witness an inversion of points of view, with tourists suddenly becoming the attraction. Often, adults and children would make joking remarks on the hairdos or clothing of visitors: 'Look at his outfit'; 'That one over there is on her way to the safari' etc. A blonde tourist is loudly saluted: 'What's up, David Beckham!' A young Indian girl is nicknamed Beyoncé. 'I make fun of them because I can't speak their language', justifies one 11-year-old girl. On other occasions, residents endow tourists with childish qualities: 'Their tongues are all curled up [when they speak], it's so cute!'; 'I love to see it when they spend the day under the rain, with those yellow raincoats looking like little chicks.' The odd gaze cast at the favela residents is often returned to foreigners whose presence is so frequent it has been incorporated into a quasi-normal state of affairs. When asked since when she first started noticing tourists in the favela, one resident replied: 'Oh, a long time ago . . . They go by freely, walk down the alleyways, among us, as if they were normal people.'

Attitudes perceived as intrusive are countered vehemently. According to Tininha, a tourist guide who worked in Rocinha for over a decade:

> Favela tourism is in fact a little invasive. Because you walk down those narrow streets and people leave their windows open . . . And there is once in a while the clueless tourist who will poke his face into people's houses! That is really unpleasant . . . A resident was cooking and the stove was right next to the window; the tourist was walking by and stuck his hand

through the window and put a lid on an uncovered pot. She went mad! And then she went like this [making the gesture of hand slap]!

Rude attitudes on the part of tourists do not need to be as explicit as that in order to provoke uncomfortable and critical reactions on the part of residents. The lines below are an excellent example. Sheila was 18 and had moved to the lower section of Rocinha when she was a teenager. She had worked as a salesperson, but was unemployed at the time of the interview:

> I've been seeing tourists since I arrived here . . . I think that guides must be getting something out of it, but not us. Yesterday, the motorcycle I was on was about to crash because their cars [the agencies'] stop in the middle of the road. Nobody says anything because we think it brings us something. No, I don't think that [favela tourism] is cool. Sometimes it is good, okay, because the place where we live is being visited, but it is also something of a drag. I saw one of them taking a picture of a garbage dump. We feel embarrassed because they'll go back to their countries and show that Rocinha is dirty, or disgusting, or whatever.

When we asked why tourists are interested in visiting Rocinha, Sheila reacted with indignation:

> Ahhh, that's what I ask myself! Rio de Janeiro is so beautiful; there are so many places to visit! It's hard to choose which one is prettiest. Why of all places do they come to Rocinha, a favela? It is obvious that it's so that they can talk about it later! Probably bad things, right? Otherwise there is no reason! They have already taken pictures of me [smiles]: once, my friend and I, we were hugging and waved at them, they asked to photograph us. Then we blew them kisses and they took the picture!

Sheila's narrative configures a relational world. It aids our perception of the possible shades between being 'pro-' or 'anti-'tourism in the favela. Being suspicious of the tourists' intentions or being bothered by certain behaviours does not necessarily imply hostility – on the contrary. We then discovered that, rather than a dichotomy with distant poles at the extremes, there is a continuum here. Residents, tourists, guides, researchers and others must constantly negotiate and renegotiate a new grammar able to cope with emotions, money, intimate lives and affairs, leisure and poverty, entertainment and violence in the touristic territory of the favela. As Heitor, a motorcycle delivery boy put it:

> Favelado ain't no sucker! We know what you are up to [Who? Researchers? Gringos? Guides? Visitors in general?]. We know that people come here to have fun, but they also want to see all our little shacks, to see the big-shot criminal.

Final remarks

Commonsense and media discourses more often than not place tourism activities in poverty-stricken areas as the perverse outcome of a despicable combination of three variables: tourism promoters' unbounded greed, tourists' morbid voyeurism, and dwellers' despairing and/or passive precariousness. This implies at least two underlying assumptions: first, that dwellers constitute a homogeneous group; second, that, unlike tourists and ourselves, who probably hail from educated segments of society, local residents are in want of reflexivity, of what Anthony Giddens (1984) has termed interpretive competence.

Residents are not so often taken as people with agency and capable of critically assessing their own situation as individuals who make choices and have a say. Seen as living in a state of resignation or ignorance, they would be accepting of the presence of tourists only because they do not apprehend its degrading character. What I have attempted to demonstrate is that these assumptions do not hold up to close scrutiny. Rather than being interpreted as a lack of reflexive competence by the inhabitants of Rocinha or as evidence of sheer ignorance, positive reactions to the tours should be placed in the long history of discrimination and stigmatization of which favelas are part. The very fact of being a tourist attraction has given those living in Rocinha a sense of importance and dignity. While mass media and several segments of the elite insist on classifying and representing the favelas as cradles of crime, tourism is seen as giving them a legitimate place on the map.

Notes

1   For a detailed analysis of the implications of using terms such as 'poverty tours' or 'poorism' to refer to this tourism phenomenon, see Rolfes (2010a).
2   The research project, 'Touring Poverty', inspiring this chapter, also included brief visits to Soweto and the Cape Flats (South Africa) as well as Dharavi (India). In Rocinha, from February 2005 to August 2009, I and my research team conducted extensive interviews with tourism promoters, guides, tourists and also souvenir producers/sellers. The research also included field observation, participant observation on different tours and the survey mentioned above. Financed by CNPq and the Foundation for Urban and Regional Studies (FURS), the research team included Alexandre Magalhães, André Salata, Andréia Santos, Cesar Teixeira, Joni Magalhães, Juliana Farias and Mariana Mendonça. I am grateful to all for their enthusiastic assistance, and especially to Palloma Menezes, Fernanda Nunes and Livia Campello, who have been 'touring' the favela with me during all these years.

Bibliography

Burgos, M. (2004) 'Dos parques proletários ao favela-bairro: as políticas nas favelas do Rio de Janeiro', in A. Zaluar and M. Alvito (eds) *Um Século de Favela*, 4th edn, Rio de Janeiro: FGV.

Carter, J. (2005) 'An outsider's view of Rocinha and people', unpublished thesis, University of Texas at Austin, Texas.

Dwek, D. (2004) 'Favela tourism: innocent fascination or inevitable exploitation?', unpublished thesis, University of Leeds.

FGV (2004) *Mapa do Fim da Fone II – Ranking Geral da Região Administrativa do Rio de Janeiro*, Rio de Janeiro: FGV.

Freire-Medeiros, B. (2006) 'Favela como patrimônio da cidade? Reflexões e polêmicas acerca de dois museus', *Estudos Históricos*, 38: 49–66.

—— (2007) 'A favela que se vê e que se vende: reflexões e polêmicas em torno de um destino turístico', *Revista Brasileira de Ciências Sociais*, 22: 61–72.

—— (2008) 'And the favela went global: the invention of a trademark and a tourist destination', in M. Valença, E. Nel and W. Leimgruber (eds) *The Global Challenge and Marginalization*, New York: Nova Science.

—— (2009a) 'The favela and its touristic transits', *Geoforum*, 40(4): 580–8.

—— (2009b) *Gringo na Laje: Produção, Circulação e Consumo da Favela Turística*, Rio de Janeiro: FGV.

—— (2012) *Touring Poverty*. Routledge: London.

Giddens, A. (1984) *The Constitution of Society: Outline of the Theory of Structuration*, Berkeley, CA: University of California Press.

IPP (Instituto Pereira Passos) (2003) *Índice de Desenvolvimento Humano (IDH) na Cidade do Rio de Janeiro*, Rio de Janeiro: IPP/Prefeitura Municipal do Rio de Janeiro.

Jaguaribe, B. and Hetherington, K. (2006) 'Favela tours: indistinct and mapless representations of the real in Rio de Janeiro', in Sheller, M. and J. Urry (eds) *Mobile Technologies of the City*, Abingdon: Routledge.

Leeds, A. (1969) 'The significant variables determining the character of squatter settlements', *America Latina*, 12(3): 44–86.

Leite, M.P. (1997) 'Da metáfora da guerra à mobilização pela paz: temas e imagens do Reage Rio', *Cadernos de Antropologia e Imagem*, 4: 121–145.

Leite, M. P. (2000) Entre o individualismo e a solidariedade: dilemas da política e da cidadania no Rio de Janeiro. *Revista Brasileira de Ciências Sociais*, Anpocs, v. 15, n. 44, p.73–90.

—— (2005) 'Violência, insegurança e cidadania: reflexões a partir do Rio de Janeiro', in Lopes de Carvalho (ed.) *Rugidos e Sussurros: Mais Promessas do que Ações*, Rio de Janeiro: IBASE.

Lopes, V. (1955) 'Duas favelas do distrito federal', *Revista Brasileira dos Municípios*, 8(32): 283–98.

Machado, D. (2006) 'Turismo de favela e desenvolvimento sustentável: um estudo do turismo de favela no bairro de Vila Canoa, zona sul do Rio de Janeiro', Master's thesis, PUC-RJ, Rio de Janeiro.

Machado da Silva, L.A. (1967) 'A política na favela', *Cadernos Brasileiros*, 9(3): 35–47.

—— (1994) 'Violência e sociabilidade: tendências da atual conjuntura urbana no Brasil', in L.C. Queiroz de Ribeiro and O.A.dos Santos Jr (eds) *Globalização, Fragmentação e Reforma Urbana*, Rio de Janeiro: Civilização Brasileira.

—— and Leite, M.P. (2008) 'Violência, crime e polícia: o que os favelados dizem quando falam desses temas?', in L.A. Machado da Silva (ed.) *Vida Sob Cerco: Violência e Rotina nas Favelas do Rio de Janeiro*, Rio de Janeiro: Nova Fronteira.

Marx, K. (1867, repr. 1984) *O Capital*, Livro 1, vol. 1, trans. Reginaldo Sant'Anna, São Paulo: DIFEL.

Menezes, P. (2007) *Gringos e Câmeras na Favela da Rocinha*. Monografia (Bacharelado), Departamento de Ciências Sociais, Universidade do Estado do Rio de Janeiro.

—— (2010) 'Tourists' photographic gaze: the case of Rio de Janeiro favelas', in R. Sharpley and P.R. Stone (eds) *Tourist Experiences: Contemporary Perspectives*, Abingdon: Routledge.

Pandolfi, D.and Grynszpan, M. (2003) *A Favela Fala: Depoimentos ao CPDOC*, Rio de Janeiro: FGV.

Pechey, G. (1994) *'Post-apartheid narratives', in* F. Barket, P. Hulme and M. Iverson (eds) *Colonial Discourse, Post-colonial Theory*, Manchester: Manchester University Press.

Pereira da Silva, M.L. (2005) *Favela Cariocas 1930–1964*, Rio de Janeiro: Contraponto.

Pimpare, S. (2008) *A People's History of Poverty in America*, New York: The New Press.

Preteceille, E. and Valladares, L. (2000) 'A desigualdade entre os pobres – favela, favelas', in R. Henriques (ed.) *Desigualdade e Pobreza no Brasil*, Rio de Janeiro: IPEA.

Ramchander, P. (2004) 'Towards the responsible management of the socio-cultural impact of township tourism', unpublished PhD thesis, Department of Tourism Management, University of Pretoria.

—— (2007) 'Soweto set to lure tourists', in A. Bennett and R. George (eds) *South African Travel and Tourism Cases*, Pretoria: Van Schaik.

Ribeiro, L.C. and Lago, L. (2001) 'A oposição favela-bairro no espaço social do Rio de Janeiro', *São Paulo em Perspectiva*, 15(1): 144–54.

Rojek, C. (1994) *Leisure and Dreamworld of Modernity*, London: Macmillan.

Rolfes, M. (2009) Poverty tourism: theoretical reflections and empirical findings regarding an extraordinary form of tourism, *GeoJournal*, 75(5): 421–42.

—— (2010a) ' Poverty tourism: theoretical reflections and empirical findings regarding an extraordinary form of tourism', *GeoJournal* (75): 421–42.

—— (2010b) 'Slumming – empirical results and observational-theoretical considerations on the backgrounds of township, favela and slum tourism', in Sharpley, P. and P.R. Stone (eds) *Tourism Experiences*, Abingdon: Routledge.

Segala, L. and Silva, T.R. (eds) (1983) *Varal de Lembranças: Histórias e Causos da Rocinha*, Rio de Janeiro: União Pró-Melhoramentos dos Moradores da Rocinha Tempo e Presença/SEC/MEC/FNDE.

Selinger, E. and Outterson, K. (2009) *The Ethics of Poverty Tourism*, Boston University School of Law Working Paper 09-29, Boston, MA: BU School of Law. Available online at www.bu.edu/law/faculty/scholarship/workingpapers/documents/Selinger EOuttersonK06-02-09.pdf (accessed 29 January 2012).

Serson, P. (2006) 'A experiência turística na favela da Rocinha: estudo de caso', Monografia de Bacharelado, Universidade de São Paulo.

Simmel, G. (*1997*) *Simmel on Culture*, London: Sage.

Souza, J. and Barbosa, J.L. (2005) *Favela: Alegria e Dor na Cidade*, Rio de Janeiro: SenacRio.

Urry, J. (1995) *Consuming Places*, London: Routledge.

Valladares, L. (2000) 'A gênese da favela carioca', *Revista Brasileira de Ciências Sociais*, 15: 44.

—— (2005) *A Invenção da Favela: Do Mito de Origem a Favela.com*, Rio de Janeiro: FGV.

—— and Medeiros, L. (2003) *Pensando as Favelas do Rio de Janeiro, 1906–2000*, Rio de Janeiro: URBANDATA-Brasil, Relume Dumará.

Zaluar, A. and Alvito, M. (eds) (1998) *Um Século de Favela*, Rio de Janeiro: FGV.

Zelizer, V. (2005) *The Purchase of Intimacy*, Princeton, NJ: Princeton University Press.

11 Slum tourism and inclusive urban development
Reflections on China

Yannan Ding

Introduction

The slum in the developing world is becoming the 'Newfoundland' of international tourism. Statistics from the most developed destinations report that slum tourism makes up quite a noteworthy fraction of the tourist trade, ranging from a few thousands to hundreds of thousands (Freire-Medeiros 2009 (Rio de Janeiro); Rolfes *et al.* 2009 and Rolfes 2010 (Cape Town); Meschkank 2011 (Mumbai)). This emerging 'extraordinary form of tourism', as Rolfes (2010: 438) puts it, has provoked a lot of scholarly interest in recent years. Special attention has been given to the production of touristic space (Allen and Brennan 2004; Freire-Medeiros 2009), the ethics debate (Butcher 2003; Briedenhaan and Ramchander 2006; Selinger and Outterson 2009) and the tour experience (Rolfes *et al.* 2009; Ma 2010; Meschkank 2011; Rolfes 2010). Slum tourism remains 'extraordinary' despite all efforts to explain it, as slums are not places normally associated with the positive connotations of tourism.

In the eyes of UN-Habitat, the slum is the 'result of a failure of housing policies, laws and delivery systems, as well as of national and urban policies' (2003a: 5). Despite the variations in physical settings and social contexts, a slum means lack of urban formalities in terms of infrastructure, social services, governance, employment etc. It embodies many of the deficiencies that come along with urbanization and development, or rather the lack of development. The cities of the developing world have to accommodate more than 95 per cent of the net increase in world population (Grimm *et al.* 2008), a pressure that results in the proliferation of slums. It is predicted that the number of slum dwellers worldwide will reach two billion by 2030 (UN-Habitat 2007).

Attitudes towards slum tourism are quite polarized. Its proponents uphold the poverty alleviation function (Rogerson 2004; Freire-Medeiros 2009), whereas critics point to the troublesome ethics of slum tourism (Marrison 2005; Weiner 2008; Williams 2008; Rolfes 2010). In this chapter I explore a perspective on slum tourism that tries to transcend the dichotomy by asking whether slum tourism can be an agent of development. Can slum tourism support the struggle against the conditions of segregation and exclusion that many slums suffer from? Arguably, the slum is a stage of great potential for interaction between slum tourists and slum residents. Slum tourism might provide a new route into development, especially at a time when existing agencies, such as intergovernmental organizations, NGOs etc. are having difficulties delivering effective and sustainable solutions (see Baptista in this volume). This chapter also contributes to the literature on slum tourism by highlighting the phenomenon in a Chinese context. Previous studies have focused mainly on Brazil, South Africa and India. Given China's stage of development and recent history of urbanization, it seems logical to ask if there is slum tourism in China and, if so, what does it look like? To answer these questions, it is necessary to form a comparative framework upon which slums are generalized to some extent. In this I understand slums to be a general condition of modern urbanity. In this chapter I introduce three cases of Chinese slum tourism. Together they provide a sketchy and yet panoramic view of slum tourism in China, a foundational contribution to further studies.

The chapter is organized into four parts. To begin with, I confront the ambivalences of slum tourism by relating it to the notion of niche tourism. The second section focuses on the Chinese context, the slum phenomenon, namely 'chengzhongcun' (meaning 'village amid the city'), and tourism marketing strategies and regulations in China. Third, three cases of the use of art in slum tourism and community development are showcased. The chapter finishes with some arguments on the potentials and pitfalls of slum tourism in the making of an inclusive city.

Slum tourism as niche tourism

The slum is closely associated with British urban history (Koven 2004; Gilbert 2007; Steinbrink 2012; Seaton in this volume). The recent incarnation of slum tourism began in cities in developing countries in the early 1990s. Unlike in journalism, slum tourism as a term is seldom used in the academic world. This may be attributed to the fact that the term 'slum' is contested. Given the geographical and linguistic variances across the globe, it is indeed a question to what extent the term can be considered as a universally valid description of places of urban poverty. So, for instance, travel agents often stick to the more specific 'favela tour' or 'township tour' rather than 'slum tour' to market their products. There are numerous names for slum-like communities around the world, each one embedded in its peculiar socio-cultural background. Attempts have been made to document these variations (for a table of place names equivalent to the slum, see UN-Habitat 2003b: 60–75). For the sake of cross-cultural comparative studies, it is necessary to excavate the slum from its historical background. Defining the 'global' slum, however, is not easy amid a myriad of lived experiences of what could be described as slums.

The ethics critique deserves a bit more clarification. The growing interest in slums in recent years has resuscitated all the 'inglorious associations' between the slum and its negative connotations (Gilbert 2007). This is not new. Ever since the early nineteenth century, when the word 'slum' was coined, more social and cultural layers have been added on to it such that the slum becomes a pejorative term associated with dirt, poverty and crime (ibid.). There is a danger that the misuse by journalists or social scientists of related terms, such as the 'underclass', as Gans (2002) argues, might lead to the stigmatization of certain groups and their respective spaces. The evolution from physical space to social space demonstrates how the slum is produced along with negative connotations (Steinbrink 2012).

The ambivalent nature of the slum might have led researchers to eschew the term 'slum tourism'. Instead, 'poverty tourism' is widely used; however, while this term is certainly relevant to slum tourism, the substitution is not without problems. For instance, numerous sources have confirmed that the slum is a place not only of poverty, but also of genuine creativity and entrepreneurship. Some researchers have also noted some similarities between slum tourism and 'dark tourism' (Freire-Medeiros 2009; Rolfes 2010). While the slum, despite its bleak conditions, hardly overlaps with dark tourism destinations, the two categories do converge in their concern for 'contemporary morality' (Stone 2009).

To indulge in an ethics critique may not only be unnecessary, but also distract from community development on the ground. It is unnecessary because the pursuit of a moral way of doing tourism – or for an ultimate 'Good Tourist', as Allen and Brennan put it – should be conditioned upon a world citizenship that is, however, a form of 'utopian thinking' (Allen and Brennan 2004: 183). Only a 'Good Citizen' whose interest transcends the local level and reaches the global level could qualify as a 'Good Tourist', whose actions are for the general good. Beauregard and Bounds also reject the idea of a cosmopolitan citizenship, for its 'idealism greatly exceeds its substance' (2000: 246). It is distractive because the moralized stance may underestimate 'the potential [of tourism] to address poverty and inequality' and 'the transformative economic development that could make a substantial difference to Third World societies' (Butcher 2003: 3).

Given the widely acknowledged social polarization in the developing world, Selinger and Outterson have contested that 'if it is harmful for Rocinha residents to be confronted with wealth and inequality, poverty tours are not the primary cause' (2009: 21). The fact that poverty is observed during the slum tour does not make the tourists more immoral than the social dynamics and/or the stakeholders that have created the slum in the first place. The critique of the voyeurism of slum tourists is misleading because it takes the symptom as the epidemic, and condemns the witness as the perpetrator.

Compared to conventional modes of mass tourism, slum tourism is still a minor phenomenon. Its participants are fewer, and the duration shorter. Most slum tours cater to small groups of tourists who take a short excursion into the slum. In this sense, it reflects a move, as observed by Marson, 'from the old-style standardized rigid motivations of tourists to a more unique approach where wants and needs are focused upon (and consumers are willing to pay for) experiences that may be more adventurous and meaningful' (2011: 9).

In other words, it is a shift from mass tourism to niche tourism, which is more specific and diverse. The slum itself is also a kind of niche. From a geographical point of view, the slum in China is sometimes located on the fringe of the city, and is characterized by an intermingled landscape of the urban and the rural. Indeed, the slum belongs to and depends on the city, and yet it is often not recognized as the city. The idea of the niche even goes beyond the spatial dimension. Given the close association with rural–urban migrants and social and economic exclusion, the slum is a niche not only spatially but also – and perhaps even more – in a socio-economic sense.

Contrary to the critique of voyeurism, tourism helps to 'rediscover' these forgotten places of social exclusion and spatial segregation and to make them visible. Without the tourists, the slum would only be a marginalized place in the established spatial and social order. The presence of tourists is a disturbance of the norm. It is due to the special interests of some niche-market tourists that this peculiar space of contemporary urbanity is known, seen and discussed. In this sense, I argue that slum tourism is niche tourism.

Slum and slum tourism in China: media, marketing and management

Whether slums exist in China is a delicate question. For instance, China is absent from a popular world slum-distribution map (see Ma 2010). According to the official government line, slums were phased out from Chinese cities after the socialist revolution. By securing urban employment and social housing, the eradication of the slum was hailed as a great achievement in the late 1950s. However, in reality, housing shortage remained a constant phenomenon in Chinese cities. Especially since the reforms in the 1980s, hundreds of millions of rural migrants have poured into the cities. According to UN-Habitat, China has a slum population of 178 million, which accounts for 37.8 per cent of the total urban population (UN- Habitat 2003b: 38). On the other hand, the World Bank has found that 'the slums and endemic poverty that have taken root in other countries are largely absent from Chinese cities thus far' (Yusuf and Nabeshima 2008: 27).

The type of community in a Chinese city that is most comparable to the universal idea of a slum is the 'chengzhongcun'. Wu *et al.* (2011) address the 'chengzhongcun' (in their lexicon, 'urbanized village') with the criteria of slum identification adopted by UN-Habitat and other scholars; they accept the technical use of 'slum', but refrain from generalizing, since there are significant differences between the 'urbanized village' and the slum, such as modes of housing construction and land ownership (ibid.). I agree with them that the social context in which the terms are applied should always be noted. But for practical reasons, in the rest of this chapter, 'chengzhongcun' is used interchangeably with 'slum'.

The concept of slum tourism was introduced to China by journalism at the beginning of 2007, when Lu (2007) wrote about favela tours in Rio. In general,

Chinese reports have taken a neutral attitude, since slum tourism is deemed a foreign issue, and very few have attempted to explore the link between slum tourism and the Chinese context (Tan 2009). Forms of slum tourism as they have developed in Brazil, South Africa and India (e.g. guided tours, B & Bs) do not exist in China. There are several reasons behind this.

First of all, it is very difficult for the 'chengzhongcun' to get official sanction and endorsement. Tourism in China is overseen by the tourism office, which determines whether or not a place can be a legal tourist destination. The *Management Regulations of Tourism Development and Planning*, issued by the National Tourism Agency of China, orders that 'tourism development and planning should be in accordance with national land use planning, [local] comprehensive land use planning, urban master plan, etc.' (2000: sec. 3, art. 12). Due to fast urbanization in recent decades, the 'chengzhongcun' is under constant threat of eviction and redevelopment, which rules out the possibility of long-term tourism planning. Chinese officials tend to take a developmentalist view on urban issues. Unlike the Brazilian ex-president, Lula, who openly endorsed the favela tour (Hestbaek 2010), there is virtually no support for 'chengzhongcun' tourism from higher level officials in China except for a few cases, such as in the city of Shenzhen.

From the perspective of tourism marketing, the 'chengzhongcun' does not have a strong relevance in Chinese tourism. For domestic tourists, a short excursion to the suburban countryside is widely known as 'nongjiale' ('farm joy'; see He *et al.* 2004). But in practice it is a kind of rural retreat to the agricultural village and has nothing to do with the slum. Poverty or slums have never been a principle tourist attraction of China for international tourists. Studies on the images and text in tourism promotion, such as travel brochures, reveal that the conventional attractions of China are 'ruins', 'religious sites', 'palaces', 'monuments', 'city gateways' etc. Accordingly, China is a destination to admire and meditate upon, rather than explore and discover (see Echtner and Prasad 2003). It is interesting to note that, among the travel logs on four Chinese destinations, none of the tourists mention a word about slums or urban poverty (Hsu *et al.* 2009).

That being said, however, slum tourism is not irrelevant to China. As early as the beginning of twentieth century, Chinatowns in the US had been frequented as picturesque ethnical ghettos (Williams 2009; Steinbrink 2012). There was 'ethnic slumming' in Chinatowns, but in Chinese towns there was no slumming. It's only recently that some of the Chinese urban policy makers have become interested in taking the 'chengzhongcun' into comprehensive tourism planning. For instance, in the city of Shenzhen, the redevelopment policy for 'chengzhongcuns' has set as its goal the integration of four dimensions: spatial integration, management integration, economic integration and cultural integration (Urban Planning, Land and Resources Commission of Shenzhen Municipality 2005). In terms of cultural integration, it is emphasized that the 'valuable cultural relics' and 'good native cultural traditions' shall be protected. In 2009, the municipal government of Shenzhen city issued a set of guidelines to promote creative industry developments in which the 'chengzhongcun' is given special supportive policy within the framework of urban regeneration. The 'chengzhongcun' is encouraged to diversify its function so that it can catch up with urban development, and eventually attract investors and tourists from China and abroad.

Chinese researchers have attempted to examine the chance of promoting tourism in the 'chengzhongcun'. Working on the touristic city of Kunming, Shi and Wen (2009) proposed a strategy to convert ethnic 'chengzhongcuns' into scenic areas in accordance with local tourism planning. Urban experts and journalists have long been calling for new mentalities of incorporative development that aim not only to govern but also to serve the 'chengzhongcun' (Liu 2007). Interest in the 'chengzhongcun' has increased in every level of society. People from various backgrounds, such as artists, architects, business-men and scholars, are attracted by the 'chengzhongcun'. For instance, the pion-eering Second Guangzhou Triennial of 2005, under the theme of 'Alternative: Space of Special Modern Experiments', was the first art exhibition ever to dedicate a special session to the 'chengzhongcun'.

Art-led slum tourism as an alternative

A central question for slum tourism research is concerned with the reasons why tourists want to see the slum. During their fieldwork in Cape Town, Rolfes found that 'interest in local culture and people' was ranked first in a group of six options (Rolfes *et al.* 2009; Rolfes 2010). Similarly, Ma (2010) concludes from fieldwork in Dharavi, Mumbai, that 'cultural curiosity' is the primary motivator for slum tourists. Arguably, the slum might be seen as attractive because it appears to be the 'Other' of modernity and globality (Steinbrink 2012).

Chinese tourism is deeply embedded into its historical and cultural settings. Tourism sites in China are also made to accommodate this demand; for instance, new scenic projects are chosen to promote Buddhist pilgrimages to attract tourists (Li 2003). The 'chengzhongcun' does not fit in with this 'traditional' cultural picture. Most of the 'chengzhongcuns' are former agricultural villages that were built with no anticipation of attracting tourists. The cultural capital of the 'chengzhongcun' destination can be found either in the remnants of the rural past or in some new attractions resulting from its location in the city.

In the next section, three intriguing cases of art-led slum tours in China are introduced. Clearly, they differ from the slum tourism model of some other countries. Even within China, these pioneering cases reveal how diverse the situation can be.

Huangqiao: public art and civil engagement

Huangqiao was a village in the city of Hefei in eastern China. The settlement was demolished in December 2010 to make room for a railway extension

(Gao 2010). Until then, it was home to more than 200 autochthones and immigrant peasants and their families. Immigrants and their children often suffer from discrimination. For example, as a rule, immigrant children in China do not have access to urban public schools because local regulations exclude these students or allow admission only on the basis of an extra fee, which is often beyond the means of their parents. Therefore, the illegal Huangqiao School was set up by some social activists in 2007 to provide primary and pre-school education to immigrant children in neighbouring villages.

Having witnessed the precarious condition of the school on a charity trip, some artists and social activists decided to do something to change the situation (Zhang 2010). The idea was to set one session of the Second Hefei Contemporary Art Biennial in the slum. On 8–9 May 2010, the exhibition was opened to the public in the 'chengzhongcun' under the adopted title 'Happiness Huangqiao'. Since there was no place to house cultural activities, the artists transformed the space under a viaduct bridge next to the village into a makeshift 'gallery'. They also used the narrow village lanes as well as the school playground for performance arts. In total, more than seventy artists participated in this exhibition. This extraordinary event immediately became a great success in the art history of the city. The urban middle class was fascinated by the daring idea of placing modern art in the slum. There was no effective entrance control, but estimates from local media put the visitors at more than 3,000 on the first day alone (Anon. 2010).

Due to the exhibition, Huangqiao became very popular locally. The number of visitors to the village and the school soared in the following months. Donations and voluntary services were offered by many individuals and groups. Moreover, some people who were concerned with the education rights of the immigrant children made petitions to the educational authority of the city. Interestingly, compared to the social effects resulting from the event (i.e. a few thousand people visiting a 'chengzhongcun'), the role of public art per se is rather dubious. According to interviews with Huangqiao residents and online discussions by other participants, very few of the residents were able to reflect on the artworks despite the efforts of the curators and artists to reflect on discriminative citizenship. This event could not solve the citizenship problem at large: for instance, the immigrants and their children had to move to another 'chengzhongcun' when Huangqiao was demolished. Nonetheless, all 123 students were given permission to attend public schools in neighbouring urban communities as an acknowledgement of their right to education.

Dafen: place making through art business

If art was a catalyst in the Huangqiao case, then it should be called a driving force in the case of Dafen. Art never stops in the Dafen Oil Painting Village. In a city of hundreds of 'chengzhongcuns', Dafen village is the gem of Shenzhen and a must-go for many visitors. A local urban legend says that a businessman from Hong Kong came to Dafen in 1989 because of its low rents.

At that time Dafen was still a predominantly agricultural village, like many other 'chengzhongcuns' in Shenzhen. The business started with the recruitment of a few painters to work in Dafen, and the products were then exported via Hong Kong. The painters were commissioned to make copies of well-recognized, Western oil-painting masterpieces. It turned out to be a lucrative business, such that many more businessmen and painters followed suit. At the turn of the century, original work also started to emerge in the market, and nowadays it makes a significant contribution to turnover. It was not easy to break the stereotype of copy-making, but the shift towards original works has been proved to be the right direction (Tinari 2007).

Over the last two decades, Dafen has become a node in the global oil-painting market. It is said to be home to more than 800 galleries and over 5,000 artists (Dafen Village 2008). The high demand from overseas markets for counterfeit 'masterpieces' has supported Dafen's transformation financially. The local government has made great efforts to improve the working and living environment for art workers. Start-up artists, for instance, could manage to stay in the village thanks to the affordable housing project. In 2007, the RMB100 million (roughly equivalent to ten million euros) project, the Dafen Art Museum, was completed. The scale of the museum (16,000 square metres in total) has made it probably the most sizable art museum ever built for a 'chengzhongcun'. It is public building at the extreme. 'Anyone who comes to Dafen, businessmen, art collectors or other tourists, can drop in for a visit. You can even contact the painter and settle a deal via the Museum if you are interested', said a painter in an interview (Huang 2010). Every year, tens of thousands of visitors frequent the lanes and the square of Dafen.

It would be difficult for visitors to associate Dafen with a slum. In terms of ambience, it resembles the British planning concept of the 'urban village' to some extent. Simultaneously, it is promoted as a model of urban regeneration as well as a form of 'rural tourism'. In accordance with the promotion campaign entitled '2006 Year of Rural Tourism', organized by the National Tourism Agency of China, Dafen was designated as one of the five pilot villages in the programme 'Shenzhen Rural Tour' (Wang 2006). And in 2010 Dafen was invited to participate in the Best Urban Practices quarter of the 2010 Shanghai EXPO, representing the city of Shenzhen. Dafen Art Museum was the only participating site of its kind not located in the EXPO Park in Shanghai. Recent reports continually confirm that Dafen is one of the most popular tourism destinations in Shenzhen (Dafen Village 2011).

Times Museum: an unusual perspective

The Times Museum of Guangzhou is a private art museum. It is important not least for the fact that it is the second work in China of the Harvard-based architect Rem Koolhas (Zi and Xu 2010). The museum is revolutionary in its hybrid space usage. This museum is embedded into an ordinary residential building and consists of several floors in a high-rise apartment tower. The space on different floors is connected by independent elevators, thus giving the whole museum a 'T' structure (City Pictorial 2011). It carves out certain floors to maximize the variety of viewpoints. For instance, from the windows, the balcony or the two glasshouses in the exhibition hall, 'visitors could have a bird's view of the city landscape of northern Guangzhou, which is a typical yet distinctive Chinese urban–rural coverage area' (Times Museum 2011). It is a rather euphemistic expression to call the neighbouring 'chengzhongcun' an 'urban–rural coverage area'. Typically, residential projects like the one the museum belongs to are built on the outskirts of the city for reasons of space, and yet not to exceed the affordability of middle-class customers. The compromise results in the intrusion of gated communities into the 'chengzhongcun' area. To reach the Times Museum from the nearest metro station, for example, you need to cross the lanes of the neighbouring 'chengzhongcun' (City Pictorial 2011).

Although the Times Museum is not built in the 'chengzhongcun', it provides an extraordinary way of engaging with the city. Unlike ordinary art museums, it is not just meant as an urban cultural amenity. Rather, it stands as a unique 'urban observatory' of the dynamism between the city and the 'Other'; that is, the 'chengzhongcun'. While the favela is probably the best place in Rio for beach views, in Guangzhou it is the 'chengzhongcun' that constitutes a middle-class gaze. As the city expands, the contrast and struggle between the two types of residence is jarring. Although the 'chengzhongcun' may recede in the future, at the moment the museum offers a panoramic view of the evolution of the city without the stress of going into the 'chengzhongcun' itself. Since opening in 2010, the Times Museum has quickly become a popular cultural attraction of the city, and artists such as Ou Ning and his partners have chosen it for their exhibitions on reform and rebuilding of rural communities (Ou 2011).

Towards the inclusive city

The Millennium Goal of the United Nations – improving the living conditions of 100 million slum residents – is very likely to fail. Alan Gilbert (2007) was right to be sceptical about the legitimacy of intergovernmental initiatives. There is no one single strategy for all the slum problems of the world. The formidable challenge of the slum should be addressed in many ways, and tourism might be considered as one of them. Tourists are important representatives of civil society, and the act of tourism has the potential to work as dialogue between visiting and host societies. Moreover, tourism is a performative act that engages its environment in different stages; 'the same tourist may act out a medley of roles during a single tour or holiday' (Edensor 2000: 341). If we take the slum as one of many stages for tourists, then they are able to bring something into the otherwise segregated and excluded slum community. Empirical studies have rejected the presumption that slum tourists are unwanted or not welcome. The 'friendliness of residents' is the most important impression that tourists experience (Rolfes *et al.* 2009; Rolfes 2010). Ma also observes that being 'neutral' towards the tour is the typical attitude of slum residents. They do not report resentment to the tourist – on the contrary, the slum residents expect more interaction with the tour, rather than simply feeling that tourists 'stop and look' (Ma 2010: 1). As long as the tour obtains 'community consent' on the basis of 'democratic structures', there is no reason to object to it (Selinger and Outterson 2009).

Proponents of favela tourism claim that it helps the community: '[it] not only includes sanitation systems and other basic infrastructure, but emphasizes the importance of integrating the favelas both spatially and socially' (Freire-Medeiros 2009: 581). Were we to take comprehensive integration as the target of social development, communication and contact are vital to this process. Therefore, 'being exposed', as proclaimed by the urbanist Peter Marcuse, is not a problem, but rather the first step to the 'right to the city' (cited in Horlitz and Vogelpohl 2009). The criticism of tourists' voyeurism is not always a negative matter. Writing about the curious emotion of shame, Tucker argues that it 'should be seen as positive in its reflexive and self-evaluative role' (2009: 455). In the context of international tourism, it helps tourists 'to engage ethically in "doing tourism"' (ibid.). Due to this engaging power, slum tourism has the potential to act as the stimulating agency for a more inclusive urban policy.

Discussion

In this chapter I have taken a critical look at slum tourism in China. Instead of retrieving moral critiques, I argue for a new perspective: to view slum tourism as niche tourism, a type of tourism that actively engages the slum community. The slum is the niche for the marginalized population, especially the immigrants, in the city. Slum tourism has a right to exploit this market niche as long as consent is gained from local communities. Thanks to the performative nature of tourism, the potentialities of slum tourists as the agents of inclusive development should never be overlooked. Tourism can offer a democratic approach complementary to conventional power apparatuses such as governments, NGOs and international organizations.

To demonstrate the practicability of slum tourism, I have described three cases from China here. They reveal that situations and strategies could vary greatly, and yet they share similar effects. Although it was initially organized as an art exhibition, the visitors/tourists of 'Happiness Huangqiao' were also involved in the call for education rights for immigrant children. Their participation and presence did not change much about the 'chengzhongcun' at large, but the fate of the children was indeed changed as a result of those visits. In Dafen the tourists come only after an initial period of business development. They are not the decisive force in this process, but they can help to sustain the success of Dafen and perhaps even transform it. Contrary to the rule of seeing the slum tour as a kind of urban tourism, Dafen was intentionally promoted as a rural tourism destination. It reminds tourists of its rural origin, of course, but the current situation in Dafen also reveals the diversity and complexity of 'chengzhongcun tourism', or even slum tourism in general (Frenzel and Koens 2012). The case of the Times Museum is rather ambiguous. Although it was expected to provide a unique viewpoint of urban development, the very same process of development could undermine the view in the future. If someday it is encircled by high-rise buildings, it will lose one of its most important treasures. Tourists to the Times Museum may not even be aware that they have been led into a designed spatial framework of social engagement, yet their very presence has made the 'chengzhongcun' relevant to the city.

Research agendas on the deprivation and poverty of the Global South have drifted from causal analysis of colonial and post-colonial power relationships to practical poverty alleviation strategies. In the search for able agencies in community development, slum tourism provides a valuable alternative. It is worth noting that the contribution of slum tourism is far more profound than the 'creation of full-time or casual work opportunities' (Rogerson 2004: 253). As far as China is concerned, slum tourism has been actively engaging with community developments. Besides, the Chinese case takes a trajectory that is different from some renowned cases in other countries. Nonetheless, they share some fundamental similarities. I end this chapter with a call for more studies comparing China with other countries in the Global South.

Bibliography

Anon. (2010) 'The Hefei contemporary art biennale has made several "world records"' (Hefei dangdai yishu shuangnianzhan chuang duoxiang "shijie zhizui"). Available online at http://hf.house.sina.com.cn/scan/2010–05–12/175011141.html (accessed 5 June 2011).

Allen, G. and Brennan, F. (2004) *Tourism in the New South Africa*, London: I.B. Tauris.

Beauregard, R.A. and Bounds, A. (2000) 'Urban citizenship', in E.F. Isin (ed.) *Democracy, Citizenship and the Global City*, London: Routledge.

Briedenhaan, M. and Ramchander, P. (2006) 'Township tourism: blessing or blight? The case of Soweto in South Africa', in M.K. Smith and M. Robinson (eds) *Cultural Tourism in a Changing World: Politics, Participation and (Re)presentation*, Clevedon: Channel View.

Butcher, T. (2003) *The Moralisation of Tourism: Sun, Sand ... and Saving the World?*, Abingdon: Routledge.

City Pictorial (2011) 'The Times Museum of Guangdong: suspending on the air, hidden in a residence' (Guangdong shidai mushuguan, xuanzai ban'kong, cangyu minjian), *City Pictorial* (Chengshi Huabao), 273/4: 98–101.

Dafen Village (2008) About Dafen (Guanyu Dafen). Available online at www.cndafen.com (accessed 8 June 2011).

—— (2011) 'Dafen oil painting village nominated for the best cultural tourism route' (Dafen youhua cun ruxuan zuijia wenhua lvyou xianlu). Available online at www.cndafen.com/shownews.asp?id=753 (accessed 8 June 2011).

Echtner, C.M. and Prasad, P. (2003) 'The context of third world tourism marketing', *Annals of Tourism Research*, 30(3): 660–82.

Edensor, T. (2000) 'Staging tourism: tourists as performers', *Annals of Tourism Research*, 27: 322–44.

Freire-Medeiros, B. (2009) 'The favela and its touristic transits', *Geoforum*, 40: 580–8.

Frenzel, F. and Koens, K. (2012) 'Slum tourism: developments in a young field of interdisciplinary tourism research', *Tourism Geographies*, 14(2): forthcoming.

Gans, H.J. (2002) 'Uses and misuses of concepts in American social science research: variations on Loïc Wacquant's theme of "Three Pernicious Premises in the Study of the American Ghetto"', *International Journal of Urban and Regional Research*, 21(3): 504–7.

Gao, C. (2010) 'Solution for the education of the 123 students in Huangqiao School guaranteed' (Huangqiao xiaoxue 123 ming mingong zinv shangxue you zhuoluo). Available online at http://ah.anhuinews.com/qmt/system/2010/11/19/003479945. shtml (accessed 14 December 2010).

Gilbert, A. (2007) 'The return of the slum: does language matter?', *International Journal of Urban and Regional Research*, 31(4): 697–713.

Grimm, N.B., Faeth, S.H., Golubiewski, N.E., Redman, C.L., Wu, J., Bai, X. and Briggs, J.M. (2008) 'Global change and the ecology of cities', *Science*, 319: 756–60.

He, J., Li, H. and Wang, Q. (2004) 'Rural tourism in China: a case study of Nongjiale in the Chengdu metropolitan area', *Mountain Research and Development*, 24(3): 260–2.

Hestbaek, C. (2010) 'Rio Top Tour helping favela business', *The Rio Times*, 12 October 2010. Available online at http://riotimesonline.com/brazil-news/rio-business/poverty-safari-or-fabulous-favelas> (accessed 30 August 2011).

Horlitz, S. and Vogelpohl, A. (2009) 'Something can be done! A report on the conference "Right to the City, prospects for critical urban theory and practice"', Berlin, November 2008, reprinted in *International Journal of Urban and Regional Studies*, 33(4):1067–72.

Hsu, S., Dehuang, N, and Woodside, A.G. (2009) 'Storytelling research of consumers' self-reports of urban tourism experiences in China', *Journal of Business Research*, 62: 1223–54.

Huang, J. (2010) 'The road towards art and internationalisation of a village in the city' (Chengzhongcun de yishuhua he guojihua zhilu), *Chinese Cultural Daily* (Zhongguo Wenhua Bao), 11 November.

Koven, S. (2004) *Slumming: Sexual and Social Politics in Victorian London*, Princeton, NJ: Princeton University Press.

Li, Y. (2003) 'Development of the Nanshan cultural tourism zone in Hainan, China: achievements made and issues to be resolved', *Tourism Geographies*, 5(4): 436–45.

Liu, Y. (2007) 'Focusing on the slum from the perspective of culture services' (Cong wenhua fuwu jiaodu guanzhu chengzhongcun), *Shenzhen Business Daily* (Shenzhen Shangbao), 11 September 2007.

Lu, Y. (2007) 'Step into the favela of the second largest city in Brazil, Rio de Janeiro' (Zoujin baxi di'er da chengshi liyuereneilu de pinminku). Available online at http://gb.cri.cn/14558/2007/01/31/1865@1430137.htm (accessed 12 June 2011).

Ma, B. (2010) 'A trip into the controversy: a study of slum tourism travel motivations', 2009–2010 Penn Humanities Forum on Connections. Available online at http://repository.upenn.edu/uhf_2010/12 (accessed 8 June 2011).

Marrison, J. (2005) 'Wise to the streets', *The Guardian*, 15 December. Available online at www.guardian.co.uk/travel/2005/dec/15/argentina.buenosaires.darktourism? INTCMP=SRCH (accessed 30 August 2011).

Marson, D. (2011) 'From mass tourism to niche tourism', in P. Robinson, S. Heitmann and P. Dieke (eds) *Research Themes for Tourism*, Wallingford: CAB International.

Meschkank, J. (2011) 'Investigations into slum tourism in Mumbai: poverty tourism and the tensions between different constructions of reality', *GeoJournal*, 76: 47–62.

National Tourism Agency of China (2000) *Management Regulations of Tourism Development and Planning*, Bejing: National Tourism Agency of China.

Ou, N. (2011) 'Bishan project at Guangzhou Times Museum' (Bishan jihua zai guangzhou shidai meishuguan). Available online at www.alternativearchive.com/ouning/article.asp?id=834 (accessed 22 June 2011).

Rogerson, C.M. (2004) 'Urban tourism and small tourism enterprise development in Johannesburg: the case of township tourism', *GeoJournal*, 60: 249–57.

Rolfes, M. (2010) 'Poverty tourism: theoretical reflections and empirical findings regarding an extraordinary form of tourism', *GeoJournal*, 75: 421–42.

Rolfes, M., Steinbrink, M. and Uhl, C. (2009) *Townships as Attraction: A Case Study on Township Tourism in Cape Town*, Potsdam: Universitätsverlag.

Selinger, E. and Outterson, K. (2009) 'The ethics of poverty tourism', *Boston University School of Law Working Paper No. 09–29*. Available online at www.bu.edu/law/faculty/scholarship/workingpapers/2009.html (accessed 22 May 2011).

Shi, M. and Wen, Z. (2009) 'A tourism-led urbanization approach to the 'chengzhongcun' regeneration in Kunming' (Kunming chengzhongcun gaizao de lvyou chengshi hua tujing), *Science & Technology Information* (Keji Xinxi), 34: 389–90.

Steinbrink, M. (2012) 'We did the slum! Reflections on urban poverty tourism from a historical perspective', *Tourism Geographies*, 14(2): forthcoming.

Stone, P.R. (2009) 'Dark tourism: morality and new moral spaces', in R. Sharpley and P.R. Stone (eds) *The Darker Side of Travel: The Theory and Practice of Dark Tourism*, Bristol: Channel View.

Tan, S. (2009) 'Show off happiness in the slum' (Zai pinminku shai xingfu), *New Weekly* (Xin Zhoukan), 295: 70–3.

Times Museum (2011) 'About us'. Available online at www.timesmuseum.org/about (accessed 12 June 2011).

Tinari, P. (2007) 'Original copies: the Dafen oil painting village', *Art Forum International*, 46: 344–51.

Tucker, H. (2009) 'Recognizing emotion and its postcolonial potentialities: discomfort and shame in a tourism encounter in Turkey', *Tourism Geographies*, 11(4): 444–61.

UN-Habitat (2003a) *The Challenge of Slums: Global Report on Human Settlement 2003*, Nairobi: UN-Habitat.

—— (2003b) *Slums of the World: The Face of Urban Poverty in the New Millennium?*, Nairobi: UN-Habitat.

—— (2007) *Slum Dwellers to Double by 2030: Millennium Development Goal Could Fall Short*, Nairobi: UN-Habitat.

Urban Planning, Land and Resource Commission of Shenzhen Municipality (2005) 'Comprehensive plan for "chengzhongcun" regeneration of Shenzhen municipality: 2005–2010' (Shenzhen shi chengzhongcun (jiucun) gaizao zongti guihua gangyao (2005–2010)).

Wang, Y. (2006) 'Chengzhongcun' joins special tourism routes (Chengzhongcun chengwei tese lvyou xianlu), *Southern Metropolis Daily* (Nanfang Dushi Bao), 9 March 2006.

Weiner, E. (2008) 'Slum visits: tourism or voyeurism?', *The New York Times*, 9 March. Available online at http://travel.nytimes.com/2008/03/09/travel/09heads.html?scp=1&sq=slum tourism&st=cse (accessed 12 June 2011).

Williams, C. (2008) 'Ghettourism and voyeurism, or challenging stereotypes and raising consciousness? Literary and non-literary forays into the favelas of Rio de Janeiro', *Bulletin of Latin American Research*, 27(4): 483–500.

Williams, S. (2009) *Tourism Geography: A New Synthesis*, Abingdon: Routledge.

Wu, F., Zhang, F. and Webster, C. (2011) 'Informality and "slum clearance": the development and demolition of urbanized villages in the Chinese peri-urban area', paper presented at the Annual RC21 Conference, Amsterdam, 7–9 July.

Yusuf, S. and Nabeshima, K. (2008) 'Optimizing urban development', in S. Yusuf and T. Saich (eds) *China Urbanizes: Consequences, Strategies, and Policies*, Washington, DC: World Bank.

Zhang, Y. (2010) 'The happiness between chaos and entanglement' (Fenluan jiuchan zhong de xingfu), in Y. Zhang (ed.) *Huangqiao Happiness Project: 2010 Hefei Contemporary Art Biennial: Art and Literature* (Huangqiao Xingfu Jihua: 2010 Hefei Dangdai Yishu Shuangnianzhan Yishu Wenxian), Hefei: Hefei Yunhua Media.

Zi, L. and Xu, L. (2010) 'Times Museum was actually a work of Rem Koohas' (Shidai meishuguan yuanshi kuhasi sheji), *Southern Metropolis Daily* (Nanfang Dushi Bao), 16 December.

12 Poverty tourism as advocacy

A case in Bangkok[1]

Kisnaphol Wattanawanyoo

Introduction: slum development in Bangkok

The development of large-scale slums in the city of Bangkok dates back to the 1950s, when they were predominantly formed near to big industrial developments, such as the cement-manufacturing industry (Rabibhadana 1999). Other slums formed next to traditional Buddhist temples and along the river and canals of the city, as there were still unoccupied spaces and low rental rates available. Old communities began to expand and attract more people from rural parts of the country to the capital city, mainly for work and to study. With the rapid urbanization of Bangkok city, the slums have also grown over the last forty years, and in the old historical area of inner Bangkok–Rattanakosin.

Krung Rattanakosin

Krung Rattanakosin, or 'Rattanakosin City', may be regarded as one of the most valuable cultural heritages of inner Bangkok. It covers an area of 5.8 square kilometres and includes three particular parts: the inner Krung Rattanakosin (1.8 km²), located on the east bank of the Chao Phraya River; the outer Krung Rattanakosin (2.3 km²), located on the further east bank of the Chao Phraya River; and the Krung Rattanakosin West, located on the west river bank (Thonbury) (17 km²).

The Government of Thailand has declared Krung Rattanakosin to be an area of conservation, under the responsibility of the Committee for Conservation and Development of Krung Rattanakosin and Old Towns (Office of Environmental Policy and Planning 1996). Since 1976, efforts to conserve Krung Rattanakosin have focused mainly on the promotion of green areas and open spaces, the conservation and restoration of old valuable buildings and architecture, and the reduction of building and traffic densities. Rattanakosin area is home to about twenty-one registered communities or neighbourhoods. One community (Pom Mahakan) is not formally recognized and is considered a slum by the local authority and the public. The origin of the community dates back to King Rama III of the Chakri Dynasty of the early nineteenth century, and lies behind the old Bangkok city wall. It accommodates 67 households and 269 inhabitants in total, who live in 51 houses, some more than 70 years old. The Pom Mahakan Community is located adjacent to Rachadamneon Avenue, next to the city moat (Figure 12.1). It sits in the National Heritage site of Rattanakosin, next to old temples, canals, palaces and traditional houses (Prakitnonthakan 2006). Its informal nature seems to contradict the urban development plans of the Rattanokosin area.

Rattanakosin historical district has been at the centre of urban development plans for some time. A first mega-project to develop the area dates back to 1982. As a result, during the 1980s and 1990s, the landscape of Bangkok

Figure 12.1 Existing Pom Mahakan community and the old city wall
Source: photo by Kisnaphol Wattanawanyoo.

became a contested terrain where contrasting and conflicting ideals and representations of urban life and its organization were debated. This was symbolized in the conservation master plan that was released in 1995. It views 'historic' Rattanakosin as a stage of objects expressing in architectonic and visual form the authorized memory of the city (Askew 2002). More recent master plans were geared towards the development of tourist attractions in the area, and the development of luxury shopping centres. Since then, local residents have experienced a range of changes, often including the clearance of old housing and communities. A variety of projects that were developed in the most recent Krung Rattanakosin master plan impacted on the local community. For example, the plan included decisions to conserve and improve the Mahakan Fortress and the Phra Nakhon gate and wall (Figure 12.2). The scenario for the Inner Rattankosin zone made no provision to allow for the continued residence of the people who still lived and worked there (Askew 2002).

The Bangkok Metropolitan Administration (BMA) has also enacted a pilot project in which parts of the Pom Mahakan community next to the old fortress were cleared to make way for a park during the year 2002–03 (Figure 12.3). The community protested and 'shut itself off' to the public, but nevertheless failed to resist the BMA. Century-old wooden houses were destroyed in the process of clearing one third of the community. In contrast to the recognized communities, Pom Mahakan inhabitants have no legal right to the land. However, the community has been rooted there for over 100 years and has witnessed the eighteen-year marathon struggle to assert the community's right

Figure 12.2 The vision of the master plan emphasizing Krung Rattanakosin's heritage with the promotion of green areas and open spaces: views and vistas for a 'touristic background'

Source: Office of Environmental Policy and Planning (1996).

Figure 12.3 The new community plan and existing new park by the BMA
Source: Bangkok Metropolitan Administration.

to stay. The Pom Mahakan community is perceived as an eyesore in the light of the adjacent National Heritage site by the BMA (Chaiyaset 2004), which thus continues to pursue the removal of the community. However, such plans have met with scepticism and resistance, and several Bangkok governors have failed to find a solution for the conflict between urban development plans and slums in the area.

The invisible wall versus the invisible community

For some time, the community has worked with NGOs and academic institutions to protect its existence. Members have lobbied the BMA by designing their own development plans in which the new park could coexist with the community, which would take a role in maintaining the park. Community members participated in meetings and discussions, and suggested different views and ideas. Their plan (in consultation with Silpakorn University) was rejected by the BMA, and the community still faces eviction. Despite the daily struggle to maintain its existence, the community has also lived a normal life, largely hidden by the wall behind which it settled.

Our intervention into the conflict came with some bias towards protecting the community. One of the key concerns was related to its visibility as part of Bangkok's heritage. In this context, the 'discovery' of the community as an attraction by backpacker tourists offered, in our view, an interesting avenue for exploring the potential of developing a heightened sense of its value by both the city administration and inhabitants. Following meetings with the community, we came up with a proposal that tackles the invisibility of the daily life of the community while highlighting the historical heritage of the area and using the wall, based on the simple assumption that there must be a way for this conflict to be reconciled without an eviction of the community.

'Invisible Wall' (2010) by the Urban Media Society

In 2006 this project started with '(RE) Writing City', an initial event for public participation and awareness in collaboration with various organizations, such as academic institutions, the media, artists, architects, planners, activists and the affected communities around the Rattankosin area. The event included an art exhibition/installation, workshops, lectures, seminars, discussions and performances, and proved to be highly critical of the top-down approach of city planning pursued by the BMA.

Following up on this initial project, in 2009 the Urban Media Society (UMS) was formed and collaborated with the Pom Mahakan community. As a result of this collaboration, network-building continued and resulted in a steady expansion of our critical activities. The starting point of this work was and is to demand democratic approaches to planning. In an ever-changing urban environment and society, which impacts on the quality of life of everybody, planning cannot be pursued in a hierarchical manner. To be successful and sustainable, planning needs to incorporate people from the bottom up.

Our proposal and main message

The proposal was based on seven key dualities that structure the conflict of urban development we are facing in the case of the Pom Mahakan community: visible/invisible, physical/virtual, presence/absence, old/new, still/moving, appearance/disappearance and continuity/discontinuity.

Our proposal was to create a visual intervention on the old city wall of inner historical Bangkok (Figure 12.4). Telling the stories of the urban communities and their histories, we projected moving images on to the city wall. Our idea was to provoke and raise the awareness of an urban narrative of this area and the existence of a small community living behind the wall. During daytime the slum may seem lifeless and invisible, as if nothing happens. But, as night

Figure 12.4 'Invisible Wall' (2010) – UMS participation in mAAN*Y 2010 design
competition in Singapore

Source: author.

falls, our intervention was designed to appear and to show the presence of
the community behind the wall. This was aimed to make people aware of a
small neighbourhood behind the wall through multimedia projections and
moving images.

Over two months of preparation and collaboration with the community, the
UMS team encountered some difficulties in dealing with public space. We
intentionally wanted to install our visual projection on the real 'heritage wall',
but due to heritage regulations we could not do as we planned. We had to adjust
the screening and project the visual images on the other side of the community
– perpendicular to the existing wall and facing the new park made by the BMA.
The content of the screening was based on the narratives created by one UMS
member: Aphiwat Saengphatthaseema (a documentary film maker), together
with the community.

At the Loy Krathong Festival[2] on 19–21 November 2010, the entries into a
visual diary and stories from the community were communicated to the public
and passers-by (Figure 12.5). Some of the people went to buy fireworks – one
of the Pom Mahakan community's popular products – and thus had a chance
to view the projected images. While some just ignored the projections, many
became curious and stayed on for some time. The show also resulted in
increasing discussions over the fate of the community (Dumrongkwan n.d.).

Conclusion

We intended to draw some attention to the community and the fact that the
city was pursuing a problematic policy of 'creative destruction' (Harvey 2003:

Figure 12.5 Realisation of the 'Invisible Wall' projects – on the Loy Krathong
festival nights. Two screens form a visual diary of the Pom Mahakan
community. This is from the existing new park, which used to be a part
of the community.

Source: photo by Kisnaphol Wattanawanyoo.

26) in the Krung Rattanakosin Master Plan. The shows also heightened the
levels of participation by the community. Likewise, more tourists became
aware of the community, and the first guided tours emerged afterwards.
Similar developments have taken place in other communities and slums of
Bangkok, such as Nanglerng and Banglumpoo. These have been organized by
the communities themselves and, sometimes, with support from the government and NGOs. More mainstream commercial tour operators have so far not
been involved. Other communities have also opened up the idea of community
tourism. They bear and share cultural values, lifestyles and the low-profile
architectural heritage.

Whether this new kind of slum tourism will be well received by the
mainstream tourism industry and society remains to be seen. The growing
attraction of the Pom Mahakam community is, however, indicative of the
potential of tourism to highlight the value of 'alternative' heritage. While we
consider that the community has a right to its place regardless of its ability to
generate tourism revenue, this is clearly an important bargaining tool in the
ongoing conflict with the BMA. In this way, tourism may help these informal
communities to stay.

Notes

1 I would like to thank the following people for their support and collaboration: the Pom Mahakan community, the Urban Media Society (UMS), the modern Asian Architecture Network-Youth (mAAN*Y), re:ACT Singapore, and the School of Architecture and Design, King Mongkut's University of Technology Thonburi.
2 Loy Krathong Day is a popular festival in Thailand, celebrated on the full-moon day, of the (usually) twelfth lunar month. During that period, the water level is high enough for floating a 'krathong' – a traditional lotus-shaped banana leaf vessel – on the river. This is in common with the similar Hindu-Brahman belief of paying respect to the water goddess.

Bibliography

Askew, M. (2002) *Bangkok: Place, Practice, and Representation*, London: Routledge.

Chaiyaset, P. (2004) 'Pom Mahakan: the production of space', unpublished thesis, Thammasat University, Bangkok.

Dumrongkwan, K. (n.d.) 'Pom Mahakan community: countdown towards the "like to do" development versus the beginning of "righteous" existence'. Available online at www.greenworld.or.th/greenworld/local/1051 (accessed 22 December 2010).

Harvey, D. (2003) 'The city as body politic', in J. Schneider and I. Susser (eds) *Wounded Cities*, Oxford: Berg.

Office of Environmental Policy and Planning (1996) *The Master Plan for Conservation and Development of Krung Rattanakosin*, Bangkok: Office of Environmental Policy and Planning.

Prakitnonthakan, C. (2006) *Old Wooden Houses of Pom Mahakan Community*, Research Report, Bangkok: Research and Development Institute, Silpakorn University.

Rabibhadana, A. (1999) *Slum: Knowledge and Truth*, Bangkok: TRF.

13 Curatorial interventions in township tours

Two trajectories

Shelley Ruth Butler

Introduction

Every township tour in South Africa tells a story. The stories are powerful, particularly because they are illustrated by panoramic views of informal settlements, glimpses of interiors of private homes, classrooms of children dressed smartly in uniforms, or plastic sundries artfully arranged on a cloth spread out on the pavement or rough ground of an informal market. The stories are persuasive because audiences are immersed in them, in a bodily sense, as they listen and look, but also touch objects and people, smell unfamiliar odours, and sometimes taste a 'strange brew' (Butler 2005). As such, the creators of township tours and their guides are involved in acts of curation, of presenting the 'world as exhibition' (Mitchell 1989). Exhibitions 'entail the bringing together of unlikely assemblages of people, things, ideas, texts, spaces, and different media' (Basu and Macdonald 2007: 9). While exhibitions are typically associated with the hermetic world of museums and galleries, increasingly they occur in vernacular spaces, whether these are public spaces formally demarcated as heritage sites, or informal venues, such as a display of photographs in a community centre. Exhibitions can be created for locals, outsiders or both, and they can involve processes of local and national self-representation. Tourism has emerged as a powerful force in exhibition making; it immerses audiences 'in situ' in environments such as townships in ways that museums increasingly aspire to do (Kirshenblatt-Gimblett 1998).

In this chapter, I explore this notion of curatorship in relation to township tours. In response to critical assessments of township tours offered by academics and journalists, as well as by tour operators and tourists, I will propose two 'curatorial interventions' that seek to shift power dynamics inherent in township tourism. While this is an imaginary and conceptual exercise, it is grounded in my ethnographic research on township tours, as well as in museum studies and critical theory. As I will show, township tours are complex cultural productions situated at intersections between education and entertainment, gravitas and adventure, responsible tourism and desires to encounter 'difference', and between community development and the market economy.

The interventions that I propose are offered as catalysts for reflection and dialogue with guides, as well as with other critics and consumers of the tours.

My premise is that township tours have symbolic and economic consequences that matter especially for locals, but also for visitors. Therefore, the creation of township tours entails responsibility. This recalls the late-fourteenth-century etymology of the term 'curator' (*curatus*), when it was primarily associated with 'caring for' and 'being responsible for' others. Yet, judging by critiques levelled against township tourism, the question of care is not always well handled. My curatorial interventions respond to three critiques that are often made of township tours: they are voyeuristic, to the point of mimicking safaris (Carroll 2004); they reproduce colonial stereotypes of Africans as 'traditional' (Witz *et al.* 2001); and, finally, they offer little economic benefit and support for marginal communities (for example, Rogerson 2004, 2005; Briedenhann and Ramchander 2006). I will begin by showing how and why township tours – even those whose operators have good intentions – are implicated in these problematics. Following this, I will propose two curatorial interventions that seek to destabilize the township tour structures and dynamics that I've described. The first intervention attempts to shift the conditions of encounter between tourists and local residents, so that the discursive and economic interests of hosts are prioritized. The second intervention proposes a change in the route of township tours, with the goal of showing how townships are an integral part of South African cities, as opposed to being conceived of as marginal and exotic spaces. Finally, I will discuss potential problems associated with each curatorial intervention. This will shed light on the challenges of reforming township tours given the symbolic and political economy within which they are enmeshed.

On safari: exposure and inequality

Voyeurism is the most common critique levelled against township tours. The basic structure of any township tour involves busing tourists to and through the townships. Residents of townships recognize that vans and buses carrying tourists through their townships imitate safaris. They complain of 'a baboon attitude' and of feeling as though their home is being treated like a zoo (Mackey 2000). These metaphoric associations are heightened because of the intersecting legacies of racist evolutionary theories and imperial museological practices that conflate non-western others with the natural and animal world (Butler 2002; Mackenzie 2009). This is not simply a theoretical legacy, but one that is embedded in everyday material culture, whether this be through outmoded dioramas in natural history museums or postcards and tourism brochures that depict Africans as 'traditional' and 'tribal', as existing beyond the reaches of modernity, industrialization and post-industrialism.

Township tours expose people's everyday lives to public view, with the worst-case scenarios verging on 'social pornography' (Kirshenblatt-Gimblett 1998: 54). My own worst-case experience of this kind occurred in 2004, when two tour guides (one a local resident) took a small group of tourists to an informal settlement on the edge of the township of Soweto, where we visited a family with a very disabled child. The goal was to raise donations for the child, but the visit was deeply troubling, as it drew heavily on tropes of pity, charity, helplessness and paternalism. While it is true that bus tours also travel through wealthier parts of the city (en route to the townships, for instance), they do not enter these residential neighbourhoods to look 'ethnographically' at how the locals live. Township tours take advantage of the lack of private space in many townships, as well as their lively sociality. As architect Lindsay Bremner writes with reference to Kliptown on the outskirts of Soweto:

> During the day, everyone is out. To stay at home is to miss out on the life of the street. Private space is small and cramped; things spill out. The prized vantage point is the street – a place to watch, view, greet, sell, and drink; to produce and reproduce the life of the collective.
>
> (2004: 523)

The classic image of a township tour is that of tourists who, encapsulated in their vans and buses, watch others, but are rarely scrutinized themselves. As tourists busily take photographs, they enact what Johaness Fabian, in the context of his critique of anthropology, calls the 'denial of coevalness' (1983: 31). This is a distancing process, in which subjects are placed 'in a Time other than the present of the producer of anthropological discourse' (ibid.: 43). A parallel dynamic occurs in township bus tours in relation to the tourist cum adventurer cum ethnographer. At stake is the denial of shared, intersubjective time (ibid.). As the tourist passes through the township, he or she is para-doxically distant and intimate, removed and invasive.

These parallels between tourism and classical anthropology are most obvious when tours focus visitors' attention on exotic sites of difference: scenes of women carrying children in wraps on their backs; a glimpse of initiates pre-paring for rites of passage; traditional dance performances; the outdoor cooking and selling of 'smilies' (sheep heads) and other livestock that are not consumed by most westerners; 'ethnic crafts'; and a visit to a 'sangoma' – a traditional healer. Such tours are critiqued by public historians who note that any pretence of an educational tour that focuses on the apartheid past invariably gives way to stereotypes of townships as an 'extension of the rural village in an expression of timeless ethnicity' (Witz *et al.* 2001: 285).

Township tour operators and tourists are aware of the moral dilemma poised by voyeurism with regard to township tours in South Africa, as is the case with comparable favela tours on the outskirts of Rio de Janeiro (Butler 2010; Freire-Medeiros 2010; Rolfes 2010). In response to the anxiety and guilt associated with township tourism, tour operators promise that their tours will be conducted with sensitivity. The visibility of this claim in township-tour brochures and websites has increased in the post-apartheid era, alongside the rise of 'alternative tourism'. The latter can be defined as 'forms of tourism that are consistent with natural, social and community values, and which allow both hosts and guests to enjoy positive and worthwhile interaction and shared experiences' (Eadington and Smith 1992: 3). Brochures promise interaction, experience and intimacy: 'join us on an intimate voyage of discovery' says the well-respected Cape Town company Legend Tours. Increasingly, brochures depict locals and visitors in a shared social space, usually in restaurants. Brochures (and tourists) also circulate photos of residents and visitors with linked arms, smiling for cameras, not unlike a family snapshot. Tourists are also encouraged to visit and join families and communities in townships, by choosing a tour that includes 'walkabouts', in order to visit markets, homes, hostels, shebeens and restaurants, by staying in a local B & B or, most recently, by going on a bike tour of Soweto (Soweto Bicycle Tours 2012). In each case, the tourist body is no longer 'protected' inside a bus; rather, the emphasis is on insertion into the fabric of daily life. Such reforms suit the post-Fordist service economy, in which middle-class tourists reject mass tourism in favour of alternatives such as eco-tourism (Munt 1994). In this economy, township tour companies try to brand themselves as alternative, niche projects, even as they become mainstream. As township tour companies compete against each other, each tries to position itself as being really alternative, a strategy that hints at the fragility of the tours as they become more popular.

However, as John Hutnyck (1996) points out with regard to comparable tourism forms in Calcutta, walkabouts, and other initiatives that are meant to diffuse voyeurism, often intensify problems of exposure that are already experienced by poor communities. Because the tourist economy ensures that the 'customer' remains emotionally comfortable (Tyson 2008), potentially difficult issues in encounters with poverty are suppressed. Instead, visitors gaze with respect and curiosity, and buy souvenirs knowing that they are contributing to the local economy and community development initiatives.

The first curatorial intervention that I propose disrupts this service economy, so that the emphasis becomes one of township residents looking at, and interviewing, tourists, as opposed to the reverse. It fits into a post-colonial tradition of 'reversing the gaze' (Ashcroft 1999: 229), as well as that of critical pedagogy, which examines power relations that are erased by celebratory images of global citizenship and rainbow nations (Giroux 1992). My second curatorial intervention also responds to the problem of voyeurism, but is theoretically informed by critical white studies, which attempt to make visible categories of social life that are unmarked and dominant (Frankenberg 1992; Mackey 2002). Finally, I am cognizant of critiques that point to the limitations of township tours as a local 'pro-poor' development strategy. Though township tourism is a growing segment of the cultural tourism market, township residents do not benefit greatly from this. Since the global tourist industry is characterized by 'leakage' problems, the majority of what international tourists spend on their visits to 'the South' does not go directly to local communities. This structural problem is intensified in South Africa, given the domestic tourism industry's racial stratification. Despite the post-apartheid era's focus

on reconstruction and reconciliation, as well as on black economic empowerment, blacks in the tourism industry work in the lowest paying and least stable
jobs (Rogerson 2005). There is little training and/or support for emerging black
entrepreneurs (Goudie *et al.* 1999) and a lack of community consultation about
township tourism (Briedenhann and Ramchander 2006). My interventions
cannot reverse these inequalities, though they may serve to make them visible
and difficult to accept.

Curatorial intervention one

When You Come Here: a photography project

Photography by visitors is a prevalent activity during township tours, as is
the case with favela tours (Freire-Meideiros 2008). Tourists seek out panoramic shots of informal settlements, close-ups of signs of the exotic, such
as a sangoma's herbal medicines, and photos of local people. Replicating the
'I was there' trope of anthropological fieldwork, tourists take many photos of
themselves in the townships, especially alongside guides, hosts and children.
For the most part, these photos depict joy, through smiling faces, and the brief
intimacy of strangers who hold hands, wrap their arms around each other's
waists, and share food and drink. As such, the photos stand as a counterpoint
to dominant cinematic and media images of townships as being overdetermined
by poverty, unemployment, crowdedness, criminality, blackness and a dis-
orderly mix of urban and rural lifeways (Ellapen 2007). For most township
tour guides, a major pedagogical goal is to dismantle such stereotypes. Thus,
even though most tourists want to witness poverty – it is the new authenticity
(Butler 2010) – they are also exposed and open to other visions of townships.
These frames include cultural vibrancy and creativity, community development
and entrepreneurial spirit, the history of apartheid and signs of middle-class
lifestyles. But, regardless of the context, tourists take photos of their hosts and
other people that they encounter. During two decades of tours since the end
of apartheid, guides have increasingly insisted that tourists ask for permission
before taking photos. Western Cape Direct Action Tours (WECAT) prohibits
the taking of photos from within the van as well as all landscape images.
Tourists must ask permission to take a photograph, and copies must be returned
to the subjects and the WECAT office.[1] This requirement makes it impossible
for the tourist to assume an invincible, panoptic point of view, in which she
or he takes photos with impunity (Kirshenblatt-Gimblett 1998). Rather, a
temporary relationship of coevalness is proposed, in which tourists and
residents share time, space and experience. Yet such encounters are always
instigated by the tourists.

If township residents hold the cameras, can power dynamics be changed?
My curatorial intervention, which I call *When You Come Here*, experiments
with this idea by enabling township residents to photograph and interview
tourists, and to exhibit the results in either material or digital form. My project

is inspired by some local precedents. For example, at Spier wine estate in 2004, the avant-garde troupe 'Third World Bunfight' presented a satiric performance in which performers, disguised as gigantic cameras on legs, 'danced' among the outdoor audience, which was largely white and included locals and international tourists (Third World Bunfight 2010). Guests reclined on couches set under trees and billowing white curtains; they sat in tree houses enjoying wine and attentive service, all in a garden and winery setting that was theatrical, serene and funky. Meanwhile, the gigantic cameras bothered, interrupted, teased and 'took photos' of their audience. The mimicry of tourist behaviour was unambiguous and the tone of the intervention was humorous.

In a different, pedagogically oriented project supported by the Getty Conservation Institute, a diverse group of youths was given cameras to 'picture Cape Town' (Younge 1996). The result is a striking collection of black-and-white photos entitled *Picture Cape Town: Landmarks of a New Generation*, which registers the mood of South Africa in transition, addressing colonial and apartheid legacies as well as glimpses of transformation. For instance, a photo by Odidi Mfenyana shows two youthful white 'ravers' with wild striped leggings, walking confidently through the township of Nyanga. The photographer loves the freedom of expression that the young men are committed to (ibid.). From a sociological point of view, their freedom to move through the township reveals a particular historical moment (Taylor 1996). Similarly, an image of silhouettes lingering at beautiful Camps Bay beach in Cape Town has a relationship to the practice and experience of democracy. 'Everyone goes to the Beach' comments the photographer Dominique Johnson (Younge 1996: 92).

The politics of social space and visual culture are felt intensely in South Africa. Thus, creative projects exploring social and physical boundaries are deeply resonant. For instance, Idasa, a democracy think-tank in Cape Town, organized a photographic and interviewing project that involved youths and commuters exploring post-apartheid segregation and prejudice, as experienced in public trains (Idasa n.d.). More broadly, collaborative initiatives involving giving disadvantaged youths cameras to evoke their life experiences were popularized during the 1990s in the United States (Ballerini 1997). Alluding to the post-colonial concept of reversing the gaze, photographer Jim Hubbard set up 'Shooting Back' projects in which children from homeless shelters and from an Indian reservation were given cameras to document their lives, in order to bring the 'cries of the economically disadvantaged to the powerful and prosperous' (Hubbard, quoted in Ballerini 1997: 161). These types of collaborative projects, which are organized by respected and socially committed photographers such as Hubbard, May Ellen Mark, Jim Goldberg and Wendy Ewald, have resulted in travelling exhibitions and coffee-table books. Asking why these projects receive widespread approval and acclaim, Julia Ballerini (1997) concludes that, despite their moments of social and political critique, the projects subtly assimilate conservative American ideology, with its emphasis on family values, self-help, volunteerism, empathy and philanthropy, as opposed to calls for government intervention.

Curatorial and editorial decisions about the public presentation of photos of marginalized subjects have also contributed to a proliferation of romantic and exotic representations of 'others', a critique that is valid in relation to township tours. Ultimately, these projects may 'serve donors more than recipients' (ibid.: 162). This is precisely the result that I want to avoid, or at least subvert, with *When You Come Here*. For this reason, I propose turning the camera towards tourists, as opposed to producing more documentation of townships. There is already a rich tradition of self-representation in the townships, including the circulation of protest art and the more recent 'high art' careers of artists such as Willie Bester and Moshewka Langa, whose work is closely connected with the materiality of township life (Williamson and Jamal 1996). Moreover, research methodologies that explore how tourists look at and photograph tourist sites and 'Others' are well established (Urry 1994; Palmer 2009; Robinson and Picard 2009). This approach enables the productive analyses of power relations, intercultural encounters, identity and place-making. Many artistic and literary productions also shed light on tourists and tourism, through satiric portrayals of prototypical 'ugly' tourists (Kincaid 1988), or via strategies of irony and juxtaposition, in order to explore different moods and contradictions that characterize tourist encounters in conditions of inequality (Phillips 1998; Tribe 2008).

My curatorial intervention departs from these various traditions, since its central activity is the creation of formal and semi-formal portraits of tourists, taken in photo studios in the townships and in public spaces that tourists visit, including community markets and tourism centres, such as Sivuyile Tourism Centre, which opened in Guguletu in 1999 and is a part of many township tour routes and includes an exhibition space. To generate income for project participants, tourists pay individual photographers directly for digital or material copies of the portraits. Before taking the portrait, the photographer or a trained researcher conducts a semi-structured interview with the tourist in English (the lowest common denominator language of township tours), with the assistance of a translator if necessary. Image and text are assembled, for instant virtual display or for exhibition in the same space where photographs are being taken. As such, the project takes place in the atmosphere of a workshop; the product evolves as more photos and text are accumulated. All project participants also have the opportunity to comment on the archive in the making, through electronic tags and post-it notes, and by literally rearranging images and texts to create different narratives. This methodology follows current curatorial experiments that are generative and participatory, rather than being authoritative and didactic (Simon 2007).

Having tourists follow the lead of their interlocutors is my primary goal. This does not mean that the project is inherently discomforting for, or antagonistic towards, tourists. In fact, given the local zeitgeist of 'ubuntu' ('humanity to others'), international solidarity and faith in tourism, such an outcome is highly unlikely. However, this is an opportunity for township residents to reverse the flow of questions. They can ask tourists about their own homes, about why they come to South Africa and the townships, about the cost of their travels and whether comparable situations exist in their own countries. Some of these topics are already raised during township tours, but typically this occurs only during conversations between tourists and their guides. In this reflexive mode, guides and tourists often reach a tacit understanding regarding the moral superiority of the choice to visit townships, which is judged in relation to the fact that most white South Africans rarely do (McEachern 2002). What are not explored, however, are more difficult issues such as the difference between demonstrating an interest in marginalized communities while on vacation, versus responding to similar issues in the context of daily life, whether this be in a setting characterized by economic segregation (as in many large American cities) or, alternatively, in a progressive, 'mixed' neighbourhood (Kopvitch 1991).

When You Come Here may initiate discussions about such difficult issues, although meanings generated by this curatorial experiment cannot be predicted. Based on my interviews with youths involved in tourism in South Africa, they are as likely to want to know about the culture of wine in France, or working conditions in the United States, as to engage in a critique of the global tourism industry and inequality. That said, exhibitions and dialogues about them are not produced in a vacuum. They are the result of particular social, political, economic, interpersonal and institutional contexts. For example, people who are investing scarce resources in township tourism express hopefulness about this growing niche market. They may discuss how difficult it is for small-business ventures with little capital to compete in the South African tourist industry, but they do not question the privilege of the tourists upon whom they depend. However, if *When You Come Here* were supported by a not-for-profit community organization with no link to tourism and the service economy, the conversations generated might be different. But given the economic difficulties that townships face, a project such as *When You Come Here* will be infinitely more appealing to locals if it can generate income, and in such circumstances critical pedagogy may have limitations. Since township residents hope to build alliances and reciprocal obligations with visitors (Butler 2005), the creation of emotional discomfort may not be a desirable strategy. Though *When You Come Here* has the potential to raise consciousness regarding power dynamics inherent in township tourism, and though it may generate modest economic and social benefits for participants, much depends on its specific conditions of production.

Curatorial intervention two

New Routes: a travelling project

Township tours make sense in the context of a journey. In Cape Town, tours begin in the centre of town and create a sense of anticipation as they move outward towards the townships, as if approaching a frontier. The spatial dynamics of the tours in the poly-centred and fragmented metropolis of Johannesburg differ slightly, as tours begin in wealthy suburbs and then move outward to townships. In both cases, however, townships are positioned as a world apart, disconnected from the heritage and social fabric of the city. This image of the townships is perilously close to apartheid ideology, which regulated racial separateness with respect to everyday social segregation, urban living and work, and the administration of rural 'homelands'. Public historian Leslie Witz (2001: 2) notes that the tours 'almost inadvertently' confirm the spatial arrangements of apartheid, 'and as a result, the city centre is associated with European heritage, while the townships are viewed as "African"'. There are at least two consequences of this spatial narrative: binary oppositions between blacks and whites and between African and European heritage are reified and simplified, and 'white' South Africa remains invisible and unmarked. (In Cape Town in the late 1990s, the inclusion of so-called 'coloured' townships in tour itineraries complicated these binary oppositions, but this was eventually discontinued due to local drug and gang issues.) While guides describe the rise of apartheid and forced removals as they travel towards the townships, the relationship between these laws and white minority rule and privilege is left largely implicit. This unmarked quality of white culture is common to settler societies in which multiculturalism has begun to displace the white elite. As Eva Mackey writes, with regard to Canada, people of dominant and unmarked ethnicities see their 'customs, beliefs, practices, morals and values as normative and universal' (2002: 157). This ellipsis informs everyday practices and ways of thinking about culture. For example, during the so-called 'Year of Cultural Experiences' in South Africa in 1997, a set of ten stamps was released to coincide with International Museums Day. The stamps represented 'culture' in terms of iconic images of tribal culture – Zulu baskets, Ndebele beadwork, a Xhosa walking stick and other artefacts held in the country's museum collections. On the one hand, this represented a democratization of culture; it is inclusive in a way that is fitting for the post-apartheid nation. Yet, there are no images or artefacts associated with European culture, which remains unmarked. Europe stands for monumental history, while Africa is vibrant culture (Butler 2002).

In interviewing guides about the invisibility of white culture, they often argue that it is not necessary to show European culture since most tourists 'see it all around' and 'already know it'. There is truth in this statement, for there is no shortage of tourism advertising that promises international tourists a seamless mix of colonial elegance and serenity alongside modern amenities. Yet, what would be involved in curating a tour to reveal what critics such as Raymond Williams and James Clifford describe as relational cultural histories? In *The Country and the City* (1973), Raymond Williams describes how rapid changes in the urban landscape of eighteenth-century London captured the attention of observers who depicted the city as a contradictory space, filled with intense contrasts between the rich and poor, and a concomitant rise in concerns with containing and expelling poor rural migrants. James Clifford's (1986, 1988,

224 Shelley Ruth Butler

2007) oeuvre similarly situates culture in relation to fields of conflict and power, whether he is writing about colonial anthropology, the museum and art world, or post-colonial identity and property negotiations. How might relational histories be translated into township tours? The tours do include moments of this kind of engagement, in which white colonial and apartheid culture is linked to histories of conflict and inequality. For instance, at the outset of a township tour in Cape Town, a guide may point to what is today known as the Iziko Slave Lodge Museum (referring to one of the earliest uses of the building), but note that for over more than three centuries it also served as government offices, the Old Supreme Court and the South African Cultural History Museum. A link between Cape Town's historic 'high culture' and the colonies' connection to imperialism, slavery and indentured labour is clearly articulated through a critical, historical reading of the surrounding bucolic, civic landscape. In another tour, a guide compares the lack of media attention paid to fires in townships that are caused by unsafe living conditions with the media spectacle that occurs when there is an occasional fire on the iconic Table Mountain, which dominates the city.

Is there a way to frame middle- and upper-class Cape Town as a source for understanding apartheid and post-apartheid culture? Ethnographers, writers and artists have succeeded in evoking a specific cultural ethos associated with the once-dominant culture of apartheid. Vincent Crapanzano, in his ethnography *Waiting: The Whites of South Africa*, depicts the 'effects of domination on everyday life' (1986: xiii), which he characterizes as a deep sense of social entrapment and a pervasive fear of others. A similar cultural ethos is evoked by South African artist Lisa Brice in her installations *Make Your Home Your Castle* and *What is a House Without an Armed Mother?* (1995), in which images of domesticity and comfort are subtly undermined by a sense of paranoia and impending violence: a soft pillow is embroidered with the words 'Alarm On?' and a blond woman who scrubs a floor wears a pretty blue dress with a matching gun tucked into her apron (in Williamson and Jamal 1996: 92). This piece was especially powerful in the context of its setting, a group show called *Scurvy* (1995), which showed in Cape Town Castle, home of the South African Defence Force. This culture of fear is also depicted by Nadine Gordimer in her post-apartheid novel, *None to Accompany Me*. A narrator reflects on houses abandoned due to white flight:

> Empty houses. FOR SALE. Estate agents' portable signs propped up at corners, arrows pointing: ON SHOW. Clues in the paper-chase of flight ... FOR SALE. ON SHOW. Are these *suburban museums*, exhibiting a way of life that [has] ended?
>
> (1995: 241; emphasis mine)

This ability to read the everyday landscape as an exhibit is demonstrated by township tours to some extent. But more can be done to render normative culture an object of critical study.

Inspired by these examples, my curatorial intervention *New Routes* seeks to trace unequal and unjust relations between communities that are increasingly separated by class as much as by race. A township tour could, for instance, follow the route of one of millions of domestic workers who commute from townships to the city, spending a great amount of time and money (relative to their wages) to do so. In the post-apartheid era, everyday life for domestics is little changed, despite the regulation of their work by a new regime (Ally 2009). A newspaper article that follows one domestic worker's commute from Soweto to a wealthy white enclave provides a narrative model for a tour (Dugger 2010). The article follows Mrs Susan Hanong, a 67-year-old woman who lives in a small home in Soweto and has worked as a maid in the northern suburbs of Johannesburg for a quarter of a century. Mrs Hanong leaves her home at 5 a.m. to spend two hours commuting to work. Her comfort has improved with the introduction of buses – a development ushered in for the World Cup – which she uses rather than the more expensive and dangerous informal taxis that are a legacy of black entrepreneurship in the apartheid era. However, concerns expressed by suburb residents about the new bus system and its effect on property values reveal a disheartening lack of empathy and sense of commonality between rich and poor. As in the apartheid era, maids remain compelling figures who are paradoxically both distant and intimately enmeshed in their employers' lives. As the reader 'follows' Mrs Hanong into her employer's home, we see her in maid's uniform, doing laundry and dishes and asking her employer's (privileged) cat, 'Why not have your breakfast?'

This genre of travelling tale is global, and compelling due to the intersection of private lives and public constraints, love, service and the market economy. A similar journey is enacted in the film *Paris, je t'aime* (2006), in which an immigrant woman arises early in her drab suburban apartment, drops her baby at an institutional childcare setting and takes a train to her employer's city home, where she cares for the latter's baby. Since this scenario is familiar globally, it is possible that enacting it as a tour could lead tourists to reflect on apartheid and post-apartheid, but also on wealth disparities or segregation in their own homes. Perhaps such a tour could facilitate consciousness building, in the sense of affecting individuals' 'identification with and awareness of the "battlegrounds" of social conflict' (McGehee and Santos 2005: 762). If this were to occur, township tourists could avoid fulfilling Zygmunt Bauman's depiction of the postmodern tourist as someone who moves through spaces that other people live in with no sense of moral proximity or responsibility. In Bauman's (1996) pessimistic vision, the tourist pays for his or her right to safety, as well as the right to not be bothered, which is the opposite of consciousness raising.

However, using rhetorical and experiential strategies of juxtaposition to inform social critique has limitations. First, a township tour that includes a stop at a 'house museum', like that envisioned by Nadine Gordimer, runs the risk of reifying binaries and promoting stereotypes. In both the apartheid and post-apartheid era, examples of images and ideologies of separateness can, for instance, be countered with other histories of resistance, collaboration across racial boundaries and experimentation with hybrid identities and lifestyles (Frederikse 1990; Martin 1996; Nuttall 2004). Thus, curation includes a responsibility: in some cases this might entail arguing a particular point of view; in other cases, it might be deemed most important to offer the public multiple points of view on a matter. Explicit and implicit juxtapositions, at least when enacted in the art world, often take on a parodic or ironic tone. In a mock event in New York in the 1960s, for instance, artist Joey Skaggs created a 'cultural exchange programme', which involved busing sixty hippies into Queens to gaze at suburban lawns and white picket fences. As in a township tour, the visitors also got off the bus to enter a local restaurant, where they were received with suspicion. In 1976, Free Flux Tours (associated with the Fluxus art movement) conducted tours in New York City that destabilized dominant practices of sightseeing by drawing attention to marginal and unmarked landscape features (Drobnick 1995). Participants in one tour admired street kerbs and cul-de-sacs in Soho; the effect was comparable to calling a series of photos of elbows and knees 'family portraits'. That said, the lack of pavements in many parts of cities in South Africa, both wealthy and poor, could tell a provocative tale about car culture and uneven civic development. These projects make use of juxtapositions and reversals in order to play with the touristic gaze. In these instances, the right to gaze is questioned through re-enactment, but is not denied. This is a classic dilemma of irony, which, as a form of 'complicitous critique' (Hutcheon 1989: 2), both subverts and challenges the conventions it questions. Arguably, my second curatorial intervention 'spreads' the touristic gaze, but does not fundamentally dismantle it.

Township tour guides do employ strategies of comparison and juxtaposition in order to create counter-images to cinematic and journalistic traditions of over-representing township violence, litter and crime (Ellapen 2007). Guides highlight middle-class and nouveau-riche neighbourhoods with private security systems in the townships. This surprises visitors and renders the landscape less 'Other'. Traditional binary oppositions between township and city are also being destabilized by popular culture and media, particularly in Johannesburg. Townships such as Soweto are celebrated for their aesthetic creativity and 'bricoleur' ingenuity, as well as for their communitarian and cosmopolitan atmosphere (Fraser 2003; Mbembe *et al.* 2004). Nevertheless, such reinventions of townships do not necessarily render them less exotic.

One wonders when a mainstream heritage tour of Cape Town or Johannesburg will ever automatically include the townships. Until then, can township tours that include the city serve as an antidote to voyeurism and Eurocentrism? In theory, my answer is affirmative. However, I am cognizant of the fact that this kind of ironic intervention may not serve the needs of township entrepreneurs who pin their hopes on the fragile economics of community tourism. My 'rhetoric of dismantlement' (Gates 1991: 34) does not serve the needs of community entrepreneurs to bring tourists to the townships in order to support the local informal and formal economy. Busing tourists into the wealthy suburbs, while provocative, deflects their attention away from township businesses and needs. As an outside curator, I also realize that my critiques of township tours may not be appreciated by some stakeholders. It is possible that my interest in subverting the ways in which townships are inscribed as sites of authentic culture and poverty, and in using tours to raise issues regarding local and global inequality and injustice, might be a privileged stance without practical application. However, I believe that a middle ground for resolving these representational dilemmas can be staked out. Success can be judged on the ways in which these curatorial interventions motivate tourists to reflect upon their subject-positions and various desires, while also encouraging the same tourists to support township residents in their entrepreneurial, creative or curatorial goals.

Conclusion

I have outlined two curatorial responses to contradictory and problematic aspects of township tours. Neither intervention rejects the notion of 'touring' per se, or the goal of creating provocative encounters in vernacular landscapes. My interventions extend and reform township tours in a spirit that is both reflexive and pragmatic. In the first instance, township residents interrupt the privileged touristic gaze by photographing, interviewing and exhibiting the tourists. In the second case, township tour routes and their narratives are changed, so that the township is understood as inextricably entwined and in conversation with the rest of the city. Poverty is understood in a broad social and political context – which is not an entirely new terrain for township tours – and township cultural styles are seen not as unchanging and exotic, but rather as integral to post-apartheid South Africa. I believe that these interventions can create space for tourists to be critical and reflexive, while also meeting local goals of interacting and exchanging with tourists in the service economy. As my curatorial interventions demonstrate, I am not willing to dismiss township tourism simply because it does not offer 'global intervention into the global balance of power, the commercial realities of the capitalist world system and the cannibalizing machine that is popular culture' (Hutnyck 1996: 222). Such a conclusion precludes the possibility that curating new tour routes and narratives can contribute to a future in which townships are viewed by mainstream tourism and media as being integral to the city.

My curatorial interventions are hypothetical, which means that I have not had to tackle pragmatic and political issues that such projects would surely encounter. I was asked by the editors of this volume to comment on the viability of these projects in the context of neoliberal South Africa. This is a challenging question that is well worth unpacking in these concluding remarks.[2] Township tourism developed during a period of political transition, in which political compromises were forged; the South African government responded to both international and internal pressures by prioritizing economic growth over more radical aspects of the ruling African Nationalist Congress platform (Murray

1994). In this ideological atmosphere, tourism was identified in government papers as a key growth industry that needed to be transformed in order to suit goals of development. Township tours fit with this agenda; while the tourism industry remains deeply unequal, both globally and nationally, township tours offer some hope to people who survive in the informal market and have a service or product that tourists might purchase. Logistically, my curatorial interventions could be incorporated into the work of a small business already operating township tours; in the language of the market, the curatorial projects would be 'value added', a new product to offer so-called alternative tourists, who seek experiences that set them apart from the masses. In the hyperinflation of township tourism, we now find alternatives to the alternative tour (Butler 2010).

I cannot, at this time, comment on the feasibility (costs and potential revenue) of the projects, but my expectations are modest given the competitiveness of the field and the seasonal and fickle nature of the market. However, while my curatorial interventions take place in the market economy, their goals are as much pedagogic and creative, as they are economic. Positioned as 'collaborative performance pieces', the interventions could perhaps attract international funding or support from museum outreach programmes. The interventions could also be linked to schools; it would be pedagogically powerful for schools that are geographically close, yet worlds apart, to collaborate and curate tours in their communities. Even if public or private funding were found, should the projects become reality, they would inevitably become tools for some stakeholders and exclude others. Having conjured these curatorial interventions, I would be disappointed to see them 'succeed' (in a market sense), but become diluted from a pedagogical point of view. These curatorial interventions, whether funded by not-for-profit or government sources, are unapologetically linked to the market economy. Here, I agree with James Ferguson's (2009) argument that kneejerk condemnations of neoliberalism risk ignoring the potential of the private sphere to be harnessed for social empowerment. One can argue that my proposed curatorial interventions contribute to the further 'privatization and commodification of global justice agendas',[3] as do township tours. Without denying the reality that poverty and social justice are commodifed and marketed for socially conscious consumers, there is a need for critical and reflexive interventions within and against this status quo.

Notes

1 Erica Lehrer, personal communication, 2008.
2 Thanks to Mary Conran, Ko Koens, Monica Patterson, Steven Robins and Bronwen Wetton for helping me to clarify these concluding remarks.
3 Mary Conran, personal communication, 2011. See also Conran, forthcoming.

Bibliography

Ally, S. (2009) *From Servants to Workers: South African Domestic Workers and the Democratic State*, Ithaca, NY: Cornell University Press.

Ashcroft, B. (1999) *Key Concepts in Post-colonial Studies*, London: Routledge.

Ballerini, J. (1997) 'Photography as a charitable weapon: poor kids and self-representation', *Radical History Review*, 69: 160–88.

Basu, P. and Macdonald, S. (2007) 'Introduction: experiments in exhibition, ethnography, art, and science', in S. Macdonald and P. Basu (eds) *Exhibition Experiments*, Malden: Blackwell.

Bauman, Z. (1996) 'From pilgrim to tourist – or a short history of identity', in S. Hall and P. duGuy (eds) *Questions of Cultural Identity*, London: Thousand Oaks.

Bremner, L. (2004) *Johannesburg: One City Colliding Worlds*, Johannesburg: STE Publishers.

Briedenhann, J. and Ramchander, P. (2006) 'Township tourism: blessing or blight? The case of Soweto in South Africa', in M. Smith and M. Robinson (eds) *Cultural Tourism in a Changing World: Politics, Participation and (Re)presentation*, Clevedon: Channel View.

Butler. S.R. (2002) 'Post-colonial challenges: reinventing museums in post-apartheid Cape Town', unpublished thesis, York University.

—— (2005) 'Sensing culture, tracing history: township tours in post-apartheid South Africa', paper presented at the Sensory Collections and Display Conference, Concordia University, Montreal, Quebec, 10–12 February.

—— (2010) 'Should I stay or should I go? Negotiating township tours in post-apartheid South Africa', *Journal of Tourism and Cultural Change*, 8(1–2): 15–29.

Carroll, R. (2004) 'Soweto is now part of the safari tour trail', *The Guardian*, 13 September.

Clifford, J. (1986) 'Introduction: partial truths', in J. Clifford and G. Marcus (eds) *Writing Culture: The Poetics and Politics of Ethnography*, Berkeley, CA: University of California Press.

—— (1988) *The Predicament of Culture: Twentieth-century Ethnography, Literature, and Art*, Cambridge, MA: Harvard University Press.

—— (2007) *Routes: Travel and Translation in the Late Twentieth Century*, Cambridge, MA: Harvard University Press.

Conran, M. (forthcoming) '"They really love me!" Intimacy in volunteer tourism', *Annals of Tourism Research*.

Crapanzano, V. (1986) *Waiting: The Whites of South Africa*, New York: Random House.

Drobnick, J. (1995) 'Mock excursions and twisted itineraries: tour guide performances', *Parachute*, 80: 31–7.

Dugger, C. (2010) 'A bus system reopens rifts in South Africa', *The New York Times*, 22 February. Available online at www.nytimes.com/2010/02/22/world/africa/22bus.html?ref=celiawdugger (accessed 21 January 2012).

Eadington, W. and Smith, V. (1992) 'Introduction: the emergence of alternative forms of tourism', in V. Smith and W. Eadington (eds) *Tourism Alternatives: Potentials and Problems in the Development of Tourism*, Philadelphia, PA: University of Pennsylvania Press.

Ellapen, J. (2007) 'The cinematic township: cinematic representations of the "township" space and who can claim the rights to representation in post-apartheid South African cinema', *Journal of African Cultural Studies*, 19(1): 113–37.

Fabian, J. (1983) *Time and the Other: How Anthropology Makes Its Object*, New York: Columbia University Press.

Ferguson, J. (2009) 'The uses of neoliberalism', *Antipode*, 41(S1): 166–84.

Frankenberg, R. (1992) *White Women, Race Matters: The Social Construction of Race*, Minneapolis, MN: Minnesota University Press.

Fraser, C. (2003) *Shack Chic: Art and Innovation in South African Shack-Lands*, Cape Town: Quivertree.

Frederikse, J. (1990) *The Unbreakable Thread: Non-racialism in South Africa*, Bloomington, IN: Indiana University Press.

Freire-Medeiros, B. (2008) 'The favela and its touristic transits', *Geoforum*, 40(4): 580–8.

—— (2010) 'Gazing at the poor: favela tours and the colonial legacy'. Available online at www.sas.ac.uk/fileadmin/documents/postgraduate/Papers_London_Debates_2010/Freire_Medeiros__Gazing_at_the_poor.pdf (accessed 8 July 2011).

Gates, H.L. (1991) 'Canon formation and the Afro-American tradition', in D. LaCapra (ed.) *The Bounds of Race: Perspectives on Hegemony and Resistance*, Ithaca, NY: Cornell University Press.

Giroux, H. (1992) 'Post-colonial ruptures and democratic possibilities: multiculturalism as anti-racist pedagogy', *Cultural Critique*, 21: 5–39.

Gordimer, N. (1995) *None to Accompany Me*, New York: Penguin Books.

Goudie, S.C., Khan, F. and Kilan, D. (1999) 'Transforming tourism: black empowerment, heritage and identity beyond apartheid', *South African Geographical Journal*, 81(1): 22–31.

Hutcheon, L. (1989) *The Politics of Postmodernism*, London: Routledge.

Hutnyck, J. (1996) *The Rumour of Calcutta: Tourism, Charity and the Poverty of Representation*, London: Zed Books.

Idasa (n.d.) *Phulaphulani! Attention Please!* Cape Town: Idasa.

Kincaid, J. (1988) *A Small Place*, New York: Farrar Straus Grioux.

Kirshenblatt-Gimblett, B. (1998) *Destination Culture: Tourism, Museums and Heritage*, Berkeley, CA: University of California Press.

Kopvitch, K. (1991) 'Third worlding at home', *Social Text*, 28: 87–99.

McEachern, C. (2002) *Narratives of Nation: Media, Memory and Representation in the Making of the New South Africa*, New York: Nova Science.

McGehee, N. and Santos, C. (2005) 'Social change, discourse and volunteer tourism', *Annals of Tourism Research*, 32(3): 760–79.

Mackenzie, J. (2009) *Museums and Empire: Natural History, Human Cultures and Colonial Identities*, Manchester: Manchester University Press.

Mackey, E. (2002) *The House of Difference: Cultural Politics and National Identity in Canada*, Toronto: University of Toronto Press.

Mackey, M. (2000) 'Festering sore lurks behind tourism', *Cape Argus*, 16 May: 14–15.

Martin, M. (1996) 'The rainbow nation – identity and 'ransformation', *The Oxford Art Journal*, 19(1): 3–15.

Mbembe, J.A., Dlamini, N. and Khunou, G. (2004) 'Soweto now', *Public Culture*, 16(3): 499–506.

Mitchell, T. (1989) 'The world as exhibition', *Society for Comparative Study and History*, 31(2): 217–36.

Munt, I. (1994) 'The "other" postmodern tourism: culture, travel and the new middle classes', *Theory, Culture and Society*, 11(3): 101–3.

Murray, M. (1994) *The Revolution Deferred: The Painful Birth of Post-apartheid South Africa*, London: Verso.

Nuttall, S. (2004) 'Stylizing the self: the Y generation in Rosebank, Johannesburg', *Public Culture*, 16(3): 430–52.

Palmer, C. (2009) 'Moving with the times: visual representations of the tourism phenomenon', *Journal of Tourism Consumption and Practice*, 1(1): 74–85.

Paris, je t'aime (2006) Film, Paris: La Fabrique de Films.

Phillips, R. (1998) *Trading Identities: The Souvenir in Native North American Art from the Northeast, 1700–1900*, Seattle, WA: University of Washington Press.

Robinson, M. and Picard, D. (eds) (2009) *The Framed World: Tourism, Tourists and Photography*, Surrey: Ashgate.

Rogerson, C. (2004) 'Urban tourism and small tourism enterprise development in Johannesburg: the case of township tourism', *GeoJournal*, 60(3): 249–57.

—— (2005) 'Unpacking tourism SMMEs in South Africa: structure, support needs and policy response', *Development Southern Africa*, 22(5): 623–42.

Rolfes, M. (2010) 'Poverty tourism: theoretical reflections and empirical findings regarding an extraordinary form of tourism', *GeoJournal*, 75(5): 421–42.

Simon, N. (2007) 'Discourse in the blogosphere: what museums can learn from web 2.0', *Museums and Social Issues*, 2(2): 257–74.

Soweto Bicycle Tours (2012) 'See Soweto bike tours'. Available online at www.sowetobicycletours.com (accessed 17 January 2012).

Taylor, J. (1996) 'The moment between', in G. Younge (ed.) *Picture Cape Town: Landmarks of a New Generation*, Los Angeles, CA: The Getty Conservation Institute.

Third World Bunfight (2010) 'See Third World Bunfight'. Available online at www.thirdworldbunfight.co.za/site.html (accessed 7 July 2011).

Tribe, J. (2008) 'The art of tourism', *Annals of Tourism Research*, 35(4): 924–44.

Tyson, A. (2008) 'Crafting emotional comfort: interpreting the painful past at living history museums in the new economy', *Museum and Society*, 6(3): 246–62.

Urry, J. (1994) *The Tourist Gaze: Leisure and Travel in Contemporary Societies*, London: Sage.

Williams, R. (1973) *The Country and the City*, New York: Oxford University Press.

Williamson, S. and Jamal, A. (1996) *Art in South Africa: The Future Present*, Cape Town: David Philip.

Witz, L. (2001) 'Museums on Cape Town's township tours', paper presented at the Museums, Local Knowledge and Performance in an Age of Globalization Workshop, Lwandle Migrant Museum, Cape Town, 3–4 August.

——, Rassool, C. and Minkley G. (2001) 'Repackaging the past for South African tourism', *Daedalus*, 130(1): 277–95.

Younge, G. (1996) *Picture Cape Town: Landmarks of a New Generation*, Los Angeles, CA: The Getty Conservation Institute.

14 Keep on slumming?

Ko Koens, Fabian Frenzel and
Malte Steinbrink

Slum tourism is a young, dynamic and expanding field of research. For a long time, few journal articles and book chapters were written about this increasingly popular phenomenon. In recent years, however, the number of publications on slum tourism has grown rapidly. This current volume, the first of its kind, together with the special issue 14(2) of the journal *Tourism Geographies*, may be seen as the culmination of this rise of interest so far. While slum tourism is highly controversial and makes for some heated debates, we believe that the increasing academic interest also has to do with more substantial implications of this form of tourism. Rather than being studied only as a particular niche or special-interest tourism, slum tourism allows for an investigation of fundamental questions in a set of diverse research areas; apart from tourism studies, this includes development studies and poverty research, and cultural as well as globalization studies.

In spite of its breadth, the literature assembled here has only begun to provide an initial comprehension of the various issues relating to slum tourism, and should be seen as no more than a foundation for further work. In fact, if it shows one thing, it is that there is still much that we do not understand regarding slum tourism. Nevertheless, we believe the contributors have made significant strides towards increasing our knowledge on the subject. One of the key problems for research relates directly to the fact that slum tourism researchers are, after all, 'professional slummers' (see Chapter 1). We have identified three key concerns in this book in regard to slum tourism, namely poverty, power and ethics. They are not only relevant to tour operators, slum tourists and local policy makers, but also to slum tourism researchers. Casting a powerful research gaze on slums and on tourists, researchers need to consider the ethical implications of their work. This includes questions about how to represent slums, poverty and tourism in ways that balance the need to make meaningful statements about these phenomena while avoiding inaccuracies and essentializing generalizations intrinsic to the term 'slum' as a universal notion (UN 2003). Great differences exist both within and between slums in different cities all over the globe. For example, the lower parts of Rocinha in Rio de Janeiro, Brazil, are not dissimilar from other suburbs – and include banks, a McDonald's and a sushi bar, for instance – while higher up on the hillside abject poverty exists. In South Africa, immense differences in income and living conditions can be observed even on the same street. Slums in various parts of the world also differ strongly depending on their local context, and are referred to by terms that seem more suited to the local situation (township, favela, 'chengzhongcun'). Not only do settlements labelled as slums differ greatly, but also tourism in these areas does. Slum tourism develops differently depending on the local settings. It thus seems to be an overarching term for various forms of tourism to impoverished urban areas that can only be meaningfully explored in situated and comparative research. Equally important is the reflection of 'local voices' (Freire-Medeiros in this volume) in participatory research practice. In this sense, slum tourism research needs to 'keep on slumming' to develop a better understanding of the complexity of the field.

As a subject, slum tourism attracts scholars from different backgrounds and fields. They may investigate similar subjects or even share concerns, but have their own way of investigating the issues at hand. This volume shows the remarkable multidisciplinarity in the field, bridging anthropology, social geography, sociology, history, literature studies, architecture and planning. The youth of the field means discourses are still fluid rather than set in stone, and there is ample room for interdisciplinary discussion and cross-fertilization of ideas.

Interestingly, much recent work has used a qualitative research methodology (Frenzel and Koens 2012). Indeed, practically all contributions to the current book are the result of qualitative work. This may be because much current work is still exploratory and best befits a qualitative approach, but it may also be that qualitative approaches may be more suitable for a fluid subject such as slum tourism, or that practical difficulties mean that it is not always possible to access the larger numbers of people that are required for quantitative work.

Looking back on the themes of the book

This book has attempted to shed light on what we consider some of the key concerns of the phenomenon of slum tourism. As previously stated, slum tourism takes place at the nexus of poverty, power and ethics, and questions regarding these themes constantly overlap in slum tourism practice. We will therefore discuss the themes here in an integrated way and highlight their relations, rather than dealing with them separately.

A first question with regard to slum tourism is the extent to which poverty is its centre of interest. Evidently, slum tourism does not take place everywhere where people are poor, and often tour operators seem keen to highlight other aspects of the slums, such as their cultural and social diversity or their value as heritage rather than poverty. Nevertheless, the findings in the current book indicate that, for a great number of tourists, poverty is the most important incentive for visiting. Meschkank (2010) discusses how tourists to Dharavi not only expect to observe poverty, but also have a negative connotation with the poverty they expect to see. Tour operators usually challenge the negative semantics of poverty and try to transform them, but they respond to the initial expectations of tourists. Poverty remains their selling point. This accords with other research on slum tourism (Rolfes *et al.* 2009; Meschkank 2010; Dyson 2012).

The contribution by Menezes (Chapter 6) is interesting in this regard, as it discusses the failure of turning a favela into an open-air museum, using it as a heritage attraction rather than a poverty destination. She finds that the project lacks 'resonance' among both local residents and tourists. Some authors in this volume, however, state that it would be wrong to suggest that slum tourism is always about gazing at poor people. Ding (Chapter 11) describes three different forms of (domestic) slum tourism in China. In two of them, poverty does not seem essential to the tourist experience. One slum attracts artists with its low rents, and this has created a tourist space that proves particularly attractive to visitors. In his other example, the slum is part of the spectacle, not so much due to its references to poverty, but more through the fact that it is different from other, more organized parts of the city. His contribution highlights the fluid boundaries when slum tourism meets with the lure of low-rent, creative neighbourhoods, documented also in many cities of the Global North (Zukin 1987; Harvey 2001). The photo essay by King and Dovey (Chapter 9) may help to further clarify such a perspective on slum tourism. They show that the attraction of the slum may not be the poverty of its inhabitants, but its informality and irregularity, creating aesthetics of the 'sublime'. King and Dovey ask, however, whether tourists who indulge in the aesthetic attraction of the slum will tend to reflect on the ethical questions evoked by the plight of slum dwellers. Therefore, poverty remains intrinsically linked to what is sought or perceived in slum tourism. In many cases, the attraction of the impoverished situation in slums is its difference or 'Otherness', and while the ways in which the slum is represented for and/or sought by tourists are diverse, poverty remains the most important signifier of difference through which slum tourism is constructed. This includes practices of 'gazing at the poor' as well as other ways of experiencing the slum.

This then leads to the problem of representing poverty. Poverty or poverty-related sights are displayed, presented and staged to become consumable in tourism. What are the ethics of such an operation? Some insights can be taken from a view into the history of representing poverty. In Seaton's contribution (Chapter 2), the link is clearly shown by referral to the notion of literary slumming. Stories of 'the poor' and 'the other half' have made attractive and successful literature, stimulating curiosity and excitement, from the seventeenth century onwards. With the emergence of social and political concerns that framed poverty in the context of the 'social question' in France in the late eighteenth century, representing and consuming poverty for entertainment became more problematic (Arendt 2006). Poverty was now a problem to be solved rather than a condition of humanity assumed to be 'natural'. Political philosophy and literature criticism became increasingly conscious of the problems of demonizing or romanticizing the poor. As Frenzel points out in Chapter 3, the problem persists in what he calls the 'global social question'.

In the case of actual tourism, literal slumming, this problem of representation is amplified by the physical proximity between visitors and visited, between those being represented and those consuming the representation. This corporal dimension evokes questions of power dissimilar to literary slumming. The critical view that slum tourists are voyeurs gawking at the poor is greatly pronounced, while such criticism is not usually levelled at people reading literature that displays the poor or who watch a film about poverty. In tourism, it seems that the issue of power is more immediate because of the physical proximity between the poor and the tourist. More research is needed to reflect the phenomenological dimension of slum tourism as a practice that brings people of radically diverging wealth close to each other. The ways in which this issue has been addressed in tourism studies is often through notions of the gaze. Non-visual aspects of the encounter have been discussed (Edensor 1998) but rarely related to questions of power and inequality.

The fact that tourists gaze at the poor, following Urry's (2002) notion of the tourist gaze, is problematic not only because tourists exercise power over the poor they look at. Rather, the Foucauldian notion of the gaze indicates that the gaze itself is a powerful construct that disempowers both the tourist and the poor (Foucault 1979). Following Urry, tourists are confined to certain preconfigured narratives and imaginaries to understand what they see when they gaze at the poor. Therefore, it seems the ethical questions about slum tourism are much more complex than criticizing tourists for their behaviour. An ethical critique should enable a reflection on the imaginaries that circulate, and the ways in which people involved in slum tourism are able to resist and transform these, including, importantly, academics reflecting on the phenomenon. Slum tourism might in this way also become a tool to empower tourists to allow for reflection and transformation on the imaginaries and discourses that govern their perception. To a certain extent, the contributions by Meschkank (Chapter 8) and King and Dovey (Chapter 9) relate to this issue by showing how tourists have agency and interpret and relate to slums according to their social preconceptions and ideas. Their discussions thus highlight that representation is a two-way process that goes beyond simply taking in what is on offer.

The issue of power between residents and outsiders should also be seen in this light. Unfortunately, very little academic research has investigated expectations, opinions and reactions by local residents. In the current volume, Freire-Medeiros (Chapter 10) and Baptista (Chapter 7) in particular address this lacuna. Their findings show how, upon closer investigation, residents are not a homogeneous, economically weak group, nor should they be seen as having hardly any agency due to their difficult socio-economic situation and lack of knowledge of tourism. Freire-Medeiros shows how opinions and interests among local residents vary greatly. Some may lack knowledge with regard to tourism, but others are very aware of how it works. Their attitude

236 Ko Koens, Fabian Frenzel and Malte Steinbrink

towards slum tourism should be seen as relational rather than simply pro- or anti-. The seemingly naive positive reactions towards favela tourism can, for example, also be situated in a long history of discrimination and the stigmatization of favela residents. As Freire-Medeiros points out, residents, tour guides, tourists and researchers all constantly negotiate and renegotiate their position when co-creating favela tourism. Baptista goes a step further in his discussion of the roles of residents, tour operators and development organizations. He shows how residents actively manipulate their tourist offerings (often related to poverty) to meet the expectations of tourists in order to increase visitation and monetary benefit. At the same time, they are hiding evidence from the visiting tourists of economic progress and social development that take place in their village.

Slum tourism can also be used as a political instrument to empower local communities. Wattanawanyoo (Chapter 12) illustrates how tourism is used to fight off local government plans for the eviction of a 100-year-old slum in central Bangkok. Highly interesting in this case are diverging notions of valuable heritage between international tourists and local elites. Wattanawanyoo reports on a project by architectural activists that attempts to harness the interest of international tourists in the slum to increase its bargaining power in conflict with local policy makers. Whether or not this fight is successful remains to be seen, but it shows that slum tourism can also be a tool for advocacy for the urban poor. Ding (Chapter 11) provides a similar example. An art exhibition that critically pointed out inequalities towards slum residents in a Chinese town succeeded in securing the provision of public schooling for the resident children. What is of particular interest here is the changing attitude of local and national governments towards slum tourism. Frenzel and Basu (Chapters 3 and 4) discuss how government and local elites often initially have negative views of slum tourism. Frenzel, in particular, relates this to the political context that surrounds the early stages of slum tourism development in a particular destination in the Global South. As slum tourism destinations develop, and tours become more commercial, slum tourism often de-politicizes. The discourses change from addressing issues of inequality and injustice to appraising cultural diversity and development as characteristic of slums. These new narratives are easier to appropriate for local policy makers. Governments in South Africa and Rio de Janeiro actively encourage slum tourism today as a means to empower local communities. Baptista (Chapter 7) points to the irony that can be found in the ethical debate regarding slum tourism here. While much of the critique of tourism has dealt with ethical issues, slum tourism is equally hailed for its ethical benefits and marketed as a form of ethical tourism.

A number of authors in the current volume take a more pragmatic view on slum tourism (e.g. Basu (Chapter 4), Ding (Chapter 11) and Koens (Chapter 5)). They argue that the negative perspectives held by outside observers (and local elites) can be detrimental, as they divert the debate away from the analysis of the current organization of slum tourism and potential developmental and detrimental issues. They highlight potential ways in which slum tourism may help in alleviating poverty, or at least increase the knowledge regarding the living conditions of slum dwellers. A great difficulty here, as Butler argues (Chapter 13), is that current tours are very much created with the tourists' interests at heart. An awareness of poverty is raised only to an extent that it does not become uncomfortable for tourists. Tour operators argue that they try to alter the negative label associated with poverty, but their desire to please tourists holds a great risk of romanticizing life in the slums. Freire-Medeiros concisely sums this up in Chapter 10 when she says: 'fighting this negative label without replacing it with a romanticized view of the conditions of living . . . seems to be as much of a challenge as it is to expose the realities of poverty without giving incentive to objectifying approaches'. The contribution of Meschkank (Chapter 8) confirms this problematic in her detailed analysis of the discursive construction and semantic transformation of poverty in tours in Mumbai. Also, Freire-Medeiros argues that residents of the favelas feel that tourism has given them a sense of importance, when mass media and local elites insist on representing favelas merely as cradles of crime. This indicates that the nexus of slum tourism and identity is not just about the slum tourists' construction of identity, but also about the identity formation of slum dwellers confronted with this form of tourism. As slum tourists view slum dwellers as their 'Other', there are indications for similar processes that reverse this gaze.

The extent to which slum tourism actually leads to poverty reduction is equally debatable. Indeed, economic benefits are difficult to assess. Koens's contribution (Chapter 5) highlights the complexity of the economic effects of slum tourism. The local setting, with particular constellations of business models and practices, needs to be considered. He discusses two townships of South Africa, where local business ownership is higher than in any of the other major slum tourism destinations. Here, local business communities are deeply fractured due to social and historical influences. Distrust, intense competition and power (ab)use among small-business owners weaken their bargaining position and hurt overall local economic benefits and the empowerment of township residents. Freire-Medeiros (Chapter 10) discusses how, in the favelas, commercial relationships between residents and tourists are sporadic and largely informal. Profits are not distributed well and money is only marginally reinvested. Furthermore, investments in local communities are practically always done by means of charity rather than through incentivizing local entrepreneurship.

Thoughts for future research

The current volume has highlighted many issues surrounding slum tourism and provided valuable new insights into this complex phenomenon. However, more unanswered questions and new paths for research have emerged. The field seems to be spreading out in a great variety of directions. It would therefore seem too early to set out a comprehensive future research agenda, which might restrict highly interesting new research. Instead, we would like to opt for a more general description of certain potential avenues for future research. These are based on, or refer to, the idea of slum tourism as existing on a nexus between the global and the local. Such a nexus can be perceived in the three main themes of the current book (poverty, power and ethics) and indeed in practically all chapters. In this section we use this global–local nexus to highlight some of the central questions that remain to be addressed.

To start with, there is a lack of knowledge of the local perspective. We know very little about how residents perceive slum tourism and to what extent they would like to get involved in or change current offerings. Contributions by Koens (Chapter 5), Baptista (Chapter 7) and Freire-Medeiros (Chapter 10) show that residents are not generally powerless and can sometimes actively manipulate tourism products. Such findings may be related to writings on tourism in Kenya, where Maasai people accommodate tourists by enacting a 'colonial' drama to fit western discourse (Tucker and Akama 2009). Also, we are largely unaware of residents' perspectives on business, or their perspectives on businesses that are (or could be) involved in the increasingly globally organized slum tourism industry. If slum tourism is to integrate more local offerings, more insights on residents' perspectives of business are required. Moreover, there is little research on the question of how value is created in slum tourism. This concerns the role of tour operators who are often criticized for being 'exploitative'. This notion assumes that tour operators appropriate value that they have not created and use a resource they don't own. Value theory might offer fruitful insights into these issues (Graeber 2001; De Angelis 2007; Harvie and Milburn 2010). This issue is closely related to remaining questions over slum tourism's role in poverty alleviation. For all the talk, there is still relatively little knowledge of what this exactly constitutes. Slum tourism research here faces a challenge that is not dissimilar to research that addresses poverty alleviation in general terms. Questions concern the measurement of poverty and its multi-dimensionality. Across the disciplines there is great interest in developing qualitative indicators of poverty alleviation to address limits of purely quantitative approaches (Scheyvens 2007; Blake *et al.* 2008; Tomlinson *et al.* 2008). Findings from the current volume (with great differences in perspective among local people) suggest that such indicators could be emerging from slum tourism research.

While the current book deals with slum tourism in the Global South, slum tourism can be seen as a global phenomenon, with similar forms of tourism also existing in the Global North. Slum tourism here (e.g. ghetto tourism or inner-city reality tourism) has received far less interest from the academic community, apart from being set in a historical perspective (Steinbrink 2012; Seaton in this volume). In addressing forms of tourism in poor neighbourhoods in the Global North, slum tourism research can develop its overlaps with questions of city regeneration and recovery, and, in particular, debates about gentrification. These debates can help to shed further light on the development of slum destinations in the Global South. In the case of Rio de Janeiro, evidently, some favelas have been subject to gentrification processes in which tourism has played a major part.

Furthermore, very little work has been done comparing slum tourism in different places. In Chapter 1 we have assembled a list of places in which slum tourism occurs, and made some suggestions on how they have influenced each other in their development. Frenzel's contribution (Chapter 3) provides a more grounded comparison of three destinations and shows that comparative research can lead to enlightening new insights into the development of slum tourism. As such, we would like to recommend the continuation and increase of such comparative research.

Related to this is a need to continue the limited amount of work that has been done in discussing slum tourism in the context of globalization. In particular, investigations into the relation between the global form and the local practice of slum tourism are needed; this also includes the question of the dynamics involved when the global form of slum tourism meets different local contexts. Further research is needed to connect globalization theories, including, in particular, literature of post-colonial critique for the explanation of, and reflections on, slum tourism.

As mentioned at the start of this section, these recommendations for further research are of a general nature and do not constitute a comprehensive list. Other, equally valid, themes and questions for future research exist and should be pursued. We hope this book will form a sound basis for a continuation of slum tourism research, so that the increasing interest of practitioners in slum tourism can be informed and challenged by an equally growing body of literature on the matter. Especially with a subject that is prone to opinionated debates, it is an important and challenging task for researchers to 'keep on slumming'.

Bibliography

Arendt, H. (2006) *On Revolution*, New York: Penguin Books.

Blake, A., Arbache, J.S., Sinclair, T.M. and Teles, V. (2008) 'Tourism and poverty relief', *Annals of Tourism Research*, 35(1): 107–26.

De Angelis, M. (2007) *The Beginning of History: Value Struggles and Global Capital*, Ann Arbor, MI: Pluto.

Dyson, P. (2012) 'Slum tourism: representing and interpreting "reality" in Dharavi, Mumbai', *Tourism Geographies*, 14(2): forthcoming.

Edensor, T. (1998) *Tourists at the Taj: Performance and Meaning at a Symbolic Site*, London: Routledge.

Foucault, M. (1979) *Discipline and Punish: The Birth of the Prison*, London: Vintage Books.

Frenzel, F. and Koens, K. (2012) 'Slum tourism: developments in a young field of interdisciplinary tourism research', *Tourism Geographies*, 14(2): forthcoming.

Graeber, D. (2001) *Toward an Anthropological Theory of Value: The False Coin of Our Own Dreams*, New York: Palgrave.

Harvey, D. (2001) *Spaces of Capital: Towards a Critical Geography*, London: Routledge.

Harvie, D. and Milburn, K. (2010) 'How organizations value and how value organizes', *Organization*, 17(5): 631–6.

Meschkank, J. (2010) 'Investigations into slum tourism in Mumbai: poverty tourism and the tensions between different constructions of reality', *GeoJournal*, 76(1): 47–62.

Rolfes, M., Steinbrink, M. and Uhl, C. (2009) *Townships as Attraction: An Empirical Study of Township Tourism in Cape Town*, Potsdam: Universitätsverlag.

Scheyvens, R. (2007) 'Exploring the tourism-poverty nexus', *Current Issues in Tourism*, 10(2–3): 231–54.

Steinbrink, M. (2012) '"We did the slum!" Urban poverty tourism in historical perspective', *Tourism Geographies*, 14(2): forthcoming.

Tomlinson, M., Walker, R. and Williams, G. (2008) 'Measuring poverty in Britain as a multi-dimensional concept, 1991 to 2003', *Journal of Social Policy*, 37: 597–620.

Tucker, H. and Akama, J. (2009) 'Tourism as postcolonialism', in T. Jamal and M. Robinson (eds) *The Sage Handbook of Tourism Studies*, London: Sage.

UN (United Nations) (2003) *The Challenge of Slums: Global Report on Human Settlements*, London: Earthscan.

Urry, J. (2002) *The Tourist Gaze*, 2nd edn, Thousand Oaks, CA: Sage.

Zukin, S. (1987) 'Gentrification: culture and capital in the urban core', *Annual Review of Sociology*, 13: 129–47.

Index